The
ARTIFICIAL
HORIZON

Mist from Vaniman's Lookout.

THREE CHILDREN WATCH AS MIST RISES FROM JAMISON VALLEY IN THE BLUE MOUNTAINS; SO DOES THE ROCK
FORMATION KNOWN AS THE THREE SISTERS. WHEN WALLACE GREEN CREATED THIS IMAGE AT VANIMANS LOOKOUT
IN 1940, HE PERPETUATED A MUCH REPEATED GAG: PHOTOGRAPHING THREE SPECTATORS IN FRONT OF THE THREE SISTERS.
A LEGEND REPORTS THAT THE THREE SISTERS ARE ABORIGINAL WOMEN WHO WERE TURNED TO STONE,
ALTHOUGH THE PROVENANCE OF THE STORY IS DUBIOUS.

The ARTIFICIAL HORIZON

Imagining the Blue Mountains

M A R T I N   T H O M A S

MELBOURNE UNIVERSITY PRESS

FOR RUTH AND BILL THOMAS,

my earliest guides

MELBOURNE UNIVERSITY PRESS
An imprint of Melbourne University Publishing Ltd
PO Box 1167, Carlton, Victoria 3053, Australia
mup-info@unimelb.edu.au
www.mup.com.au

First published 2003
Text © Martin Thomas 2003
Design and typography © Melbourne University Publishing Ltd 2003

National Library of Australia
Cataloguing-in-Publication data:

Thomas, Martin Edward.
The artificial horizon: imagining the Blue Mountains.

Bibliography.
Includes index.
ISBN 0 522 85072 3.

1. Blue Mountains (N.S.W)—Folklore. 2. Blue Mountains
(N.S.W.)—History. I. Title.

994.45

Designed and typeset by Sandra Nobes
Front cover image: Frank Hurley, *Three Sisters with mist background*.
By permission National Library of Australia
Back cover image: Thomas Mitchell, *Part of New South Wales from the Summit of Jellore*.
By permission National Library of Australia
Printed in Australia by Ligare

CONTENTS

VI

ACKNOWLEDGMENTS

MY GREATEST DEBT is to Stephen Muecke who discerned value in this project in the early days. For his inspiration, criticism and patience, my heartfelt thanks. I am indebted to Paul Carter, Paul Foss and Jennifer Isaacs for their encouragement and to the reading group consisting of Martin Harrison, Vivienne Kondos, Ruark Lewis, Andrew Lattas, Diane Losche, Ian Maxwell, Cathy Payne and Lesley Stern. Thanks to Barbara Blackman for friendship and feedback and to Roslyn Poignant for her numerous suggestions. Jim Smith shared insights and documents. John Low opened the door of the Blue Mountains City Council's Local Studies Collection. Lynette Stanger, Jean Murphy, Hugh Doggett, Gwenda Doggett, Ken Duff, Bill Boldisten, Neil Stuart and Doug Macarthur contributed oral history. Dawn Colless allowed me to quote from the story of Mirragan and Gurangatch. June Barker generously shared memories of the Gully. Gavin Andrews furthered my understanding of Bull Cave. Eve Stewart and Laila Haglund contributed memories of V. Gordon Childe while Delia Falconer and Isabel McBryde commented on that part of the manuscript. Jani Klotz, Ross Gibson, Ken Orchard, Vicky Roach, Mark Swivel, Alan Krell, Joan Kerr, Ross Mellick, Richard Byrne and Kate Low all contributed and supported. For their constructive criticism thanks to Greg Dening, Michael D. Jackson, Deborah Bird Rose and Kate Darian-Smith. Thanks also to my commissioning editor Teresa Pitt.

Parts of this book have been otherwise published or broadcast. A version of 'Morphic Echoes, Stony Silences' in Passage Four was published by *The UTS Review*, vol. 4, no. 1, 1998, and a radio adaptation titled *Stony Silences* was aired on the ABC in 1997. A radio version of

VII

'Homage to Catalina', also in Passage Four, was broadcast by the ABC in 1999. 'A Mountain Is not a Plateau', in Passage Three, was published in *Kerb*, 6, 1999.

I am grateful to staff of the State Library of New South Wales, Art Gallery of New South Wales, National Gallery of Australia, National Gallery of Victoria, Macleay Museum, Fisher Library, State Records of New South Wales, National Archives of Australia, Australian Institute for Aboriginal and Torres Strait Islander Studies and Geelong Art Gallery who responded to my enquiries. The National Library of Australia was especially generous in providing pictorial reproductions during a Harold White Fellowship in 2002.

Financial support came from the Literature Board of the Australia Council and an Australian Postgraduate Award. The high quality production was assisted by the publication subsidy programs of the Australian Academy of the Humanities and the University of Technology, Sydney.

Finally, my deepest thanks to my partner Naomi Parry, who supported and discussed the project as we prepared to submit it for publication.

VIII

Martin Thomas

At the heart of all beauty lies something inhuman, and these hills, the softness of the sky, the outline of these trees at this very minute lose the illusory meaning with which we had clothed them, henceforth more remote than a lost paradise.

ALBERT CAMUS, *The Myth of Sisyphus*, 1942

Major (later Sir) Thomas Mitchell (1792–1855) was deputy surveyor-general of New South Wales when he climbed Mount Jellore in 1828. Convict labourers cleared the summit of all but seven trees and with the aid of a theodolite Mitchell drafted this northward view of the Blue Mountains and surrounding ranges. He met local Gundungurra people during his survey but, according to his journal, none accompanied him to the summit—the Aboriginal man depicted in the foreground is probably a retrospective insertion.

INTRODUCTION

Only ideas won by walking *have any value.*

FRIEDRICH NIETZSCHE, *Twilight of the Idols*, 1889

THE VIEW FROM JELLORE

I DRIVE THROUGH a maze of logging tracks. The 'No Shooting' signs are shot to shreds. At a locked gate, the private property of some weekender, I park the car and continue on. The driveway twists through a building site, then narrows to thread its way among thick sclerophyll and steepen suddenly as it nears the bluff. By the time I reach the summit, my heart is pounding from the short but energetic climb. I gather sticks, light a fire. Behold: the country of this book.

Initially, it is the sense of layering that strikes me. Looking northwards from the basalt dome, the varied succession of range and ravine cuts lateral sections through the panorama: stepping-stones to the horizon. In front of me lie more than a million acres of dissected plateaus. They start almost immediately below with the steep and rugged ranges of the Nattai. The fabric there is richly verdant, the foliage a silken drape through which a shot of ebony completes the weave. From this foreground the colour changes with successive contours. Each layer of country brings a diminution of the darkness until finally it disappears. The blue that was always buried in the green emerges in the mid-ground and triumphs in the furthest ranges to the north. The effect is due to the fine droplets of oil produced by the unusually dense eucalyptus forests that cover the range. With any distance the horizon here is always blue.

A light snowfall comes scurrying out of nowhere, chafing my face and fanning the fire. Actuality and illusion combine in the lustrous transition from intense green to oceanic blue. The element of illusion heightens rather than diminishes the sense of majesty, which scale and distance make utterly compelling. A feeling of boundlessness is palpable here, though I need a number to give it meaning. Again training my eye on the horizon, I think of the surveyor Thomas Mitchell, who climbed up here in 1828 and also experienced the limpid purity of winter light. Through the telescopic lens of his theodolite he spied another basalt cap rising from surrounding sandstone, a mere wart on the horizon. Later he would put a name to it, for an 'intelligent native' explained that the peak was Warrawolong, 'near what we called "Newcastle"', 106 miles north.[1]

Mitchell's response to this topographical tableau was the impetus for my own excursion to the superb though rarely visited Jellore, on the southern fringe of the Blue Mountains. Camped near the base, Mitchell ascended the mount on successive days, mapping and drawing the landscape, immortalising his vision of the country and in the process leaving it physically changed. Despite the windswept elevation (Jellore is 960 metres above sea level), the fertile, volcanic soil throws up thick forest and consequent frustration to the spectator. While their master surveyed, Mitchell's convict labourers opened the view by clearing the summit of all but seven trees. Cognisant of the symbolism of his operation, Mitchell carved his name on one of the remaining trunks and nailed to it 'a copper penny piece' showing the head of King George IV.

As the placement of Mitchell's coin suggests, the dominant objective in visiting this vantage point was to integrate an expanse of unsettled territory into the imperial schema. Despite their proximity to Sydney Town, and the fact that forty years of British occupation had passed, the ranges visible from Jellore had not been mapped in any scientific way. While launching the trigonometrical method in Australia, there was also a sense of personal ascendancy in Major Mitchell's visit to Jellore in 1828. A veteran of the Peninsular War fought against Napoleon in Spain and Portugal, he mapped the battles meticulously, eventually producing a sumptuous folio that greatly pleased the Duke of Wellington. In 1827, at something of a loose end in England, Mitchell was offered the position of deputy surveyor-general in New South Wales. Though he considered the rank of deputy beneath his station, he ultimately accepted—partly in desperation and partly on the understanding that Surveyor-General Oxley, the incumbent, was terminally ill.

It was one of John Oxley's stockmen who guided Mitchell's party to Jellore. They had called upon the bedridden surveyor-general as they travelled south-west from Sydney and he confided that it would all be over in a matter of days. The distraught Mrs Oxley was already dressed in black. Mitchell took his leave, heading through the Razorback Range to reach Jellore where he could look all the way back to Sydney Lighthouse on the southern head of the harbour. 'I could see distantly with my naked eye the wall of the new gaol and with the theodolite glass, the 2 new windmills at work.'[2] He decided to fuse art and science by dividing his notebook into sections numbered by degrees and drafting a panoramic view with the aid of the theodolite. In this manner, over the four days required to clear the

3

forest on the summit, he took bearings on every discernible feature. It was a double-headed operation, laying the broad foundation for a vast and intricate survey of the colony while also producing a memorable sketch of the magnificent succession of ranges. Mitchell's journal records that he had finished the drawing and mapping when news arrived 'that Mr Oxley was dead and buried!' The surveyor-generalship, and a much anticipated career in exploration, were now his own.

A lithograph version of Mitchell's view from Jellore was included in his 1838 publication *Three Expeditions into the Interior of Australia*.[3] He was highly accomplished in the picturesque style of illustration, and the Jellore lithograph, which folds out from the book as if to approximate the expanse of country, is surprisingly convincing. A tinted version held by the National Library of Australia is even better, precisely depicting the gradations of colour that are so distinctive from the mount. The novelty of this northward aspect on the range (typically it is seen from the east or west) is powerfully and persuasively captured. From parts of the coast, from high points in Sydney, the Blue Mountains appear distinctly though undramatically: a blue and largely flattish tract of uplifted country, the terminus of the westward gaze. The French naturalist François Péron evoked it well when he wrote of 'a bluish curtain, rising but little above the horizon, and preserving a considerable uniformity'.[4]

Péron's hint of disappointment points to a distinctive trait of these plateaus known as mountains: that inside experience is incommensurate with exterior impression. Once within the range, one is amply rewarded for the lack of drama beyond it. The blue curtain admits cliff-top spectacles of deeply worn valleys and sandstone outcrops. They are ancient and affecting, capable of prompting the most extreme reactions: they can move you to tears, or love, or even—quite literally—to death. Perhaps for this reason they resist a sense of overview. Nowhere else in my travels have I experienced the immense totality that the view from Jellore affords.

To me, Mitchell's lithograph encapsulates the sense of discovery that is felt when something familiar is rendered anew. Significantly, he coupled the vista of uncharted country with what was already a familiar pictorial device in colonial art. On a ledge in the foreground, adjacent to a stump of tree, sits the figure of an Aboriginal man. His back faces the viewer as he contemplates the topographical expanse.

~

The motif of an Aboriginal figure that appears as both spectacle and spectator in colonial depictions of topography is as central to this book as the blue ranges themselves. It poses an abiding question that hangs over this country: why has the figure of the displaced person been symbolically restored to the colonised landscape and what does this motif, so pervasive, so recurrent (and by no means confined to the visual arts), reveal about the invading culture?

Certainly, a plethora of implications might be drawn from Mitchell's lithograph. A human element can provide a point of contrast to the topography; a personal presence might inject narrative to the overall image; or the precise positioning of characters can help steer the eye of the viewer through pictorial space. It must be acknowledged, though, that formal structure is replete with ideological implications, as John Barrell pointed out so memorably in *The dark side of the landscape* (1980). He describes an eighteenth-century convention requiring 'that the rich and their habitations... be illuminated, and the poor and theirs be left in the shadows'.[5] Although the placement of the Aboriginal figure in Mitchell's lithograph does not correspond to the contrast between wealth and poverty identified by Barrell, comparable issues concerning possession and dispossession are certainly implicit. With the depiction of an Aboriginal person in territory of which he has recently been—or is about to be—deprived, the claiming of land for the British Crown is rendered somewhat ambiguous.

It could be argued that Mitchell's inclusion of the Aborigine was nothing more than token colonial content for the audience back 'home', an antipodean curiosity more or less interchangeable with some example of native fauna—an emu or a kangaroo. However valid, this interpretation does not do enough to explain the complexities and ambiguities that make the Mitchell lithograph an interesting and significant reflection of colonisation at work. For example, an opposing argument could be advanced: the vision of the unclad Aborigine who contemplates a terrain with which he is obviously connected might suggest ambivalence on the part of the artist about a process of dispossession in which he is personally engaged.

As D. W. A. Baker has argued, the surveyor-general's relationships with Aboriginal people were sometimes hostile, sometimes co-operative.[6] When he was surveying around Jellore in 1828 the

5

latter seems to have been the case. The interactions Mitchell described suggest a genuine process of enquiry, even the transcription of several Aboriginal songs followed by their English translation. This is evidence of an early ethnography and it could not have taken place without a degree of mutual respect. Mitchell's notebooks of this period occasionally suggest a tacit recognition that his project of map-making and survey was a *secondary* activity. He was learning how thoroughly the features of the landscape were already named, known and schematised. He knew that he was visiting the land of Gundungurra-speaking people, the traditional owners of the southern Blue Mountains and beyond, whose territory extends through the Southern Highlands of New South Wales to somewhere near Lake George, not far from the site of Canberra. Mitchell's recognition of Aboriginal taxonomy is reflected in his frequent and sometimes fastidious use of indigenous terminology. At the beginning of his diary he refers to the mountain as 'Jellore'. Later he calls it 'Geloro', this being closer to how he heard the Gundungurra pronounce it. Whether he endeavoured to reconcile his scientific and imperial ambitions with the disruptions suffered by indigenous people is difficult to tell. Often he would do no more than observe—as when, just before he ascended Jellore, he found domiciles near his own encampment: 'huts recently left by the natives' which consisted of 'pieces of bark flattened & joined like the roof of a house so as to cover about a square yard'. What did he make of such tangible evidence that the country of his survey was someone's home?

Some days later he met the likely owners of these dwellings. One evening he was told that Moyengully, 'the king of the Nattai', had 'sat down' nearby. Mitchell was evidently aware that the tradition of sitting and lighting a fire near someone's camp was the courteous method of indicating a desire to speak. Mitchell joined Moyengully, who was accompanied by several young men, a small family and a widow with her child. Their faces were lit by various small fires, around which they reclined. Mitchell eyed their array of spears with apprehension, but quickly discovered that Moyengully's purpose was to ask him if he had a cure for a swelling on his wrist. It was the beginning of a convivial evening. The clan sang several songs—'one was what they called the Bathurst song, another the Kangaroo Song'. The 'old king added his voice occasionally to the strain'. Mitchell's attitude was apparently respectful, for he wrote how:

> One young fellow seemed one of the happiest beings I ever saw. Without any covering but a skin over his hips, he lay on his belly, on the ground, laughing heartily... His hair behind was filled with a |profusion of black Eagles' feathers, which had a very appropriate and good effect.

The following day Moyengully visited Mitchell at his tent. 'I could not resist the temptation of drawing his head, the profusion of woolly locks, seemed so very extraordinary,' he wrote, adding that he 'would have drawn the feathered dandy too' but he had already departed north towards the Cowpastures.

Mitchell recorded that Moyengully sat 'very impatiently' as he sketched. Yet the portrait, published in the same volume as the view from Jellore, is a persuasive image, revealing a self-possessed individual who looks away from the artist, to display severe dreadlocks that are certainly 'extraordinary'. It is estimated that Moyengully was born around 1800.[7] So the 'old King', as Mitchell calls him, was probably less than thirty (almost a decade younger than Mitchell himself) when the drawing was made. Still, the sense of gravitas communicated by the portrait seems beyond his years. Perhaps the disruptions of colonisation, which had included violent skirmishes between the British and the Gundungurra under Macquarie's governorship, forced early responsibilities upon him. His leadership and strength were well remembered by later generations of Gundungurra, including his nephew Werriberrie (William Russell), who in a short memoir of 1914 described him as a highly significant figure.[8] Moyengully was certainly conversant with British customs and felt that his social rank was equivalent to Mitchell's. He also believed that the making of his image necessitated some sort of exchange. Mitchell offered him a pair of convict trousers as recompense for sitting, but Moyengully refused, saying 'they were not fit for a gentleman'. Mitchell was forced to surrender a thin grey pair from his own wardrobe.

These interpersonal encounters must be kept in mind when considering the anonymous, somewhat generic Aboriginal figure who inhabits the foreground of Mitchell's view from Jellore. Whether inspired

7

by a real person or whether intended as a 'type' is impossible to determine. In that respect, a certain haziness will always cloud the picture. There is no record in the diary of any Gundungurra climbing the peak while Mitchell mapped and drew. Only years later, at the end of his life, when a committee of review was examining his department, did the surveyor-general make mention of an unnamed 'intelligent native' who had identified that distant peak as Warrawolong. Possibly Moyengully imparted this information during their discussions, and perhaps the somewhat 'woolly locks', the only personal characteristic of the foreground figure, are a muted reference to this Gundungurra 'king'.

Regardless of the artist's intention, the sense of peace with which the foreground figure sits before the landscape suggests to me a tension, a point of contrast, to the imperial presumption that the planting of flags, the making of maps or the fastening of coins to trees could offer a way of making the prospect one's own.

The Aboriginal figure, steady and continuous, stands in contrast to the bewildering visions one might encounter in the field. Take, for example, an incident dating from 1835 when Mitchell was exploring near the Darling River in western New South Wales. One frosty morning, as the foliage began to thaw, he hastened up a hillside, there to behold 'the transient vision of a distant horizon'. Here was something perceptible but fantastic: the ranges to the west, which hitherto had been no more than tiny hummocks in the distance, 'appeared raised as if by magic'.[9]

Mitchell was witnessing the prismatic effect of rising moisture, something akin to a great lens suspended in the lower atmosphere— an effect commonly known as refraction. The surveyor-general and his party had seen it previously when 'small eminences' in the distance were gloriously magnified 'like cliffs on a sea coast'. But the illusion was short-lived. 'To the astonishment of the men,' he wrote, 'all the hills, however, soon disappeared.'[10]

Astonishment had been Mitchell's own reaction when, in 1829, he was surveying a route for the Great North Road which would connect Sydney with the Hunter Valley. He was on the ranges adjoining Warra-wolong when he encountered the illusion. There, on the western horizon, he noticed 'Several gigantic ranges . . . overhanging with trees & glistening with rocks.' Staring at his notebook in stupefaction— previously he had sketched the view—Mitchell reached for his telescope, enlarged the enlargement, and watched the mountains 'change shape' until one 'fell away in the middle'.

This first encounter would set the tone for his dealings with optical illusions. On the Darling he not only observed the vision through his telescope but took readings with a theodolite, obtaining bearings on the refracted range 'from a spot whence it could be but seldom visible'. A 'mirage' was thus incorporated into a trigonometrical survey. It is an image to be borne in mind as we reconsider the unsettling of the figure in the landscape: the putative surrender of myth to science.

~

So it is that the view from Jellore, with its real yet spectral figure in the foreground, provides a path to the country of this book. I began researching the Blue Mountains because I felt haunted by that figure in the landscape. Though an individual response, I became convinced that my feelings originated from a cultural rather than a purely personal condition. For the intimation of presence to be confronted with the symptoms of absence is a troubling thing. It is sobering, for instance, to think that one could walk through half the territory depicted in Mitchell's view without discerning any trace of Aboriginal occupation. When I was sixteen I did just that. One winter vacation, I joined a friend and his brother on a hike from the town of Katoomba in the upper Blue Mountains to the Southern Highlands village of Mittagong which is not far from the meeting place of Mitchell and Moyengully. It took us a week to cover a distance that we reckoned at about 130 kilometres.

Two decades on, my memories of that journey are still wonderfully vivid. We caught the train to Katoomba, the town where I now live, some two hours west of Sydney. Then to the start of Narrow Neck by taxi where the hike began. True to its name, Narrow Neck is an elongated plateau, faced on either side by yellow cliffs, weathered and familiar—signature items in Blue Mountains scenery. The plateau, a ten-kilometre offshoot from the main east–west escarpment, is visible from the famous tourist spots of Echo Point and the Three Sisters. It drives a southern course, dividing two great valleys: the wild and wooded Jamison to the east and the tamed, much cleared Megalong to the west. As we walked the broad trail that forms a spine on Narrow Neck, it was as if two different universes were presented to our right and left.

9

Soon the vast reservoir of Lake Burragorang, Sydney's water supply, came into sight. We passed the fire tower, a landmark visible for miles, and clambered down Taro's Ladder, a series of spikes. That was Narrow Neck.

Now we were off the fire-fighters' trails and onto hiking tracks, narrow and sometimes patchy, marked on occasion by cairns or splotches of paint. When the track eluded us, we bush-bashed. Having navigated the Wild Dog Mountains, we descended to the fast-flowing channel of the Coxs, taking care to draw our water from a side creek because the river itself is badly polluted. To the murmur of river over river-stones and breeze through casuarinas, we slept a night in the valley. From there it was steep, steep climbing, up and along a ridge that led us to Mount Cloudmaker where we absorbed the panorama and signed the visitors' book that lives in a tin. Then on to the most splendid of plateaus, Kanangra Walls, a great sandstone edifice that juts into a pitted colosseum of surrounding country; terrain that is not just folded but brutally crumpled so that gullies collapse suddenly into waterfalls or narrow into deep, subterranean canyons. We slept up there at Kanangra in the Dance Floor Cave, once used by settlers for remote mountain revelries. Next morning the weather turned. Through mist and rain, we made our way round the oblong feature of Mount Colong, stayed a night at the old lead and silver mining centre of Yeranderee, now a ghost town, then headed towards Mittagong along the Water Board trails.

In the last days, as we approached the country of the Nattai, west of Jellore, much of the land was cleared for grazing. We saw wildlife as well as cattle and stinky packs of feral goats. One day we disturbed a wedge-tailed eagle feeding on a slope and we watched as it cranked awkwardly like some inventor on his flying machine, wondering whether this expert glider and hunter could ever be airborne again. Earlier, we had stopped motionless as a crack like a gunshot resounded through space. Then came a guttural moan as a huge eucalypt on the hillside opposite, dead as a fossil, chose this moment with audience to keel in a graceful arc and shatter before our eyes.

No doubt my admission that I saw no signs of Aboriginal habitation during that beautiful though physically exhausting week reveals a limited power of observation. I should have known, as I might then have guessed, that the caverns where we slept at Mobb's Soak in the Wild Dog

Mountains and the Dance Floor at Kanangra Walls have sheltered people for millennia. A careful search of such caves will often yield flakes of chert, remnants from the making of tools. I knew nothing about that, just as I had no idea that, had we strayed a few metres from the track near Kanangra Walls, we would have seen human figures, their limbs outspread, painted on the rock. These are the iconic dancing men who grace rock art sites in Gundungurra country. At Kanangra, some of the dancers are overwritten with the signatures of colonial settlers. The history builds up in layers.

All this I have learnt since. I guess I did not have an archaeologist's disposition; nor did my education, which included some practical bushcraft (without which we could never have made such a journey), prepare me in any way for dealing with the reality of Aboriginal history and heritage. A contrast to my own experience can be found in a moving comment by Eugene Stockton, a priest and archaeologist who, in the 1960s, did important surveys in the Blue Mountains, pursuing interests that had been kindled in his youth:

> As a teenager I began to find stones which did not belong to the geology of the area. These pieces of basalt and chert I learned to recognise as artefacts of a former Mountain people. Holding a stone tool in my hand I wondered at the last hand to grasp it: it was like a handshake across the centuries.[11]

Regrettably, there was nothing in my own wanderings comparable to that 'handshake across the centuries'. I knew of a few hand prints and rock engravings that survived from the pre-contact period, but these apparently isolated remnants only affirmed the expunging of the civilisation that produced them. I knew few details about the conquest of Aboriginal society. On this matter the school histories of the 1970s were guarded. But through family connections I became aware quite early of the dreadful massacres that had decimated the Aboriginal population of Tasmania. Concerning Sydney and its environs, however, imagination was forced to compensate for a dearth of data. So the bush, for all its beauty and grandeur, often had a melancholy, an autumnal quality, the origin of which seemed sketchy though somehow associated with the lack of human presence. Despite—or perhaps because of—these feelings, I found that forests and wild landscapes generally tended to

12

arouse very strong emotions. The destruction of natural environments seemed an extension of some earlier corruption.

These sentiments mark the beginning of a longstanding interest in the forms of story-telling and image-making that might facilitate, or else destabilise, one's connection with place. In an era when relationships with locality and community appear to be fragmenting, it seems essential to think in very broad ways about issues of rootedness and belonging; the ethical dilemmas, personal and collective, which must be resolved before a rightful place in the world can be assumed.

Early inklings of the study that became this book occurred when I was working as a research assistant on a project concerning pioneer women. I happened to read a poetic account, packed with incident and misadventure, of a crossing of the Blue Mountains in 1822. The author was Elizabeth Hawkins, an Englishwoman in straitened circumstances, whose husband had been appointed the first government storekeeper at the infant town of Bathurst on the western side of the range. Hawkins' account was immediately engaging, both as a literary document and as an insight into a particularly resilient woman, a mother of eight children below the age of twelve. They all made the journey in wagons pulled by recalcitrant bullocks. The drivers and servants were convicts, of whom this colonial neophyte was extremely frightened. In some ways the journey was horrific, but Mrs Hawkins still managed to maintain a sense of humour in penning her immensely detailed account, which took the form of a letter to her sister.

The Hawkins document is memorable for its sense of doubt and hesitation. This is a welcome contrast to the congratulatory bravado that typifies so many narratives of pioneering, the vast majority scribed by men. Examples of such colonial self-confidence, as well as some really brilliant topographical writing by travellers including Charles Darwin, can be found in the collection where I first read Elizabeth Hawkins' missive. This is a book titled *Fourteen Journeys Over the Blue Mountains*, edited in 1950 by George Mackaness, a distinguished anthologist and historian. As I began to research, other material and interests became prominent. So neither the Hawkins letter nor the Mackaness collection feature dominantly in this book. But Hawkins' vibrant prose, shaped by her down-to-earth slant on a line of travel so often recounted as an epiphany in British fortitude and ingenuity, was influential in steering

OPPOSITE: MYLES DUNPHY'S *Gangerang* MAP HAS AIDED BUSHWALKERS SINCE ITS FIRST PUBLICATION IN 1953. MYLES AND HIS SON MILO DUNPHY WERE PROMINENT ADVOCATES OF BLUE MOUNTAINS CONSERVATION. THIS DETAIL OF THE MAP SHOWS THE IMMENSELY PRECIPITOUS AREA AROUND KANANGRA WALLS, A FAVOURITE STAMPING GROUND OF THE DUNPHYS. THIS EDITION OF THE MAP WAS PUBLISHED BY THE COLONG FOUNDATION IN 1979.

my enquiry. So too was Mackaness' simple, elegant idea of publishing a collection of documents in which fourteen travellers describe the same route. It was a clear demonstration of how cultural responses to a landscape might provide something akin to a barometric reading of the mood and aspirations of colonial and, by implication, postcolonial society.

In Passage One I describe growing up in a Sydney suburb where the horizon of the Blue Mountains served as an inconspicuous though influential presence. That I was drawn to the mountains is not surprising. They affect the lives of Sydneysiders as strongly as the more celebrated coast and harbour. They provide the drinking water and influence the climate and air, containing the humidity and pollution that build up pressure on the plain. Reaching about a thousand metres above sea level, the Blue Mountains are a cool antidote to the steamy, sub-tropical metropolis, attracting more visitors in winter than in summer. Occasionally they are blessed with a dusting of snow. Offering both the lure of quietness and physical adventure in a landscape shrouded in mystique, the mountains are frequently a place of escape or refuge, just as they serve as an attraction for travellers from around the globe. Inevitably, this makes them the source of an endless stream of image-making: photographs, postcards, calendars, videos, paintings, and lashings of miscellaneous kitsch. Thus the mountains have a double presence: semiotic and topographical. Their influence is certainly uneven, but the possibility exists that the mountains can be felt, anywhere at any time, across the globe.

~

I was living in a warehouse in inner Sydney when my research began in earnest. It was a light-filled space with windows facing west. Were it not for the intervening buildings and Central Railway Station, I might have seen the mountains. My desk was positioned in front of a window. Beside it hung a colour reproduction of Eugène von Guérard's 1862 painting of Weatherboard (now Wentworth) Falls.[12] This romantic landscape captures just the top of the waterfall as it tumbles into Jamison Valley. The density of the rainforest and a portion of the rectangular massif of Mount Solitary are visible in sunset light. Once again, the pictorial foreground provides the glimmer of a narrative with the inclusion of a human figure. And again the figure is an Aboriginal man, this time with a snake at his feet, and poised as if for combat.

It was several years before the original painting came into public ownership and I could view it at the National Gallery of Victoria in Melbourne. On the large canvas I could see how the snake, easily missable in the reproduction, had a disconcerting presence. Other quite lovely details became apparent: the variegated effect of dappled light across the landscape, and the wily presentation of the artist's signature—inscribed as a graffito on a rock of his own painting. Back in Sydney, however, I had little choice but to make do with the tiny reproduction, a virtual window in my urban world, which seemed to signal all sorts of possible directions. The vista itself was becoming a familiar backdrop, for my parents had recently bought a cottage at Wentworth Falls, a few minutes' walk from the scene of von Guérard's painting. Now I had a regular place where I could work and walk. Thus began a process of immersing myself in both the country and the images it has spawned, a process that I don't think will ever stop. My commitment to the project gradually strengthened; the labyrinth became denser, more intriguing. Eventually I settled in Katoomba, making a home in the place itself.

15

~

This is a study that does not sit comfortably within a disciplinary niche. Suggesting possibilities for both narrative and movement, it does not attempt to order the past according to some model of cause and effect. Acknowledgment of the literary basis of history, however, does not downplay its role in the conveying of truth. On the contrary, it emphasises a facility for grappling with manifestations of truth that are almost unapproachable from other avenues. Deliberating on subjects such as the meaning of the snake in von Guérard's painting or the colonial conceit that the main path across the Blue Mountains, an Aboriginal route for millennia, was *discovered* by a trio of white men in 1813 convinced me that my cultural survey of the landscape would yield a heterogeneous array of myths. Investigating further, I found the subject of myth increasingly intriguing and ever more inseparable from the imaging and imagining of land. Authentic details from the ancient Aboriginal mythology came to my attention and, as I discuss in Passage Four, so did various legends that purported to be Aboriginal but which were probably the inventions of white people. Here was a perplexing, but to me very revealing, genre—what might be termed 'mythical myths'.

As I began to consider these stories, I became convinced that the relationship between myth and historical events was crying out for investigation. Rather than endeavour to expose or deconstruct myth, I would attempt an analysis that acknowledged its power and potency. The supposition that myth can be banished by the bright light of reason exemplifies the danger of scientific methods in the study of culture. If myth is to be discounted as mere error or falsehood, what is being said about systems of thought that make no claim to know the world as a scientific object? Should 'the Dreaming' of Aboriginal epistemology— a vast network of narratives and traditions founded on myth—be written off as some primitive fancy? Of course this has been done often enough in the past, though these days such cultural chauvinism is, one hopes, less acceptable. The legitimacy of Aboriginal world views has won acknow-ledgment, even prestige, in certain quarters of society. Unfortunately, this has encouraged very little recognition of the degree to which the beliefs and values of what is called 'Western society' are themselves founded on myth. As we will see, this can be said even of the doctrines that have been most influential in 'rationalising' the world. There is a mythical foundation to science itself.

My study, I came to realise, would examine the relationship between myth and society. As a form of collective imaging, myth can be seen as an active force that inspires action and activity, thereby influencing human destiny and the social pattern. Myths can be read in the way dreams are read: as an index to the hopes, fears and temperaments of those who have brought them into being. In this way, my study draws from the human experience of a particular landscape. Being a place where local, regional and global forces continue to interact, I have attended closely to the meeting of cultures and the consequent impact on their mythological orders. I have done this not to produce a local or Aboriginal history (never my objective) but, on the contrary, to interrogate the culture of my own people, the 'arriving ones' as we might call ourselves, in the hope of thinking constructively about the ethical challenges of inhabiting this colonised country. The presentation and narration of this history, if that's what it is, have been shaped by the country, drawing inspiration and warning from the symbol of the labyrinth, the most pervasive colonial metaphor for the topography I have studied. My framework is not strictly chronological; it travels through space and time in its use of juxtaposition; it allows my experiences to surface among those of others; it is composed of essays and fragments that take as their subject a place or narrative. One of Nietzsche's meaty aphorisms gave momentum to the writing: 'Only ideas *won by walking* have any value.'

The pleasure of the labyrinth (in contrast to its primal terror) involves movement, points of contrast, interconnection, an attention to the path itself. As a narrative model it encouraged the emergence of a series of voices that take on such disparate subjects as the story of a racetrack near my own back yard, a treatise on suicide or the request by the explorer Gregory Blaxland that the governor lend him a surveying instrument called an artificial horizon. The jazz musician Bruce Cale once said that his musical interest in bi-tonality is connected with his childhood in Katoomba 'where it was once possible to hear the music from three dance halls intermingling—as often as not in different keys'.[13] In this spirit I hope for a reader who is also a listener, attentive not only to the reflections but to the juxtaposition of echoes and reverberations that run through the Blue Mountains labyrinth.

This book, then, draws from the collective cultural memory though it does not purport to be a cultural history of the Blue Mountains. Nor is it an art history or an ethnographic study. It has elements of all of these, and might contribute something to various disciplines. But the process of writing was more quixotic. If I look for a metaphor of how I was inspired and influenced by my materials, it cannot be drawn from some disciplinary code. Of such things one can only be suspicious. My methodology developed from a practical craft, my activity as a radio-maker, which evolved over the period of the book's writing. The idea of making a recording, of capturing in real time the speech and ambience of a moment, of returning to that moment, listening and re-listening, until details I did not hear in the first instance become clear and imbued with their own logic like the brush strokes of a painting: here was a distantly attainable ideal that might guide my encounter with the stories and images that bring the country into being.

ARTFULLY CONSTRUCTED WALKING TRAILS ENHANCED THE ATTRACTIVENESS OF THE BLUE MOUNTAINS AS A RESORT FOR TOURISTS. SCULPTED INTO THE ESCARPMENT, THEY FREQUENTLY EMPHASISED THE VERTIGINOUS QUALITY OF THE LANDSCAPE. THIS PHOTOGRAPH SHOWS A SECTION OF THE NATIONAL PASS AT WENTWORTH (PREVIOUSLY WEATHERBOARD) FALLS WHICH OPENED IN 1908. TAKEN BY AN UNCREDITED PHOTOGRAPHER, IT WAS INCLUDED IN *Tours in New South Wales*, A GUIDE FOR MEMBERS OF THE BRITISH ASSOCIATION FOR THE ADVANCEMENT OF SCIENCE WHICH MET IN SYDNEY IN 1914.

Passage One

THE FALSE HORIZON

The health of the eye seems to demand a horizon.

RALPH WALDO EMERSON, *Nature*, 1836

OVERTURE

the view was

boundless as

the ocean

JOHN OXLEY,
*Journals of Two
Expeditions*, 1820.

THEY ARRIVED ON the eastern seaboard of Australia, looked to the ranges in the west and saw a horizon that was always blue. The colour of sky—and distance—the blueness, like the horizon itself, is endlessly deferred the closer you get. Shades of green enmesh you as you move towards it: the bluish and olive greens of eucalyptus and acacia, the dry, yellow greens of clumpy grasses, the verdant green of temperate rainforest and waist-high fern. Yet come to some vantage point, an opening in the trees, and the blueness beckons in the distance, urging you on. It is this forceful presence of something intangible that suggests a connection between the blue horizon and things remembered. Both are shaped by the landscape of experience. Both are as elusive as they are illusory. Yet, indisputably, they are there.

The process whereby memory is triggered by the view to the horizon sits a little oddly in a culture where memory is more often associated with reflection. Think how frequently the pool and polished surface appear in war memorials and other intentionally mnemonic structures. Likewise, turn the pages of an album, read the words or photographs, and surely you will find your posture is curled in towards your self. Hence the friction between the outward gaze to the horizon and the essentially inward process of seeing the world in a watery surface.

This friction was vividly symbolised in the era of the scientific revolution when Europeans endeavoured to locate themselves in space and time with a hitherto undreamed-of specificity. As the girdles of longitude and latitude tightened round the globe, the difference between the outward and inward gaze was vividly symbolised by a scientific instrument known as a 'false', or 'artificial', horizon.

This instrument was a simple thing, its main component being mercury, that remarkable substance which among alchemists had stood for metamorphosis and the physical origin of all the metals. John Webster, an alchemist scholar, poetically described mercury as a 'metallick body' that could 'neither be hammered, nor fluxed, or melted. . . As water is amongst other things, so is this amongst Metal.'[1] With its concept of symbiotic harmony, alchemical cosmology proposed that metal molten in the forge becomes a form of mercury, just as mercury's liquidity anticipates the solidity of other metals. How appropriate, then, that as the years unfolded, and alchemy underwent its own metamorphosis—giving ground to empirical science—the unforgeable metal should provide the reflective surface between earth and heaven, between sea and land.

The pool of mercury in a false horizon was contained in a shallow vessel covered by a roof of glass. Designed to exclude the very murmur of a ripple, it combined mirror and spirit level in a single object. The surveyor using the false horizon would position it so as to capture the reflection of a star. Then he would measure the arc between the star and its reflection using another instrument, the sextant (which is really a telescope mounted on a very accurate protractor). This was achieved with considerable precision for the star was aligned with the silken cross-hair made from spider's web that was strung within the sextant. The purpose of this ritual was to calculate the 'actual' elevation of the star. The scientific surveyor, like many wayfarers before him, invoked the heavens in locating his temporal position.

The false or artificial horizon is appropriately named, for its purpose is to negate the inconstancy of the terrestrial horizon, to replace it with an acknowledged falsehood—a horizontal line. Working with methods that were first adopted for the spherical perfection of a world at sea, the surveyor must negotiate the lumps and irregularities of land. In this regard the sea captain is fortunate indeed: the view from an ocean-going ship gives a constant horizon; there are no depressions or mountains that will alter, by some degree, the apparent elevation of a heavenly body. The unique problem of the landed surveyor is that the interfering topography (the very thing he has come to measure!) must be burnished into smoothness. That is the peculiar role of the artificial horizon. For if the surveyor measures the angle between the star and its mercurial reflection and then divides it in half, the resulting figure is the elevation he would get if the world were a perfect sphere. The outward gaze, whereby vision terminates at the horizon, is thus substituted for a reflected image in a toxic surface. The scenario is worthy of Narcissus. Watching the stellar body through his lens, aligning the enlarged surface of its reflection with the cross of spider's web, the surveyor might briefly, if ineffectually, possess the star, translating its eternal brightness to a virtual zone; an enclosed image in a tube; a fleeting conjunction of retina and glass.

~

In the surveyor's vessel, mercury disperses to form a plane and thus anticipate the triumph of Euclidean geometry, with its idealised forms, over the lumps and bumps of country. While synthesising the outward gaze to level the irregular world, mercury would also help the surveyor to apprehend his vertical position—measured, of course, as height above the sea. The mountain barometer is a thin glass tube marked with gradations and housing a reserve of mercury. Confined in this narrow enclosure—unable to disperse—the volatile liquid leaps upwards, not outwards, and from its motion the surveyor will calculate the degree of elevation.

For John Oxley, the mariner who became surveyor-general in the colony of New South Wales, mercury was a reluctant servant. Travelling inland in 1817, he considered himself

> so unfortunate as to find the barometer broken, the horse which carried the instruments having thrown his load in passing the swamps: every precaution had been taken in the packing to prevent such an accident.

Then, a few months later:

> An accident happened to the vessel containing the mercury of the artificial horizon, by which the greater part was lost, leaving scarcely sufficient for use. It had been a matter of surprise to me that such a misfortune had not occurred sooner, the box containing the instruments, &c., being so shaken by the horse.[2]

Little wonder that his successor, Thomas Mitchell, commissioned a servant with the sole responsibility of carrying the mountain barometer.

Oxley, an habitual seaman, who calculated his latitude and longitude whenever weather permitted, regarded the artificial horizon as an essential part of his baggage. But at the blue horizon where I started, there lies a stranger story. The Blue Mountains, as the range to the west quickly became known, had both lured the British and stopped them in their tracks. When the colonist Gregory Blaxland instigated yet another of his unofficial expeditions, the one that would cross the range in 1813, he petitioned Governor Lachlan Macquarie for a loan of an artificial horizon. The matter became something of a grievance in the ensuing years as the travellers lobbied to supplement the thousand acres they were each rewarded for crossing the range. One of Blaxland's companions—it must have been William Wentworth or William Lawson—had suggested he 'should apply to His Excellency to lend us a false horizon for which I did apply but was refused'.[3]

Yet why should the governor accede to his request? He had no sextant or astronomical tables, without which an artificial horizon is supposedly useless. This was, after all, the plain Mr Blaxland, grazier and purveyor of meat, whose exploration was anything but philosophical in intent. Rather, it was a sign of desperation in a man whose land was already overstocked. He had substantial holdings in the country between range and coast, the future site of the Sydney metropolis, to which they gave an English county name, the Cumberland Plain. By 1813 much of the soil was trampled and impoverished by deforestation and a mere two decades of inappropriate use. A plague of caterpillars had struck in the spring of 1810, drought the following year. In February 1811 rain brought relief, but the caterpillars burgeoned once more. The following year was dry.[4] Bitten by drought and bug, Gregory Blaxland, the man whose business the earlier and subsequently deposed governor, William Bligh, derided as 'so speculative as to care for nothing but making money . . . of buying as cheap as they can and selling dear',[5] would launch a mission that transcended the horizon, giving access to territory that Macquarie punningly christened 'West-more-land'.[6]

23

~

Mercury, like Hermes, was the messenger of the gods. He was also protector of traders and thieves. Perhaps he should have been there on Blaxland's journey. Whatever their reason for wanting an artificial horizon, the explorers' tiff might point to a major truth about the land itself. There is a correspondence between the work of the instrument and the play of the mind's eye. It reminds us that the meeting of vista and visitor *always* involves artifice. It is bathed in cultural expectation. This reality, and the kinds of imaginative leaps that follow from it, form the subject of this first passage, which provides an overview of the country and offers a re-telling of that most enduring colonial myth, the 'First Crossing' of the Blue Mountains in 1813. Few stories could provide more convincing testimony of how, when looking out, we do create an artificial horizon.

I

THE EDGE

The myth of pure,

untouched nature

was inaugurated

at the moment

of its decline,

expressed by the

new conflict

between nature

and technology

at the interior

of the sublime.

ALLEN S. WEISS,
Unnatural Horizons,
1998.

DRAWN TOGETHER BY the mystery of the wilderness, a crowd is gathered—pilgrims from around the world. We have entered a sanctuary, a shrine to a venerable (if vulnerable) Nature, her space redolent with symbol and myth. Speaker unseen, a voice thunders godlike through the darkness. Prepare yourself for the journey ahead, through a 'wild and dangerous labyrinth'.

The icons of Australian fauna appear as overblown apparitions—a koala munching gum leaves, a scampering wallaby. The paradox of the platypus is near at hand. Every sensation, every sound, is amplified in this environment; each detail more than alive. Feel the lurch in stomach when a rock climber, hanging on to little more than grit, makes his way up a sheer arête, a sword of sandstone to menace the sky. 'This is the old world,' the voice insists. 'When Europe was young, this was ancient.' Toehold by handhold, the climber persists in his game against gravity; nears the top.

Departs the labyrinth?

Down at her belay point, a long-haired Ariadne feeds out thread.

With a sweep, my gut jumps backwards, pinioned by a centrifugal movement that propels me into an airborne spiral to turn and turn again around the climber like the nightmare in Hitchcock's *Vertigo*. Hijacked in this perpetual holding pattern, how could one ever touch the ground?

'The Edge' is the well-chosen title of this filmic sanctuary, and without apparent irony its promoters claim that here, 'in one of the world's most technologically advanced cinemas', you can have the 'ultimate Blue Mountains wilderness experience'.[7] It's a grand claim that mere celluloid can provide the 'ultimate' experience of this indisputably grand landscape; that a film can surpass the age-old, if prosaic, action of stepping outside and seeing it for yourself. But John Weiley's motion picture is not easily outdone in terms of grandiosity. With a seventy-millimetre print, a six-storey high screen, the ability to magnify by 452 times, it provides a roller coaster of a trip through valley and cataract, collapsing rapidly from helicopter view to time-lapse imagery, from macro to micro, from forest glade to overarching panorama, replete with nubile maidens, hair aflow and legs projecting from their harnesses, abseiling into coal-dark clefts.

The spectacle that is *The Edge* screens numerous times daily at the customised Maxvision cinema in Katoomba, geographically central to the country it purports to describe. The seating is sharply raked and uncomfortably close to the screen, which measures eighteen metres high and twenty-four metres wide. This is site-specific cinema, viewable only in this location (unless you count the video diminutive which, with T-shirts and glossy booklets, is part of the merchandising package). As a marketing phenomenon, *The Edge* is brilliant: the perfect antidote for tourist operators who know all too well the vicissitudes of Blue Mountains weather. By locating the experience of travel in an armchair habitat, *The Edge* gives superfluous confirmation—for a generation raised in the theatre of wildlife documentaries—that the penetrating gaze of the camera is infinitely superior to that of the naked eye.

If art derives strength from synthesising its own process and the object it seeks to evoke, *The Edge* rates poorly. Anyone who has spent time in this country and attempted to unravel its subtleties—then had the meditation broken by a low-flying helicopter—will attest to that. Its claim to the 'ultimate' experience could almost be forgiven if it were nothing more than an adman's hyperbole. Instead, it's the very basis of the film. Because *The Edge*, with all its thrills and spills, its conviction that digital sound and high-fidelity visuals are *the* key to apprehending something as down-to-earth as a tract of land, is not only an attempt to lure an audience in a 'market environment' of competing attractions (understandable if not entirely laudable), but foremost it's a film with a 'message'.

While the veneration of nature is often religious in aspiration—tapping, perhaps, the very roots of divine intimation—*The Edge* thumps its gospel of environmental purity with all the smarminess, all the uptight sanctimony, of the worst television evangelist. Environmental degradation, we are told, started with the arrival of Aborigines. 'All of the very large animals soon became extinct and since the arrival of Europeans another one hundred species of plants and animals have vanished.' Following a creek now, the airborne camera hovers at the brink of a waterfall. I think I recognise it as Wentworth Falls—though it's hard to tell. The narrator (Hugo Weaving) continues the species spiel as we begin to teeter: 'Five thousand more are now close to the edge of extinction.'

This is the apocalyptic edge of the film's title—a motif repeated *ad nauseam* throughout its 35-minute duration as it leans out over clifftops, drops away with abseilers, penetrates the limestone bowels of the earth. It is a swirling, dizzying picture of the mountains that manages to include a few revelations among the clichés. A section of the film, really its inner core, shows intriguing footage of the *Wollemia nobilis* (Wollemi Pine), the remarkable 35-metre tree that scientists had previously known only through fossils. They thought it had been extinct for sixty million years, a theory disproved when a grove of these trees was discovered in a northern Blue Mountains canyon in 1994. The specific location is virtually a state secret, and although the tree is being commercially propagated it will be many years before the lay person can see mature specimens in the flesh. The Wollemi Pine was hailed as the botanical discovery of the twentieth century, and certainly it would be difficult to identify a more potent symbol of the ruggedness of the range. To think that here, within a hundred kilometres of Sydney, exploration and discovery can still go on!

The survival in an isolated canyon of a 'fossil species' like the Wollemi Pine might attest to the strength, the tenacity, of natural phenomena. But in *The Edge* it is the extreme vulnerability of the tree, the need for secrecy about its location, that is driven home. There is certainly no acknowledgment that the discovery of the pine might facilitate a comeback. With all the attention heaped upon it, there will be no lack of buyers when the tree comes onto the market. Through human intervention, the Wollemi Pine will become more populous than it has been for millions of years.

~

In 1999, while introducing a collection of essays about art and nature, I wrote of the doubt 'that represents the really difficult legacy of what is termed (albeit loosely) "environmental awareness"'. This, I suggested, 'is a paradigm, utterly unique, where confidence in the productivity of nature, its Hydra-like propensity to sprout life at every severance, has entirely bottomed out'.[8]

The Edge is completely typical in this regard, appearing as a homage to wilderness while adopting a tone of admonition rather than celebration. The sense of vertigo is everywhere apparent. A fall of cosmic dimension could be imminent. Or has it already occurred? For all its glory, the 'wilderness' depicted here is only an atavistic relic—a teasing reminder, as the narrator puts it, of 'a flood of creativity that continued until the arrival of mankind'.

Both 'wilderness' and 'mankind' get poor treatment in this argument, which is perhaps influenced by Tim Flannery's more subtle ecological history, *The Future Eaters* (1994). Should human impact be regarded as the erasure of creativity? Is nature so hypersensitive that its process halts with human arrival? Is there ever a moment when the work of 'mankind' becomes a part of nature? There is an extraordinary collision of self-denial and egocentrism in this eminently Cartesian fallacy. It is also poor observation. Organisms might thrive in spite or in light of human intervention. Ask the eucalypts that regenerate with fire. Ask a leech. This is not to deny the evils of pollution, loss of species, environmental degradation. It is simply to argue that an insurmountable gulf between humanity and nature is inscribed in this world-view.

In contradistinction to the schism between humanity and nature documented in *The Edge*, the recently approved World Heritage nomination of the Greater Blue Mountains specifically highlights the 'outstanding natural and cultural values' of the area. 'Through their scale and symbiosis with the City of Sydney,' declares the citation, 'the Greater Blue Mountains exemplify the links between wild places and human aspirations.' While the 'crux' of the World Heritage listing was the 'outstanding universal significance of eucalypt-dominated vegetation, of which it represents the best single example', the nomination placed great emphasis on the long history of community involvement in protecting and nurturing this unique environment.[9] Of course this includes the labour of the Aboriginal inhabitants who, according to the official figures, have occupied the mountains for at least 14 000 and perhaps as long as 22 000 years. European arrival irrevocably disrupted the traditional lifestyle of the Blue Mountains Aborigines. But the economic exploitation that contributed to their uprooting (logging, mining and farming for the most part) scarcely affected significant tracts of this wild country. Frequently, the land was just too rugged to be profitable. Where exploitation did occur, much of it was wound back during the later twentieth century when conservation objectives gained priority. There are presently eight national parks or reserves which combine to form more than one million contiguous hectares of protected land.

This means, of course, that the greater part of the Blue Mountains is completely uninhabited. But ribbons of development do exist along the two roads that cross the range. In total, there are 26 townships inhabited by more than 72 000 people. The population is growing rapidly as the highway improves and industry in western Sydney, with attendant employment opportunities, continues to grow. Most of the towns are situated along the railway and the Great Western Highway, which follow the main east–west ridge (the route used by the Blaxland party). A few villages plus various orchards, mainly apple, sit along the secondary route, parallel and to the north: Bells Line of Road. In the farms and often renowned gardens of those who live here, one can find an enormous range of responses to the soil, the climate and the aesthetics of this unique landscape. In the shaping of the ground, the choice of plantings, the placement of species both indigenous and foreign, a great and complex history of how an arriving culture has attempted to habituate itself is written upon the earth.

Naturally, the human dimension of the Blue Mountains landscape gets very short shrift in a film like *The Edge*. Those who fill their gardens with azaleas are mocked, and even that well-trammelled Australian term *the bush* is gently chided. This was the language of insensitive newcomers who could not see the wilderness for trees. Yet why should the term *wilderness* supersede *the bush*? The latter has the merit of being a linguistic adaptation: a derivation of the Dutch term *bosch*, it denotes in colonial idiom country that could never be described as 'park' or 'wood'. In Australia, just about any place that is not a city might be classified as bush. 'Wilderness', by contrast, is a word laden with old-world symbolism, a foreign import if ever there was one. The etymology of the term brings associations that the makers of *The Edge* may not enjoy. Jerome Rothenberg says of wilderness that '"Wildness" and "be*wild*erment" are its cognates', and behind them lie '"wold" or "*wood*land," which was also Middle English jive for "madness", "wildness of the mind"'.[10] The American writer John Brinckerhoff Jackson has argued that 'wilderness' is closely connected with the term *forest* which arrived in England with the Norman Conquest and the rage for hunting game:

> Wilderness thus became the domain of the nobility, an environment where they alone could develop and display a number of aristocratic qualities. Friction arose between the peasants—inhabitants of open, unobstructed outdoor spaces—and the noble occupants of the forest, and that friction persisted as long as the peasant felt excluded from a portion of the landscape that he believed was his by right of heritage.[11]

Several salient points can be drawn from Jackson's analysis. At one level he is pointing to a substantial tradition in which 'wilderness' has functioned as a key term in legitimising or *naturalising* territorial dispute. This process of 'naturalisation' is actually a distinct form of intervention. Occurring in places where the erstwhile inhabitants have been removed, the wilderness area is managed in such a way that it conforms to a preconceived notion of untrammelled nature. An insight to the preconceptions underlying 'wilderness values' can be gleaned from these comments by Dr J. Mosley of the Australian Conservation Foundation which date from 1965:

> If the country within the reserve is to invite the visitor to wander where he will and present a challenge to route-finding skills, it must be kept as wild as possible. The landscape should exude an atmosphere of countless freedom. Any attempt to influence movement is clearly incompatible and these areas should be kept trackless, hutless and bridgeless.[12]

That Mosley's nostalgia for an extensive, uninhabited tract of land has dangerous precedents is discussed most tellingly in the critique of wilderness advanced by Marcia Langton, an Aboriginal anthropologist. Langton has identified the veneration of wilderness as an extension of the doctrine *terra nullius*, the assumption that the indigenous occupants of Australia had no legal tenure of the land on which they lived, which was declared legally invalid by the High Court of Australia in its Mabo judgement of 1992. As Langton describes it, 'Where Aboriginal people had been brought to the brink of annihilation, their former territories were recast as "wilderness."'[13]

This view is shared by many Aboriginal people. Deborah Bird Rose, a non-indigenous anthropologist, describes how, when travelling in the Northern Territory with Daly Pulkara, a traditional owner, she and Pulkara stopped to look at 'spectacular erosion' in the Victoria River District. Pulkara drew a distinction between the 'quiet country—the country in which all the care of generations of people is evident' and 'the wild': 'a place where the life of the country was falling down into the gullies and washing away with the rains'.[14] For many Aboriginal people, wilderness offers no cause for fond nostalgia. Rather, it represents a tract of land without custodians. The intense pain of finding his country bereft of occupants was movingly described by Jimmie Barker when, in the 1960s, he returned to the long-abandoned camping ground on the Culgoa River in New South Wales where he had lived with his mother's people, speakers of the Maruwari language, half a century before. 'I went around to the old, familiar spots, standing here and there, thinking of the times when all was laughter. Now so silent. I could not but shed a tear in memory of the past.'[15]

2

LOOKING

OUT

I HAVE MOVED, rapidly perhaps, from Blaxland's interest in a false horizon to the images of wilderness being projected in *The Edge*. Such contrasts, which juxtapose themselves with the forcefulness of a film-maker's edit, mock the historian's contrivance of chronological order. To wander the country, to enter the archive, is to encounter an archaeology deliciously entangled. As Walter Benjamin once put it, the past 'can be seized only as an image'.[16] This is what strikes me as I approach the landscape that forms the subject of this book.

This study of the Blue Mountains is a contribution to the growing literature of place and landscape that has given rise to such 'landmark' histories as Simon Schama's *Landscape and Memory* (1995). In Australia, where a fraught history of territorial conquest continues to make its mark on political life, and where the unique qualities of the topography still induce both marvel and bewilderment, the land itself has a troubled primacy. Hence the emergence of notable Australian landscape studies that precede Schama's: works such as Paul Carter's 1987 study of language and cartography in colonial Australia, *The Road to Botany Bay*; Stephen Muecke's collaboration with Paddy Roe and Krim Benterrak, *Reading the Country* (1984); and Eric Rolls' great tribute to the Pilliga forest, *A Million Wild Acres* (1981).

The symbolic potency of land in the Australian experience is re-flected in the readiness with which it provides raw material for the iconography of nationhood, surfacing frequently in attempts at self-definition. Australians are assiduous in acquiring land. A block in the suburbs is almost a necessity, a block in the country a common dream. Yet much of the colonial mythology depicts a land that is dry, harsh, unforgiving and difficult to understand. There is a problem of occupancy. How on earth to make this home?

A book like Schama's, based on the European experience, appears at a time when the idea of a 'cultural landscape' is gaining credence among geographers and historians. This concept, now fundamental in many areas of heritage management, acknowledges that landscape is not the work of unaided nature; it is the outcome of myriad decisions: whether to build, plant, clear, make a track, leave it alone. These decisions are mediated by the images we make of it, the images of other landscapes, other places, the myths or narratives we bring to country. In an influential essay, W. J. T. Mitchell has described landscape as the

IMAGE-MAKING BRINGS
A RITUALISTIC QUALITY
TO THE LANDSCAPE
ENCOUNTER. THIS PHOTO-
GRAPH BY G. A. DRUCE,
TITLED 'TRACK TO LINDA
FALLS', DATES FROM 1912.

31

'"dreamwork" of imperialism', disclosing 'both utopian fantasies of the perfected imperial prospect and fractured images of unresolved ambivalence and unsuppressed resistance'.[17] As the inspiration for an infinitude of inscriptions, as the open-air depository for as many more, the Blue Mountains are a living text. Accepting that the landscape is a dreamscape, a question arises. How to draw a history out of dreams?

~

The photographer Tracey Moffatt cites as a truism about Australia that, no matter how much you try to reinvent yourself, 'your suburb never leaves your system'.[18] My home suburb, a place in north-west Sydney called West Pennant Hills, received its name, as I was taught, from having been a signal station during the infant days of the colony of New South Wales. Our elevated district was visible from both Sydney Town on the shore of Port Jackson and the river settlement of Parramatta to the west. I was told that when the governor travelled between these centres, a distance of fifteen miles, flags would be raised and the message relayed via Pennant Hills that he was on his way. I was taken to Old Government House at Parramatta, a heritage exhibit, and could imagine the scurry of convict wenches making beds and puffing pillows that would break out whenever that sententious pennant had been sighted. They might even have filled the copper for the Governor's Bath-house, an adjoining historic site that I visited and carefully examined.

Perhaps I experienced a vague sense of civic pride at the part played by our locality in these matters of state. But I don't remember it. In the main, the protagonists of our history lessons—explorers, circumnavigators and agriculturalists—seemed no more real than the painted figures cut from cardboard that we inserted in our dioramas. It seems the past was not adequately explained. Somehow it did not ring true. When I heard much later that the name 'Pennant Hills' had nothing to do with pennants or signal stations and was in fact named after the naturalist Thomas Pennant, I was not exactly surprised. In fact, I began to find some meaning in the story, acknowledging there is a truth to myth.

The elevated Hills district of Sydney has left a very particular legacy. My thoughts on history and time find focus in the contrasting views from two vantage points at Thompsons Corner, my local stamping ground. The first, just opposite the school in fact, was Mount Wilberforce Lookout, a sloping park of some hectares that terminated in a patch of weed-infested bushland. Meeting the westerly horizon was the object of the lookout—the pale ribbon of the Blue Mountains. The range was true and untrue to its name. Due to the light or climate and to the vapour exuded by eucalyptus trees (the causes are still debated), the range was invariably blue. Mountains, however, it is not. Geologically, the escarpment is a series of sandstone plateaus. Arthur Phillip, first governor of the colony, had visited the site of West Pennant Hills in 1788, the founding year of settlement, and named the raised basalt summits Carmarthen Mountains. The rest he called the Lansdowne Hills.

Unfortunately for Phillip, these names never stuck. The term *Blue Mountains* emerged from the colonial vernacular, eventually becoming official. While plenty of Aboriginal names for particular features and localities do survive, that of the range as a whole does not seem to have been recorded. So we are landed with the mountainous misnomer which might reflect an awareness that the plateaus—flattish up top though bounded by cliffs—seem bigger than they are.

This sense of distortion could account for the common misconception that the Blue Mountains are part of the geographical feature known as the Great Dividing Range. In fact, the Blue Mountains run parallel to the Great Divide, which is so named because it separates the coastal flowing rivers from the inland ones. All the precipitation that strikes the Blue Mountains eventually flows to the east. The fact that different sections of the same river system were discovered and named in isolation adds to the confusion. On descending the mountains on the western side, motorists of today cross Coxs River. An hour earlier, on the eastern side, they had crossed it as the Nepean, by then a broad channel indeed. Collecting run-off from the western slopes, the Coxs cuts a crooked horseshoe of a path through the southern Blue Mountains, gathering the waters of major tributaries like the Wollondilly and Kowmung as it goes. In the course of its travels the name changes from Coxs to Warragamba. Then it merges with the Nepean, assuming that name, as it exits the range on the eastern side where it turns northwards to flow along the Blue Mountains' edge. Downstream (further north), another Blue Mountains river, the Grose, joins the system. This is a fairly modest river, which runs through a tremendous east–west gorge that almost cuts the Blue Mountains in half. Having collected the Grose, the Nepean finally becomes the Hawkesbury, a name it manages to keep until it meets the ocean north of Sydney at Broken Bay.

Narratives of exploration form an important part of Australian culture. When I attended primary school in the 1970s, I was taught about the 'riddle' of the mountains: the fact that from 1788 until 1813 they presented, to quote from a marvellous children's book, 'an insurmountable barrier that limited the extent of the settlement at Port Jackson'. Despite numerous attempts 'to cross the dizzy heights and treacherous ravines, each one had been beaten back, the gallant explorers

33

glad to escape with their lives'.[19] For one whole generation, expansion to the west was thwarted.

The distance, the blue haze, the knowledge of those obscure attempts to solve the 'riddle', combined with faint memories of early holidays in a house crammed with ancient furniture and stories from my mother about catching the Blue Mountains steam train, gave the view from Mount Wilberforce an aura of the past.

This could not have been more different than the view from Dame Mary Gilmore Park. Very close to the other, but providing a south-easterly vista, it revealed the highrise skyline of central Sydney. It represented a future, both personal and collective, just as surely as the Blue Mountains symbolised the past.

Both parks are named after people who could easily be described as visionaries. The evangelist William Wilberforce is remembered for leading the campaign against slavery in Britain, while Mary Gilmore, a poet and early champion of Aboriginal rights, has been venerated as a stateswoman of Australian letters. Gilmore lived for almost a century—from 1865 until 1962. Raised near the southern New South Wales town of Goulburn, she spoke with exceptional clarity about events that, although never raised in recitations of the 'First Crossing', were the corollary of opening up Australia as an agricultural centre. She was one of the very few white people of her era who were willing to speak openly about Aboriginal massacre, as is demonstrated in this extraordinary passage:

> I have seen a curl, the curl of a child's hair lying in the hollow of a man's hand, and the man who held it looked from it to the curls on my head. Something was said; because it was beyond me to grasp its full significance I cannot remember its words. But I can reach its meaning now, though the words are not there, nor even the clear tones of the voices. And I feel my father's arm about me, his hand on my head, and I know that he would have seen every black in the country shot before such a curl as that should be taken from my head. Indeed, I know that it was the sight of that curl helped him to endure, in common with all other men of the day, what actually the need of the times compelled.
>
> It was then that the men said in fear; '*If once the blacks procure arms . . .*' So the poor black had to die before arms became his

possession; before women had to be shut in a room fearing the firing of a roof, fearing the failure of their men's limited ammunition, and having for their only comfort the knowledge that, when the time came, enough bullets would be saved for each of them and their children; as I knew they would be saved for my mother and me.[20]

Pennant Hills was a conservative district where the petit-bourgeoisie and nouveau-riche would jostle for quarter-acre blocks, the most desirable of which overlooked the less well-to-do suburbs of Carlingford and Dundas. I therefore found it odd that parks in this locality had been named after an anti-slavery crusader and a socially active poet who had even participated in William Lane's New Australia project, a utopian venture in Paraguay. Social activism and poetry were low on the community agenda in Pennant Hills.

I have since learned that Mount Wilberforce was named by 'the flogging clergyman' Samuel Marsden, a chaplain and magistrate in the early colonial years. Marsden adored the New Zealand Maoris, to whom he preached the Scriptures, and despised the Australian Aborigines with equal passion, explaining their 'weakness' and 'vices', according to Manning Clark, 'as a special punishment . . . for the role of their ancestors in that terrible drama between God and man in the garden of Eden'.[21] George Caley, the botanist, had fiery altercations with Marsden. On one occasion he had Caley's Aboriginal manservant imprisoned for refusing to guide a party of soldiers and settlers who were seeking 'to apprehend the natives by force in the night'. Caley complained to his patron, Sir Joseph Banks, that 'This gentleman [Marsden] said there never would be any good done until there was a clear riddance of the natives.'[22]

Marsden was among seven missionaries who in 1799 were each granted a hundred acres of land in the district of Pennant Hills. Marsden's tract was situated at the top of the hill, which he promptly cleared of forest to make way for crops and sheep. Believing that 'material advance was a proof of the genuineness of his personal sense of salvation', his farming interests developed rapidly, and by 1827 his holdings totalled 3631 acres by grant and 1600 by purchase.[23] He named the Pennant Hills property after William Wilberforce who had supported his admission to Cambridge and persuaded him to accept an assistant chaplaincy in New South Wales. Marsden's tribute to Wilberforce is

35

both ironic and intriguing, for it suggests that he too associated the view of the Blue Mountains with an aspect of his past.

I wonder whether our quarter-acre block, with white house staring blankly at its neighbours, was part of Marsden's original title? This was not the sort of information that anyone seemed to know. Our local myth about the signal station infused the sense of locality. The real events had always happened somewhere else. Despite the obvious reality that our place must have been something before it became a suburban garden, the system of erasure that had transferred Aboriginal land into farm, housing estate and whatever else in between had itself attained invisibility.

With a transition such as the walk I occasionally made between the Wilberforce and Gilmore vistas, time is tentatively crossed. Of course it is not the time travel of H. G. Wells' fantasy, but a perceptual journey—a play of the senses. To me it expresses a fundamental divide in the mental geography of Australia. Ours is predominantly a coastal culture, orientated towards the sea. The inland, the ranges, lie behind us. The land mass broods and beckons behind our backs. The significance of the range, its dialectical opposition to the coast, is humorously but tellingly evoked by David Foster who, like Delia Falconer more recently, made his first novel, *The Pure Land* (1974), about a postcard photographer in the Blue Mountains. In a more recent book, *The Glade within the Grove* (1996), Foster describes the Blue Mountains as 'the sea's antithesis':

> The sea is a continuum in time and space, and we know the sea. And whether we are viewing the Aegean, the North Sea, or the Tasman Sea . . . the sea is a lifeline to us, and a highway, and a familiar face, for any sea is every sea.

Where the sea is familiar, he didactically declares, the Blue Mountains are:

> correspondingly alien, and the well-adjusted Sydney child should aim to spend as much holiday time at Echo Point as on Manly Pier. Not before Manly Beach is uplifted and petrified—rather like one of its own ageing showgirls—can the two be reconciled, except through the agency of *mist*, which, as the sea's Cimmerian benison to its hinterland, confers on these Blue Mountains a sense of familiarity that gladdens and relaxes the hearts of those who dwell here.[24]

~

Wilberforce and Gilmore were starting points. But every lookout leads out onto another. The fenced vantage points within the mountains have names like Echo Point, Sublime Point, Inspiration Point, Princes Rock. You do look outwards—but also downwards. The sandstone cliffs cut a crooked amphitheatre; below, a sea of trees. These valleys, gorges, are the opposite to mountains—a far-fetched antipodean inversion. Instead of gazing or climbing skyward, the path goes down.

This negotiation with the perpendicular epitomises so much of travelling through the range. A byproduct of this is a perennial drama of incident and accident played out on the tourist trails, along the cliffs favoured by rock climbers and within the canyons. But in the early nineteenth century the road itself was rude enough to provide drama aplenty. (Even today it is the biggest killer.) After Blaxland, Lawson and Wentworth made the crossing, George Evans, the surveyor, followed their route and pushed it further, becoming 'completely entangled among the hills' when he hit the Great Divide, but pushing on until he reached the eventual site of Bathurst.[25] In the process he marked the route for a road that Macquarie insisted be suitable for a four-wheel carriage or cart.[26]

ROAD AND RAILWAY PROVIDE EASY ACCESS TO THE CLIFF TOPS. FROM THERE WALKING TRAILS, SOME SCULPTED INTO THE SANDSTONE, ZIGZAG DOWN THE ESCARPMENT. THIS PHOTO BY ERN MCQUILLAN WAS TAKEN IN THE 1960S.

Started in July 1814, it was built by some forty convicts led by a free settler, William Cox, who had been a paymaster in the army.[27] Cox's eye for an orderly column of figures was turned now to the land itself. The surveyor's chain—a measure of sixty-six feet—would beat the country into order. The convicts measured as they built the road, marking trees at the end of each mile. Cox fed them on pickled pork, counting the pieces in each barrel, supervising the flow of tools, animals, provisions, men. An efficient but laconic leader, he recorded setbacks and achievements with dispassion, including a disruption on 26 August when a sergeant died. Cox ordered a coffin, despatched the corpse to Windsor and 'Wrote to the Governor for another sergeant.'[28] Within six months the road was completed. At 101 and a half measured miles from Emu Plains to Bathurst, this was an amazing accomplishment. But Cox had on his side the ultimate inducement: a pardon from servitude at the end of the line. The convict workers were building for their lives.

I doubt that the majority of those who used that hastily built road in the ensuing years were greatly concerned with the aesthetics of scenery. The Blue Mountains were something you crossed. When Thomas Mitchell was called upon to survey the goldfields of New South Wales in 1851, he expressed incredulity at the crowds of miners on the mountain road. In one of the most intriguing images of westward migration, he described 'their overloaded carts, which some pushed from behind, others drew in front harnessed to the shafts'. Some months later he counted seven hundred miners in a day's travel along the western highway, all en route to the diggings.[29]

That the Blue Mountains were a conduit to somewhere else held true for much of the nineteenth century. When George Mackaness published his collection of travellers' accounts from the period 1813 to 1841, he called it *Fourteen Journeys Over the Blue Mountains of New South Wales*. The title reflected the period. All fourteen travelled *across* the range. None went there entirely for its own sake. There were some, like Charles Darwin, who took their time and visited certain scenic points (of which he provided superb descriptions). A nascent tourism can be discerned in the records and activities of naturalists, artists and other gentile travellers.

More typical, however, were people like Elizabeth Hawkins and her family. With her husband, Thomas Hawkins (who was to become the first government storekeeper in Bathurst), she left England in 1821, bringing her aged mother and eight children, the oldest less than twelve. Elizabeth's experience of the landscape during an eighteen-day journey had moments of appreciation. She describes 'small shrubs, many of them blooming with the most delicate flowers, the colours so beautiful that the highest circles in England would prize them'.[30] But there are no grand panoramas. Her narrative, like many of the paintings of the period, is centred firmly on the road.[31] The steepness of the ascent at Lapstone Hill, the stubbornness of the bullocks that refuse to haul, the wagon teetering on rises and bends, her worldly possessions hung in the balance—these are the matters that preoccupy the pioneer mother. Concerning the descent on the western side, notoriously bad until Mitchell safely re-routed it in 1830, the normally loquacious Mrs Hawkins was briefly lost for words.

> I had better stop. I leave it to your imagination. I feel it out of my power to give a proper description of it. I have offered the pen to Hawkins, but he refuses. I tell him I must take a leap from top to bottom, but that he will not allow, so I must write on as well as I can.[32]

From Elizabeth Hawkins' motherly perspective, the sensory world of bellowing bullocks, convict profanities, bugs in the bedding, food and provisions takes precedence over any intimation of the picturesque. Gregory Blaxland, when he took the trouble to describe the view, declared himself 'much disappointed' by scenery now regarded as the finest in the mountains. He complained that it 'has the appearance of having acquired its present form from an earthquake, or some other dreadful convulsion of nature'.[33] These are startling comparisons to the contemporary ethos in which picture-making, mainly in the form of photography, is the dominant ritual of visitation in this part of the world. Certainly, there are intimations of it among early colonial travellers, the people like Darwin who could afford to take their time. Governor Macquarie wrote glowingly of landscape 'as romantically beautiful as can be imagined' when he inspected William Cox's newly finished road with an entourage that included the artist John Lewin.[34] But notions of the picturesque—always subjective—did not come automatically to the Australian landscape. Barron Field, a colonial judge and poet, is another traveller represented in the Mackaness collection.

His name, unpromising for a commentator on landscape, did not disqualify him from recording the most sardonic reflections.

> The King's Tableland is an [*sic*] anarchial and untabular as any His Majesty possesses. The Prince Regent's Glen below it (if it be the glen that I saw) is not very romantic. Jamison's Valley we found by no means a happy one. Blackheath is a wretched misnomer. Not to mention its awful contrast to that beautiful place of that name in England, *heath* it is none. *Black* it may be when the shrubs are burnt as they often are. Pitt's Amphitheatre disappointed me. The hills are thrown together in a monotonous manner, and their clothing is very unpicturesque—a mere sea of harsh trees.

Field's encounter with disordered 'wilderness' was redeemed, however. He saw a green valley from the western extremity of the range, Mount York. The 'earliest burst of Christian transalpine country, as seen from the beginning of this mountain, is very beautiful. The sight of grass again is lovely.'[35] Such expressions of relief and familiarity are common in the narratives of those pioneering days. For Elizabeth Hawkins it was represented by the meeting with a soldier and his wife who had settled near Coxs River. 'She was both clean and civil. Hearing of our coming she had proceured [*sic*] a bucket of milk, and never was anything more enjoyed.'[36]

~

During the nineteenth century the perception of the Blue Mountains in European consciousness underwent a profound shift. From being a barrier, then a conduit to the anticipated riches of the interior (land, gold, bountiful harvests), finally, in the wake of the railway that led to the upper reaches in 1867, the Blue Mountains became an object of beauty and contemplation to a greater populace. So complete is the transition that only a handful of the millions of tourists who now visit the region each year would ever think to extend their trip to the small and dignified city of Bathurst.

THE WESTERN RAILWAY REACHED THE UPPER BLUE MOUNTAINS IN 1867 AND WAS THEN CARRIED ON TO BATHURST. THE STEEP DESCENT ON THE WESTERN SIDE OF THE RANGE NECESSITATED THE FAMOUS ZIG-ZAG RAILWAY, DEPICTED HERE IN VOLUME III OF ANDREW GARRAN'S *Picturesque Atlas of Australasia* (1886).

It is in this transition—an ongoing process whereby the distinctive topography of the Blue Mountains has been mapped as an object of curiosity and desire for visitors from around the globe—that the landscape is established as a field of veneration and a shifting pattern in aesthetic sensibility is demarcated. While expressing much about attitudes to nature in the wake of modernity, that transition says plenty more. It opens up the 'dreamwork' of country, a continuing and collective process of making narratives and representations that contribute to the endless rebuilding and modification of the landscape; representations that reveal perceptions of mortality, divinity, otherness, the place of history, the history of place—and especially the fraught legacy of colonisation.

The distinctive manner in which particular landscapes assume portent at particular times was described by Thomas Hardy, arguably the greatest landscapist in English literature, when he established the rugged heath of Egdon Moor as the scene for *The Return of the Native* (1878). Arguing that ideas of beauty match the temper of their epoch, Hardy suggested that the changes witnessed by his generation (the perennial subject of his novels) had induced a 'recently learnt emotion' that would eventually force a re-definition of beauty in nature. In words now especially brilliant for their power of prognostication, Hardy questioned whether:

> orthodox beauty is not approaching its last quarter. The new Vale of Tempe may be a gaunt waste in Thule: human souls may find themselves in closer and closer harmony with external things wearing a sombreness distasteful to our race when it was young. The time seems near, if it has not actually arrived, when the chastened sublimity of a moor, a sea, or a mountain will be all of nature that is absolutely in keeping with the moods of the more thinking among mankind. And ultimately, to the commonest tourist, spots like Iceland may become what the vineyards and myrtle-gardens of South Europe are to him now; and Heidelberg and Baden be passed unheeded as he hastens from the Alps to the sand-dunes of Scheveningen.[37]

Hardy sets something of the tone for the project here. Through a reading of the land and the mythology it has inspired, a cosmology of the colonial imagination can be charted.

IT WAS 1788, the first year of British occupation, when the governor and his party stood at Pennant Hills and looked towards the blue horizon. Alluring and frustrating, the range—wrapped in its cloak of illusory colour—would serve as both the object and the limit of colonial vision. The tension was latent as convicts, soldiers, a few voluntary settlers began to clear the forest and make their mark.

The majority of the thousand souls who disembarked from the British fleet had no idea of their position on the globe. Map-making was a hidden art. Hence the growth of an alternative cartography where, for convicts, the blue curtain of the Blue Mountains might represent the threshold between servitude and a better world. Dreams of a utopian settlement beyond the range prompted escapes and disorder. A war of words ensued. Successive governors would emphasise the danger, the impenetrability, of a labyrinthine topography that so often formed the last line of defence for a regime that was, at root, a prison without walls. But I pre-empt my argument. For the moment allow the gaze to rest upon the line. Think of how it figured in crossings both real and projected. Pause, if only for a moment, at Emerson's dictum 'The health of the eye seems to demand a horizon.'

A crucial aspect of Blue Mountains folklore is encapsulated in a 1958 comic-strip rendition by Arthur Hudson of the 'First Crossing'. Governor Macquarie gazes anxiously at the mountains through an open window and opines to Captain Antill by his side, 'We've got to cross them I tell you.' The colony, the caption explains, is seemingly 'doomed' for 'although more people arrived every year, the vast Pacific hemmed them in on one side and the mysterious, unconquered mountains on the other'.[38] This is very much the tale I remember from the 1970s. The colony was stretched like a membrane to the point of bursting.

It is sobering to realise that the colony numbered just 13 116 people in 1813, the year of the Blaxland journey.[39] Even by the standards of the period, the Sydney Basin could hardly have been 'full' since between 1812 and 1821 a further 228 000 acres on the Cumberland Plain were issued to settlers. The problem that beset those graziers who searched for greener pastures was a combination of drought, pestilence and mismanagement, to which can be added an obsessive reliance on beef. The geographer T. M. Perry stated it economically when he wrote that the 'need was not for land, but grass'.[40] While true so far as it goes,

THE IDEA THAT SYDNEY IN 1813 WAS PACKED TO THE POINT OF BURSTING HAS CONTRIBUTED TO THE MYTH OF A 'FIRST CROSSING' OF THE MOUNTAINS. ARTHUR HUDSON'S COMIC STRIP DEPICTION DATES FROM 1958. THE STORY WAS STILL CURRENT WHEN I ATTENDED PRIMARY SCHOOL IN THE 1970S.

this statement ignores the fact that the connection between land and capital was already well established in the colony. Obtaining land was often the means to rapid, sometimes instantaneous, acquisition of wealth.

Today a population of four million is sprawled none too closely across the Sydney Basin—and it continues to grow. The social memory of the three explorers travelling westward, responding to collective need and transforming the landlocked colony into a nation-in-embryo, must be read against Macquarie's coolness towards the Blaxland expedition, his refusal to lend the artificial horizon. As Blaxland explained in a letter of lamentation to Sir Joseph Banks, the governor's conduct before and after the 1813 journey had been 'perfectly inexplicable'. Blaxland complained that both the pass down the Blue Mountains and the river on the western side had been named after the road-builder William Cox, 'who only followed our steps'.[41] He was seriously concerned that posterity might not know of his contribution. In the governor he had discerned 'a reservedness in his manner which I could not account for'.[42]

The tension between grazier and governor is evidence of the visions and expectations that so often stood in conflict as they looked towards the west. It was anything but a uniform view. The desire of men like Blaxland, Lawson and Wentworth to further their already generous holdings suggests a point of origin for the idea of a membrane bursting, of settlers and livestock surging west. Compare it, however, with Macquarie's order upon completion of Cox's road: 'no person, whether Civil or Military, shall attempt to travel over the Blue Mountains, without having previously applied for and obtained permission in the prescribed form'.[43] Macquarie, in keeping with this vision of a controlled economy of movement, a regulated landscape (typified by the Georgian architecture and town planning of his years in office), voiced to the Earl of Bathurst the sanguine hope that the western district bearing his lordship's name should be limited to fifty 'Sober, Industrious Men, with Small Families' each to be granted between fifty and a hundred acres.[44]

The historian Heather Goodall has written of the nostalgic longing for the world of the yeoman farmer, 'a largely imaginary pre-industrial Britain', that became widespread in England in the wake of the French Revolution. Many of Australia's rulers thought of the colonies becoming what Britain had supposedly been: a myriad of 'interlocked freehold cultivated farms, all embedded within a network of church and administrative structures.'[45]

Macquarie, as a proponent of this vision, found little to admire in the Blaxlands. While Gregory and his older brother-cum-business

THESE ADVENTURERS WERE MOVED TO RE-ENACT THE 'FIRST CROSSING' IN 1951, CELEBRATING AN UNRELATED ANNIVERSARY—THE FIFTIETH YEAR OF AUSTRALIAN FEDERATION. THEY ATTRACTED ENORMOUS CROWDS BY TRAMPING ACROSS THE BLUE MOUNTAINS, PARADING THROUGH TOWNSHIPS AND VISITING SACRED NATIONAL SITES (INCLUDING THE CORRIDOR OF OAKS AT FAULCONBRIDGE WHERE EVERY AUSTRALIAN PRIME MINISTER PLANTS A TREE).

GAZING TOWARDS THE
WEST, THESE BUSTS OF
BLAXLAND, LAWSON
AND WENTWORTH WERE
INSTALLED AT MOUNT
YORK TO CELEBRATE
THE EXPLORERS'
ACHIEVEMENT IN
CROSSING THE BLUE
MOUNTAINS.

46

partner, John, made a killing with their farms, stockyards and butcheries, the governor was determined to encourage a colonial agriculture based on the cultivation of grain. Macquarie's arrival in 1810 had been preceded by serious floods on the Hawkesbury River which resulted in a scarcity of wheat. Macquarie utterly deplored the Blaxlands for eschewing wheat in favour of land-hogging beasts. Instead of 'setting a good example of an improved stile [sic] of farming and agriculture, they have turned their whole attention to the lazy object of rearing of cattle', he complained to the Earl of Liverpool.[46] Elsewhere Macquarie described the brothers as 'lazy discontented Drones'.[47]

To understand Macquarie's tone and his probable suspicion of Blaxland's endeavour to cross the Blue Mountains—a self-initiated and financed enterprise—it is necessary to review the exceptional circumstances that preceded Gregory's arrival in Sydney in 1806. The Blaxlands were completely unlike the numerous and often penniless emigrants who headed to the colonies to make their fortune. The family had been affluent landholders in the south of England for many generations. The brothers' assets upon John's departure in 1806 amounted to £30 000.[48] While their interest in New South Wales was cultivated by Banks, a personal friend, it has been said that John Blaxland's decision to emigrate was made 'because his farm resources, even when swollen by wartime prices, were inadequate for his pretensions'.[49] Gregory and John secured an exclusive agreement with the imperial government whereby land, convict labour and free passages to Sydney were issued in return for agricultural investment in the colony. It being 'deemed expedient', in the opinion of Viscount Castlereagh, 'to encourage a certain number of Settlers in New South Wales of responsibility and Capital, who may set useful Examples of Industry and Cultivation from their property and Education',[50] the home government promised John Blaxland some 8000 acres if he invested an amount of £6000.[51] The agreement with Gregory was proportionate: 4000 acres in return for a £3000 investment.[52] To Macquarie these favours went 'far beyond what any other persons have been ever indulged with'.[53]

Despite these favourable conditions (at a time when grants to ex-convicts, the 'yeoman farmers', rarely exceeded 100 acres), neither brother could substantiate his investment. There are strong grounds to suspect that they never committed the promised sum. This accounting failure was part of a pattern in which relations between the Blaxlands and the colonial administration were often strained. They had fallen out with Governor Bligh who alleged that John 'was so indiscreet . . . as to unite with his brother and write to me for permission to carry on a distilling'—a practice which, though illegal, Blaxland thought Bligh might like to join as 'part of the firm as he was pleased to term it'.[54] Of course, Bligh's opposition to the traffic in spirits being conducted by the colony's officers, the so called 'Rum Corps', was a major contribution to his ultimate undoing in New South Wales. Having narrowly survived Fletcher Christian's mutiny on the *Bounty*, Bligh suffered another deposing at the hands of Major George Johnston who led the military coup of January 1808, an action that the Blaxlands vigorously supported.

Surviving the aftermath of the rebellion, the Blaxlands got everything promised in their letter of agreement signed in London, though Macquarie issued the land grants through gritted teeth, emphasising to Liverpool, the minister then responsible for New South Wales, the imprudence of encouraging 'this description of persons called *Gentlemen Settlers* by extraordinary concessions', who had nonetheless become 'the most discontented unreasonable and troublesome persons in the whole country'.[55] Gregory had been granted 2000 acres known as Mersey Farm, another 2000 called Lee Home, and a further 280 acres

that he called Villiers Farm. Blaxland represents something of a prototype
for the large-scale colonial grazier, his fortune based on an expanding
network of properties seized from Aboriginal owners without recompense. The desire to expand further inspired some earlier missions along
the Warragamba River. On one occasion he had been accompanied
by 'two natives' who:

> proved but of little use; which determined me not to take them again
> on my more distant expedition. Very little information can be
> obtained from any tribe out of their own district, which is seldom
> more than about thirty miles square.[56]

It is inconceivable that Aboriginal knowledge would have been so
limited. Later travellers, such as Mitchell, received enormous assistance
from Aboriginal guides on journeys spanning thousands of kilometres. In
Blaxland's case it is overwhelmingly evident, from the manner in which
he lived and travelled, that he had neither the diplomatic skills nor
cultural awareness to establish a relationship and negotiate appropriate
terms of employment with an indigenous guide (typically a man) who
was both willing and qualified to lead a journey through the country of
his neighbours. Despite various opportunities, the Blaxland team refused
to engage with the Aboriginal people they saw and heard during the
1813 journey.

That Blaxland found his 'two natives' unhelpful by no means
proves their ignorance of the country. It is more likely to have been a
deliberate refusal to share the knowledge. Blaxland is praised for his
perspicacity in following ridge lines instead of rivers (always easier in
sandstone country). In so doing he avoided the most densely populated
parts of the mountains—river valleys such as the Warragamba that were
fertile and full of wildlife, which expeditions before Blaxland's had
'proved' uncrossable. In truth, the Gundungurra people had few reasons
to support—and very good reasons to hinder—an incursion into the
mountains and the land beyond.

Blaxland's partners on the 1813 journey both had interest in land.
Lieutenant William Lawson had trained as a surveyor in England, entered
the New South Wales Corps as an ensign and arrived in Sydney in 1800.
His agricultural interests had started modestly in 1807 when he bought
a small farm between Sydney and Parramatta where he kept six horses,

three bulls and fourteen cows. He too supported Bligh's overthrow and was appointed aide-de-camp to Major Johnston (the self-appointed lieutenant-governor), a position that was accompanied by a considerable rise in fortune. He was granted 500 acres at Prospect, the eventual site of his forty-room mansion, Veteran Hall.[57]

The third member of the expedition was certainly the most remarkable. He was the son of the surgeon D'Arcy Wentworth, of noble Irish stock. It is noted in no less a source than the *Australian Dictionary of Biography*, which provides entertaining reading on both father and son, that the older Wentworth 'proved as popular with the female sex as he was asserted to be with general company'.[58] Travelling as a surgeon on a convict transport, D'Arcy became involved with one Catherine Crowley, transported from England for stealing 'wearing apparell', by whom he sired William Charles, the first of the three sons he acknowledged. They reached Sydney in 1790. William Wentworth's later, highly illustrious career as a grazier, barrister, politician, co-founder of Sydney University, writer, publisher, nationalist and propagandist for Australian immigration —a sort of demagogic all-rounder—did most for the rise of the 'First Crossing' as a metaphor for nationhood and has sometimes prompted the belief that he was its leader.

At twenty-three years of age, Wentworth was actually the most junior member of the expedition. In 1813 he was at something of a loose end in Sydney, having returned there after schooling in England. His father, a remarkable man in his own right, had worked as principal surgeon in the colony, living with Crowley as his de facto wife. For this he was shunned by colonial society where the distinction between convicted and 'free' was fundamental. Indeed, it was sometimes assumed that D'Arcy had himself been a convict, a claim that is almost true. As William learnt later in life—to his absolute mortification—D'Arcy had been tried four times in England for highway robbery, although each time he had been acquitted. With the possibility of further charges pending, he had decided on a voluntary rather than a forced expatriation to New South Wales where he was to hold, among other official positions, the post of superintendent of police.[59]

In his lengthy poem *Australasia* (1823), William Wentworth referred to the shame of convict origins, anticipating a moment when 'this early blot,/Amid thy growing honors, be forgot'.[60] Publishing titles such as

Australasia and *A Statistical, Historical and Political Description of the Colony of New South Wales* (1819) which encouraged emigration to Australia over America, Wentworth dominated the Australian scene as an individual both immensely talented and strangely flawed. The distinction between his own self and the nation he anticipated seems ill-defined. Here was a character in whom collective anxieties were deeply inscribed in his own experience. Though slighted by the colonial elite, Wentworth 'was no leveller, no democrat. Men must be free, but free to rise—and his own family especially'. Macquarie reacted against the ostracism suffered by the Wentworths, evidently regarding this young man, a convict's son educated in England, as exactly the kind of 'native Australian' who deserved encouragement. He appointed him acting provost-marshal in 1811 and allowed him a land grant of 1750 acres on the Nepean River.[61]

~

Blaxland, Lawson and Wentworth are invariably remembered as a trinity: a symbolically laden number in Christian theology, and one that appears in other aspects of the mythological construction of the Blue Mountains. To Henry Kendall, who would celebrate the trio in his jingoistic poem 'Blue Mountains Pioneers', they became the 'dauntless three'.[62] They were not, however, a threesome at all, for the party included four servants, five dogs, and four horses. This was a collaboration between animals and men. Among the latter was James Burns, selected by Blaxland, who was probably key to their success. While it is traditional to imagine the explorers venturing into virgin country, their own journals indicate the extent to which, as they traversed the range in May 1813, they were entering an inhabited realm. This was brought home on the third day of the month-long return journey. Entering a large tract of 'forest land, rather hilly', they 'found a track marked by an European by cutting the bark of the trees. Several native huts presented themselves at different places'.[63] By this date the colony was anything but sharp in demarcation. There were convicts, escaped or emancipated, and free settlers too, who chose to live beyond the bounds of settlement, some joining the blacks. By profession a hunter of kangaroos, James Burns was one of those people who had lived out on the edge. Although his contribution is played down by

EUGENE STOCKTON, AN
ARCHAEOLOGIST AND
ROMAN CATHOLIC PRIEST,
PUBLISHED THIS MAP
SHOWING ABORIGINAL
ARCHAEOLOGICAL SITES
IN HIS BOOK *Blue
Mountains Dreaming*
(1993). SHOWING
EVIDENCE OF ABORIGINAL
HABITATION ALONG THE
MAIN EAST–WEST ROUTE,
IT BELIES THE CONCEIT
THAT ABORIGINES DID
NOT CROSS THE RANGE.
MORE THAN A HUNDRED
ADDITIONAL SITES HAVE
BEEN IDENTIFIED SINCE
THE BOOK WAS
PUBLISHED.

Blaxland and the others, its significance is revealed in the records of
D'Arcy Wentworth's police fund. Burns was the recipient of a £10
payment 'in remuneration for his services as a guide to the Party who
lately crossed the Western Mountains'.[64]

In acknowledging the value of Burns' assistance or the reality, a
platitude really, that the main east–west ridge through the mountains has,
for millennia, been an Aboriginal route (a network of art and camping

sites confirm what would logically be inferred[65]), we encounter the fullness with which this historical event has entered the domain of myth.

~

In an inspirational study of mythical knowledge, Ernst Cassirer argued that: 'knowledge does not master myth by banishing it from its confines. Rather, knowledge can truly conquer only what it has previously understood in its own specific meaning and essence.' Cassirer was at pains to emphasise that myth was not the antithesis but 'the actual point of departure for all science, the immediacy from which it starts.'[66] Just as it would be jaundiced, indeed 'unscientific', for a historian of science to sever chemistry from its alchemical roots, we would be stripping history of its flesh, the very stuff that gives it life and interest, if we were to ignore the mythical and linguistic associations that accompany an act as apparently simple as pouring mercury into an artificial horizon.

Hence, in seeking to re-tell the most hackneyed event in Australian history—the 1813 crossing of the Blue Mountains—I am endeavouring not to break from historical events but rather to show how myth and history are constantly entwined. Of interest is every factual detail that might be recovered: the landholdings of the explorers; the role of Burns; the tiff with Macquarie. Each has its place. Yet history, like science, cannot ignore its roots in the storytelling tradition, cannot ignore the ways in which myth is the stuff of history, providing the impetus for historical events.

For Nietzsche the relationship between myth and history was fraught with danger—but history, not myth, was the corrupting influence. He regarded myth as a vital and powerful force—integral to the creative aspirations of humankind—but warned how, in the process of becoming history, it petrifies and crumbles: 'one begins nervously defending the veracity of myths, at the same time resisting their continuing life and growth'. The narrative construction of the 'First Crossing' is consistent with Nietzsche's comments. He claimed that it is 'the lot of all myths to creep gradually into the confines of a supposedly historical reality, and to be treated by some later age as unique fact with claims to historical truth.'[67]

In re-visiting the myth and history of the Blaxland crossing, it is worth contemplating the view to the horizon once again. This enables us to consider the mythical dimensions that have been obscured as a monocular account of the crossing has been eroded ever deeper into the historical landscape. We might think about the act of looking west in terms of its symbolic richness: how an orientation aligned with the setting sun would acquire its own cosmic grandiosity, establishing a 'psycho-geography' (to use the terminology of Allen S. Weiss[68]) in which the moment of sunset—the visible merging of solar orb and terrestrial horizon—marked the line of colonial advance. In this westward path, delineated by the setting sun and the inevitable advent of night, there are intimations of the melancholy that still flavours the Blue Mountains—what the poet and librarian John Low has called 'the dark side of the Mountains'.[69]

The history of suicide from scenic lookouts, or more distant experiences where convict dissidents were publicly executed in sight of the range (a futile attempt at preventing further escapes), serves to affirm this aura of mortality. But the westward view is also redolent with associations that are different, indeed opposite, to the necessity of death. Connotations of transcendence are suggested by the sun itself. The Christian deity retained some echo of Apollo, the sun god of the Greeks. Add to this the symbolism of the horizon, meeting place of earth and sun, which marks the limit of the human gaze yet has long been paradoxically regarded as a point of infinitude. We still honour the convention when we focus a camera on a distant object, turning the lens to 'infinity'.

The sense of infinitude beyond the horizon materially affected a multitude of lives as the conquest of the west unfolded. Here was a powerful metaphor that influenced nearly all the actors in this story. Macquarie called the country 'West-more-land' while, Blaxland wrote of the 'unlimited pasturage' that they discovered.[70] The faith in endless space beyond the horizon was seemingly unbounded. Wentworth, when he returned again to England to study law, wrote to Lord Bathurst offering to explore the Australian continent from the eastern to the western coast. Declaring 'that there is no mean betwixt success and death', he offered to carry out this perilous mission for no more recompense than a grant of land—'a speck out of the almost endless millions of acres' he would have to traverse.[71]

Such a vast complex of associations is opened up by the vista to that blue horizon. It stands as both object and metaphor—itself a lens that magnifies, distorts, filters; always emphasising the lie of the land and the play of the mind. This quality is encapsulated in a watercolour by Major James Wallis who painted *Hawkesbury and Blue Mountains, from Windsor* in 1815, two years after the Blaxland expedition.[72] As explained in an inscription on the painting, this view of two gentlemen on a hill, who gaze out to river and range, was drafted with a *camera lucida*. This means that Wallis employed the prismatic drafting instrument, one of the precursors of the modern camera, which attracted much interest from optical designers in the course of the nineteenth century. As John Hammond explains, it was tricky to use, the draughtsman's eye needing to be:

> placed so that the centre of the pupil was directly above the edge of the prism. A reflection of the object or view was seen by half of the eye and the pencil point by the other half. As the images fused on the retina it was possible to trace the outline of the reflection.[73]

I can think of no image that expresses more succinctly the fusion of art, technology and perception that would make the Blue Mountains in every sense an artificial horizon.

~

54

Gregory Blaxland never took up his thousand acres west of the Blue Mountains. Instead he exchanged it for land south of Sydney which was subsequently sold.[74] Macquarie obstructed Blaxland's plans for expansion, refusing to allow him to take his stock into the interior.[75] Their feud continued and Blaxland did everything in his power to erode Macquarie's administration.

As a hero of the 'First Crossing', Blaxland was the dourest of the three explorers. The historian Jill Conway described him thus:

> Always a man of moody and mercurial character, Blaxland devoted his colonial activities almost entirely to the pursuit of his economic interests, and his diaries do not suggest great attachment to the colonial environment beyond what was suggested by the hope of personal gain.[76]

His description of the 1813 journey, the most comprehensive to be handed down, is distinguished by the distance on its subject, by its tone of removed austerity that makes this journey, of all journeys, such a disturbing choice for elevation to national myth. In a gesture uncommon in journals of exploration, Blaxland adopted the style of the memorialist and wrote entirely in the third person. Never, in the body of his text, is there acknowledgment that *I, Gregory Blaxland, am a* participant *in these proceedings*.[77] The published version of 1823, now a bibliographical curiosity of enormous value, corrects a few details here and there and scales down immoderate estimates of height, but it repeats a mistake in the original where, in referring to a *tract* of country, Blaxland uses the spelling *track*.

Perhaps one can make too much of these simple slips of pen or tongue. Or maybe not. Blaxland's preference for 'track' over 'tract' suggests a leaning towards the white page, an expanse of blankness, where—although surrounded by the palimpsest of country—he would *make* a mark, not *read* one. He avoided contact with Aborigines at all stages of the expedition. Never would he seek a native name. And despite the abundance of sights, smells and sounds that would inevitably present themselves on such a journey, he completed the journal with the following recollection:

> they heard a confused noise arising from the eastern settlements below, which, after having been so long accustomed to the death-like stillness of the interior, had a very striking effect.[78]

It is difficult to imagine a lack of sound as the explorers ventured into the range in May 1813, climbing the steep and forested escarpment, the domain of bell-birds and lyre-birds, an acoustic so different from that of the plain below. It is sometimes surmised that the party had direct Aboriginal guidance or that they followed a traditional track. The journal suggests, however, that neither is strictly true. Burns, a white man, was evidently the principal guide, though he gets scant credit in the journal. The party frequently met with impenetrable scrub. Blaxland makes much of the labour with which

> they proceeded to cut a path through the thick brush-wood, on what they considered as the main ridge of the mountain, between the Western River and the River Grose; keeping the heads of the gulleys, which were supposed to empty themselves into the Western River on their left hand, and into the River Grose on their right...They now began to mark their track by cutting the bark of the trees on two sides.

55

Following this principle, keeping to the ridge, they probably travelled much of the way along a route parallel to that favoured by Aboriginal travellers. It is also possible that Aborigines, whose movement would have been dispersed—burning, hunting and foraging being integral to their way of walking—left no *singular* path that the explorers could follow with their horses.

On 20 May, the tenth night of the journey, Blaxland relates how:

> the dogs ran off, and barked violently. At the same time, something was distinctly heard to run through the brush-wood, which they supposed to be one of the horses got loose, but they had reason to believe afterwards, that they had been in great danger; that the natives had followed their track, and advanced on them in the night, intending to have speared them by the light of their fire, but that the dogs drove them off.

This is the climate of suspicion that distinguished the journey as they cut their trail, marked blazes on trees and treated as *tabula rasa* this land already inscribed. One day 'they heard a native chopping wood very near them'. Then they saw 'the fires of the Natives' in the valley below, then others 'more in their direct course'. Within three weeks they had crossed the range, descended to a grassy meadow by a river and reached the terminal point of their mission: an Aboriginal camp, very recently abandoned, where fires still smouldered. The ground was strewn with flowers of the 'honey suckle Tree' from which the 'natives' had sucked the nectar. The party's provisions were by now almost exhausted and clothes and shoes were worn. All were suffering from complaints of the bowel. On the first day of June they turned for home. Macquarie marked their accomplishment by naming a hump-shaped hill near Coxs River 'Mount Blaxland' and its two adjoining peaks the 'Lawson Sugarloaf' and the 'Wentworth Sugarloaf'. 'They are mere hummocks—lumps of sugar,' wrote Barron Field in his imperious style. Since Blaxland, Lawson and Wentworth were 'exclusively entitled to the merit of exploring this pass over the barrier mountains of the colony', they should 'have been more substantially rewarded, than by a mere grant of one thousand acres each . . . and the sugar-plum of a name'.[79]

~

The western land of barking dogs, thudding axes, running river, admirable meadows, smouldering fires and flowers of sustenance was translated in memory to a place of 'death-like stillness'. The governor may have denied Gregory Blaxland the artificial horizon, yet he carried it with him, perfected it in his mind, just as he replaced the palimpsest of country with a blank slate on which to inscribe his unique and uniform track. In the liquescent surface of his mind's eye, Blaxland reflected his own desire. Dangers and advantages attend this process. Despite the material benefit of clearing away and marking anew, the Blaxland experience opens up a most fundamental question. To what extent can life proceed when it fails so categorically to open itself to the ways of an other? The least remembered detail of our well-remembered traveller is the manner of his passing. Gregory Blaxland committed suicide in 1853.

57

Two Aboriginal figures inhabit the foreground of this early painting of Sydney Harbour with the Blue Mountains in the distance. Although unsigned, it is attributed to the surveyor George Evans. In late 1813 Evans transcended the horizon he had previously painted. Following the blazes of Blaxland and his party, he led the team that established the route for a road to Bathurst.

Passage Two

SHADES OF BLUE

So bewildering were the maze's paths that even Daedalus could scarcely find his way back to the entrance.

PENELELOPE REED DOOB, *The Idea of the Labyrinth*, 1990

OVERTURE

IN THE MID to late 1990s, the popular lookout at Echo Point, Katoomba, near the Three Sisters, was regularly attended by an Aboriginal busker named Goomblar Wylo (Paul Shillingsworth) who painted himself with ochre, dressed in a loin cloth and played didgeridoo. For a few coins he would allow himself to be photographed in front of the sublime vista. One day I spoke to him about his activities. At one level, he explained, this was just a way of making a living. But Goomblar was also convinced of the political import of what he was doing. Although he makes no personal claim to the country of the Blue Mountains (he originates from the far north-west of New South Wales), he considers his performance a political act which reminds visitors of the area's original occupation.

Goomblar Wylo's decision to assume tribal dress and perform in the foreground of the landscape provides a contemporary perspective on a range of issues. They are addressed here in the form of three essays, two of which concern topographical scenes of the Blue Mountains: an 1809 watercolour attributed to George Evans, where the range is visible from Sydney; and a sequence of views of Wentworth Falls by Eugène von Guérard originating from a visit to the site in 1859.

Like Thomas Mitchell's view from Jellore, the Evans and von Guérard paintings feature Aboriginal figures in the foreground. The

IN THE 1990S GOOMBLAR (AKA PAUL SHILLINGSWORTH) WOULD ASSUME TRIBAL COSTUME AND PERFORM DIDGERIDOO AT ECHO POINT NEAR THE THREE SISTERS. HIS DESIRE TO ESTABLISH AN ABORIGINAL PRESENCE AT THIS WELL-KNOWN TOURIST HAUNT RESONATES WITH THE WORKS OF NINETEENTH-CENTURY LANDSCAPE PAINTERS WHO PLACED ABORIGINAL FIGURES IN THE FOREGROUND OF THEIR COMPOSITIONS.

Goomblar Dreaming

first essay considers the relationship between this human presence and the terrestrial horizon. The second examines the varied depiction of Aboriginal people in von Guérard's landscape painting and how the increasing frailty of his Aboriginal figures responded to the dispossession he witnessed. In his major Wentworth Falls painting of 1862, one of his last to depict an indigenous person, the Aboriginal man is being menaced by a snake at the edge of a cliff. Exploring the nuances of this scenario and how they reverberate in von Guérard's later versions of the view, these studies from visual records establish the ground for an exploration of the labyrinth as myth and metaphor which forms the third component of this passage.

61

I

TOWARDS

THE

HORIZON

WATERCOLOUR WAS A favoured medium among early colonial artists to whom we are indebted for the extraordinarily thorough visual record of the early years of Australian settlement. I have long been fascinated by an early depiction of the vista from Sydney to the Blue Mountains, a painting by George Evans. He was the government surveyor who followed the blazes of Blaxland and company, extending their line to the site of Bathurst. It was some years earlier, possibly in 1809, that he painted the blue horizon.[1]

There are two very similar versions of this painting, both held by the Mitchell Library in Sydney. Richard Neville, the pictorial librarian, laid them flat on a storage cabinet for me to view. One painting, signed by Evans, is grossly faded to a dull tan. The second, unsigned, but attributed to him on the basis of compositional and stylistic similarities to the other, is utterly pristine. The colour is sensuous, still moist, it seems, on the fibrous surface of wove paper. Moving between this and the degraded version, the irony is palpable. Light is the condition of vision and therefore painting—but also the agent of corruption. The watercolour, cocooned in darkness and thus deprived of the audience necessary to complete it, is the version that survives intact, the colour undiluted. Ultimately, I can feel only gratitude that both are extant, expressing in their difference the process of time's ferment and the arbitrary manner in which objects survive or don't survive to fashion our perception of the past.

The Evans views were 'taken' (the term predates the camera) from the southern head of Sydney Harbour—the district east of the settlement that William Wentworth eventually acquired and called Vaucluse. The foreground is a grassy bank, green leaning towards charcoal in its hue, with the harbour, enclosed and lake-like, dappled by uneven light in differing shades of blue. Sydney is whitewashed, gleaming in the distance; windmills are visible on the outskirts of town. So are the gallows on Pinchgut Island. Beyond the settlement, the hinterland is a paler green, and then at last the blueness of the range. Two Aboriginal figures in the right foreground—one seated, the other standing—attend to their modest fire. They seem oblivious to everything beyond.

Most art scholars agree that the mid-ground is the intended focus in topographical landscapes. As Gordon Bull explains, 'the viewer's eye is at first carried rapidly from an insignificant foreground space to the horizon; that journey is then repeated more slowly to take in the details of the midground'.[2] Evans' adoption of a viewpoint that placed Sydney Harbour in the mid-ground, flanked at the rear by the settlement, is predictable. British influence, the result of maritime supremacy, is established as the predominant sphere of interest in the landscape. The foreground and horizon are the peripheral elements of the painting. They tell different stories though they are intertwined.

~

From parks, houses and offices, from just about any elevated point in Sydney, you can see the Blue Mountains. Phillip and his officers viewed them from Pennant Hills when they gave the names Carmarthen Mountains and Lansdowne Hills. Consistently visible, they were the inspiration for escape and speculative explorations. But the mountains seem to have evaded pictorial representation until William Westall, an artist on the *Investigator*, sketched them in pencil in 1802. Two years later (by then in Asia), he pulled out his brushes to produce in watercolour a topographical scene that extends to the blue horizon. Both Westall and Evans depicted harbour and township and both had Aborigines in the foreground (unlike Westall's original drawing which is inhabited only by native vegetation). Evans painted dark, fairly featureless individuals, while Westall showed a romantic couple, Grecian in build, their gaze meeting across a clearing.[3] The timing of Westall's works coincides with two of the more extensive Blue Mountains explorations: Barrallier's of 1802 and Caley's of 1804. The latter was in part a scientific mission—carried out by Banks' collector of specimens. As European knowledge was extended, the Blue Mountains found their entree into the world of paint.

The tardiness with which a view, apparent on a daily basis, should enter the realm of pictorial representation is testimony to the way in which an understanding of the horizon—and thus the sense of New South Wales as a visual environment—was dependent on the scope of colonial aspirations. There was a considerable gulf between what was visible in the phenomenal world and what should be *made visible* in a work of art. It is conceivable that an unstated prohibition was at work here, preventing the depiction of a possible destination for escapees.

Viewed sequentially, the pictorial record of the colony can be likened to a round of golf in which the strokes lengthen rather than

THE WESTERN SKYLINE—VISIBLE ALMOST DAILY—TOOK FOURTEEN YEARS TO FIND ITS WAY INTO PICTORIAL REPRESENTATION, DESPITE MUCH ARTISTIC ACTIVITY IN THE COLONY. WILLIAM WESTALL'S SKETCH IS THOUGHT TO BE THE FIRST VIEW OF THE BLUE MOUNTAINS FROM SYDNEY. IT WAS DRAWN IN 1802, THE YEAR HE SAILED WITH MATTHEW FLINDERS TO CIRCUMNAVIGATE AUSTRALIA. WESTALL EVOKED THE 'NOBLE SAVAGE' WHEN HE ADDED ABORIGINES TO THE FOREGROUND OF THE WATERCOLOUR VERSION.

contract as the game progresses. Each view projected a ball or arrow that marked the territory from which the next view would be taken. Early images of the settlement—a watercolour by William Bradley, a drawing by John Hunter—reveal a smattering of huts around the harbour, always taken from the ships themselves. The drawing boards had barely been unpacked. These terms were reversed in the early 1790s, as the cleared land along the foreshores provided access points for eastward vistas of the harbour. The horizon had broadened. This eastern view was especially favoured by Thomas Watling, a convict whose penchant for making likenesses had led to his transportation as a forger. He rarely neglected to include a vessel in his images, and through this emphasis on arrival and departure he suggested the tenuousness of settlement in these early years. That state of ambiguity is suitably expressed in his drawing dated 1793–95, *Sun-Rising—Going out of Port-Jackson Harbour*, where new sunlight on the fledgling settlement illuminates a departing ship. The Union Jack is flapping in the breeze.

The eastward views of Watling and a host of contemporaries marked out the area on South Head where Evans and Westall would take their westward views in the early 1800s. In 1809 John Eyre drew the first panorama of the settlement. By this time, the sense of visual space was becoming increasingly encyclopaedic. When the mountains were crossed and Cox's men completed the road, views back to the settlement, or to the new farmland in the west, would in turn become the objects of desire—the mid-ground of topographical landscapes.

In the preserved version of Evans' painting, Port Jackson ripples blue and lake-like, a watery path along which the eye can tread its way to Sydney Town bathed in light. The hinterland is green, the mountains blue. They appear as they should, it seems, but the Aborigines, perched about the orange flame, are not quite right. The fire emits a greasy smear of smoke which hangs like a veil above the water, refusing to disperse. It was the last thing to be painted into the landscape. As the product of the Aboriginal figures, there's a suggestion that they too are insertions into the scene.

The French artist J. Alphonse Pellion, who sailed with Louis de Freycinet's vessel *L'Urainie*, travelled to the Blue Mountains during their Sydney sojourn in 1819. Pellion left the first identified portraits of Blue Mountains Aborigines. Published in two engravings, they are fairly

The French artist
J. Alphonse Pellion met
and sketched several
Blue Mountains
Aborigines when he
visited Sydney and
environs with Louis
de Freycinet in 1819.
He names the subjects
as Hara-o (left) and
Karadra.

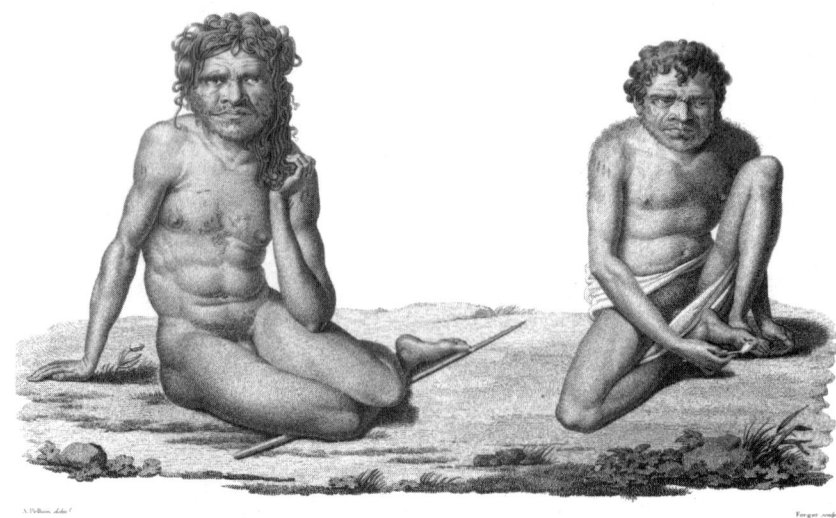

66

sympathetic depictions, with some of the subjects actually named. For this they sit at odds with most of the British productions. While some of the earliest colonial artists—including Thomas Watling and the mysterious figure known only as the Port Jackson Painter—had drafted attentive portraits of Aborigines, this practice declined in the decades after 1800. Aboriginal figures, especially when they appeared in scenes of landscape, rather than portraits, became a form of marginalia, authenticating the exotic location and providing a symbol of 'savagery' against the backdrop of the new 'civilisation'. According to Bernard Smith, they 'become stereotypes' 'and are found in drawing after drawing'.[4] Smith documents a process in which, by 1812, portraiture of Aborigines had disintegrated into a form of caricature, typified by the work of a convict, T. R. Browne, with its grotesque figuration and derogatory titles like Hump-back'd Maria, Long Jack and Pussy Cat.

Of course, there are exceptions to this convention. Thomas Mitchell's portraits come to mind. There are others that have emerged since Bernard Smith published his conclusions in 1960. An album of fine watercolours by Joseph Lycett, returned to Australia in 1972, depicts a varied and always active vision of Aboriginal life and culture—of fishing, hunting, ceremony and song. Sometimes there are traces of settlement in the background, but never are these figures mute witnesses to European invasion.[5] Yet such work is comparatively rare, even in terms of Lycett's own opus. In the vast majority of views being painted, drawn and engraved, the indigenous figures of the foreground are as disconnected from the world as the streaky smoke in Evans' painting.

A most intriguing aspect of so many of these images is their refusal to acknowledge that colonialism affects the world it touches. The emergence of Aborigines as pictorial symbols anticipates (incorrectly) their disappearance. The nostalgia for visualising the wild man, in his loin cloth, leaning on a spear, coincided with the processes of profound transformation that followed the seizure of Aboriginal land. The symbolic Aborigine became a mark of stasis in a climate where everyone was forced to adapt. There is little intimation here of the manifold strategies adopted by the Sydney Aborigines as they dealt with their situation; no acknowledgment that a pidgin language was called into being. As early as 1796 David Collins was describing a communication between Aborigines and settlers in which 'nothing but a barbarous mixture of English with the Port Jackson dialect is spoken by either party'.[6]

This deletion of historical experience suggests a situation in Australia similar to that discerned by Octavio Paz in America: the terrain was treated as 'geography, pure space, open to human action'. Historical obstacles such as indigenous societies were 'erased from history' and 'reduced to a mere act of nature'.[7]

Certainly, the figures in the Evans painting appear as agents of nature rather than culture. There is no evidence that they have adapted in response to the gleaming settlement in the mid-ground, nothing to suggest they have learnt a pidgin tongue. They are exemplary cases of what the anthropologist Johannes Fabian describes as *allochronism*—the refusal in Western culture to acknowledge traditional people as contemporary beings.[8] The 'posited authenticity of a past (savage, tribal, peasant) serves to denounce an inauthentic present'.[9]

Reviewing the pictorial legacy, Aboriginal presence in the landscape appears shadowy, peripheral and out of time. Ultimately, it becomes impossible to disconnect such imagery with a grim prophecy that might well have been self-fulfilling: that Aboriginal Australians were doomed to extinction. Admittedly, any human figure can be interpreted as a symbol of mortality in the landscape. The suggestion is reinforced

67

because foreground and horizon, the 'marginal' elements of pictorial space, share a dialectical relationship which contrasts human temporality with those suggestions of infinitude already discussed. But the conventions for depicting Aborigines were distinctive. Rarely are they seen as social actors. Their passivity, their resistance to change, the frequency with which they huddle round campfires oblivious to the fences that divide their territory—all are evidence of the way in which anxieties about mortality were scripted according to racial suppositions, enforcing one of the most pervasive if unacknowledged traits in Australian culture: that Aborigines have long represented to Europeans the face of death within the landscape.

The racial theories often associated with Darwin could not have proliferated in the way they did if they had no grounding in social memory and experience. Darwin himself, when he crossed the Blue Mountains in 1836, observed 'a score of black aborigines' near Emu Plains, 'all partly clothed and some could speak a little English', but none within the range itself.[10] The absence (perceived or actual), the altered circumstances and the often degraded living conditions of Aboriginal fringe dwellers combined with other factors to reinforce notions of racial demise. Aboriginal death was not merely anticipated—it was prominent in the reality of colonial life. I have quoted the testimony of Mary Gilmore in which the image of a lock of hair triggers the confession that her father and his kin had been killers of blacks. Here was a situation in which the face of the other revealed the murderer within the self. I have also told how Jimmie Barker, visiting a campsite of his youth, heard silence where once 'all was laughter', a grim ricochet of Blaxland discerning 'the death-like stillness of the interior' when he recalled the expedition that terminated at a functional Aboriginal camp.

But no foundational event could more strongly emphasise the tragic association between Aborigines and death than the smallpox epidemic of 1789. The First Fleet annalist Watkin Tench described it in the following terms:

> Repeated accounts brought by our boats of finding bodies of the Indians in all the coves and inlets of the harbour, caused the gentlemen of our hospital to procure some of them for the purposes

of examination and anatomy. On inspection, it appeared that all the parties had died a natural death: pustules, similar to those occasioned by the small pox, were thickly spread on the bodies; but how a disease, to which our former observations had led us to suppose them strangers, could at once have introduced itself, and have spread so widely, seemed inexplicable.[11]

It is impossible, really, to acknowledge fully the devastating impact of the disease. Beaches and caves were littered with corpses. There was no one to bury the dead. The community of Colebee, a prominent figure around Sydney, had only three survivors. Some commentators estimate that over half the Aborigines of the wider Sydney region were lost in the epidemic.[12] David Collins described how a young Aboriginal man then living with the settlers was taken to the harbour to look for his companions.

> [T]hose who witnessed his expression and agony can never forget either. He looked anxiously around him in the different coves we visited; not a vestige on the sand was to be found of human foot; the excavations in the rocks were filled with the putrid bones of those who had fallen victims to the disorder; not a living person was any where to be met with. . . . He lifted up his hands and eyes in silent agony for some time; at last he exclaimed, 'All dead! All dead!'[13]

Painful as it is to recall these shocking events, I believe it is necessary if an object like the Evans watercolour is to be understood in its complexity. The enclosed, pool-like depiction of the harbour makes it a mnemonic object; the imposition of Aboriginal campers on a scene where in all probability none was sighted makes poignant the loss of life, the social memory of a harbour littered with corpses, which marked the appropriation of this territory as a deathly transaction.

A painting like this is both an act of erasure and a memorial object. It sends a wash of colour across the surface of the country that might position the Aboriginal subjects as nothing more than relics on the scene but which also, by contrast, might insist on the enduring tradition of attachment to country, allowing the viewer to turn the lens and contemplate what the foreground figures would have seen as they had looked towards the west.

Thus we must acknowledge the Aboriginal names for this expanse of country. To the traditional owners of the region, the Sydney basin, the Cumberland Plain, was frequented by people who spoke varying dialects of a language no longer used but referred to as 'Darug'. Within Darug, like its neighbouring language groups (sometimes referred to as 'tribes'), were sub-groups consisting of fifty to sixty people who formed bands or clans and who lived, foraged and hunted together. They were each known by a particular name which was often that of the locality they owned, served and guarded.[14]

Darug territory extended from Broken Bay in the north to Botany Bay in the south where it bordered with a language known as Dharawal. Darug included most of what we see in the Evans water-colour: Port Jackson (Sydney Harbour), Parramatta and the other areas immediately occupied by the British in the 1780s–90s. Darug speakers left an impressive and distinctive legacy of rock art in which human, animal and mythical figures are engraved onto sandstone platforms. Such art exists along the eastern stretch of the main east–west ridge through the Blue Mountains, presumably made by the clan identified by Jim Kohen as the Oryang-Ora (or Aurang).

West of the Blue Mountains is the territory of Wiradjuri-speaking people—a vast area that covers much of the present state of New South Wales. To the north of Darug lies Dharkinjung; and inland, immediately south of the ridge travelled by Blaxland—the part of the Blue Mountains visible in the left hand side of the painting, is the land of the Gundungurra.[15] Inevitably, given the disruptions forced by colonisation, some of these boundaries are subject to conjecture.

The terrain of this study is principally that of the Darug and Gundungurra, totally distinct peoples each with their own language, traditions and appearance. The Gundungurra were described by colonials as short and muscular. Some had never seen a white man before Francis Barrallier entered their territory in 1802. Upon contact, he noticed that unlike the Darug who lived without clothing, these 'mountaineers' wore a mantle 'of skins of various animals sewed together'.[16]

George Evans traversed the land of Darug, Gundungurra and Wiradjuri when he headed west in late 1813 and transcended the horizon he had previously painted. He was a better artist than he was writer, as he himself suggested:

TRADITIONAL BOUNDRIES
OF THE
GUNDUNGURRA NATION

NEW SOUTH WALES
SCALE 1:1 000 000

71

I am now 98½ measured Miles from the duration of Mr Blaxland's excurtion [*sic*]; most part of the distance is through a finer country than I can describe, not being able for want of Language to dwell on the subject, or explain its real and good appearance with Pen and Ink, but I assure you there is no deception in it.[17]

Assisted by the redoubtable kangaroo hunter, James Burns, Evans and a few convicts were laying the route for William Cox's road.

Evans quickly crossed the Blue Mountains and found a rivulet which he wrote as 'Riverlett' (it became the River Lett)—and it was then that he became 'entangled among the hills' of the Great Divide. Having disentangled himself, he continued westwards, hauling enormous fish from the inland flowing river, and writing rapturously of 'the finest grass intermixed with variety of herbs; the hills have the look of a park and Grounds laid out: I am at a loss for language to describe the country'.

Frequently, he saw smoke from the Aboriginal fires that had shaped the country, but he found it 'strange we have not fell in with the Natives; they are near about us as we find late traces of them; I think they are watching us'. Then, some days later, he saw 'some Natives coming down the Plain...the poor Creatures trembled and fell down with fright'. He gave them fish, some fish hooks, twine and a tomahawk. The two women were blind in the right eye. When he climbed back into the Blue Mountains he discovered that the Aborigines had fired the country.

72

> Flames rage with violence through thick underwood...Bad travelling...the Bushes here are worse than if their leaves had not been consumed; they catch my Chain which makes the measuring very fatiguing; also tears our clothes to pieces, and makes us appear as Natives from black dust off them. The Marks in the Trees are burnt out; therefore am obliged to go over them again.

Both sides could play at wiping the country clean.

THE EVANS WATERCOLOUR opens up the conceptual foreground for that great landscape painting of the Blue Mountains, Eugène von Guérard's *Weather Board Creek Falls, Jamiesons Valley, New South Wales*, painted in 1862.[18] Von Guérard was visiting the Blue Mountains in December 1859 when he lodged at an inn known as 'The Weatherboard' which had begun to accommodate a few sightseers among the multitude crossing the range. Von Guérard walked the one-and-a-half miles to the waterfall, which was to be renamed in 1879 to honour William Wentworth. There he made a pencil sketch which served as the preliminary drawing for the painting exhibited in Melbourne three years later. At its first exhibition, the painting was warmly applauded by Melbourne's small circle of art critics, and von Guérard was sufficiently encouraged by its success to paint a smaller but similar version titled *The Weatherboard Falls* in 1863.[19] 'The title is not romantic, but the picture is eminently poetical,' wrote the critic for the *Illustrated Melbourne Post*, when describing the 1862 canvas.

> This is distance, there are rocks, there is falling water, and that is all. But the effect is grand and imposing beyond conception. It gives you the idea of eternal solitude, and perpetual exclusion from civilised life. The far extending summits of those peculiar, level, ranges, so characteristic of Australian landscape, convey the impression of vast space. The blue vapour that hangs over the valley and reaches up well nigh to the brown of the mountains, has an aerial quality about it, quite startling. You seem to breathe the pure cool air, as it comes swelling up from the deep-down gorges below, whose impenetrable gloom is almost awe inspiring.[20]

In planning his sunset painting, von Guérard stood at one of the most famous tourist spots, a place I have visited countless times. This vista is a short walk from my parents' house and even closer to the mansion, formerly derelict, that in its heyday was home to Vere Gordon Childe, a protagonist in the later pages of this story. The lookout is some hundred metres from the house. Like George Evans I am nearly lost for words when I try to describe the view. This is how it seemed to Charles Darwin who visited in 1836:

> By following down a little valley and its tiny rill of water, an immense gulf is unexpectedly seen through the trees, which border

2 VON GUÉRARD'S SHADOW

looking back I beheld the thick body of a huge snake sinking beneath the trunk of a fallen tree. I had not moved many steps before another crossed me. Not admiring such company I retraced my steps, and sat down near my horse to gaze on this dismal scene…Once or twice I started up, under the idea that the blacks were near.

GEORGE HAMILTON,
The Journal of an Overlander, 1836–45

the pathway, at the depth of perhaps 1,500 feet. Walking on a few yards one stands on the brink of a vast precipice, and below is the grand bay or gulf (for I know not what other name to give it), thickly covered with forest. The point of view is situated as if at the head of a bay, the line of cliff diverging on each side, and showing headland behind headland, as on a bold sea-coast. These cliffs are composed of horizontal strata of whitish sandstone; and so absolutely vertical are they, that in many places, a person standing on the edge, and throwing down a stone, can see it strike the trees in the abyss below. So unbroken is the line, that it is said, in order to reach the foot of the waterfall, formed by this little stream, it is necessary to go a distance of sixteen miles round. About five miles distant in front, another line of cliffs extends, which thus appears completely to encircle the valley; and hence the name of bay is justified, as applied to this grand amphitheatrical depression. If we imagine a winding harbour, with its deep water surrounded by bold cliff-like shores, laid dry, and a forest sprung up on its sandy bottom, we should then have the appearance and structure here exhibited. This kind of view was to me quite novel, and extremely magnificent.[21]

Just where von Guérard did his sketch is difficult to determine. The most significant difference between the initial drawing and the painting of 1862 occurs in the foreground. The tilted and inhospitable boulders which start near the bottom of the page, leading the eye towards the precipice, have been flattened, suggesting a stage-like appearance. The valley itself has been compressed, enabling its most dramatic elements to fit within the pictorial frame. The Aboriginal figure stands against this backdrop on one of the stage-like outcrops near the cliff edge. His back is turned upon the valley, though he does not meet the gaze of the viewer. He is preoccupied with his private drama. A boomerang is poised in his right hand and a spear is held in the left.

When the painting was first shown at the Victorian Exhibition of Fine Arts, the figure, if it attracted notice, was treated as a decorative flourish. The *Argus*, absorbed by nationalist objectives, claimed that 'We do not require either the description in the catalogue, or the presence of the aborigine in the landscape, to assure us that the subject is racy of the soil.' The Aborigine was pure ornamentation in a scene that was already

primitive—where the cataract tosses 'its wealth of waters wastefully into an invisible abyss'.[22] The critic for the *Illustrated Melbourne Post* was the only commentator who considered the specific detail of the figure to be worthy of notice, writing:

> There is nothing to break the solemn repose of the scene, save a dusky savage starting at the sudden appearance of a large snake, gliding from beneath its thick concealment of stones and grass.[23]

The snake and Aborigine are diminished by the imposing scenery. But this does not satisfactorily explain why their combative pose attracted so little interest among von Guérard's contemporaries or the manner in which it has been ignored by subsequent interpreters. Perhaps there has been a reluctance, in the context of realist expectations about landscape painting, to grapple with the anthropomorphic symbolism of the painting. The evocation of a sunset scene, and the proximity to the precipice of Aborigine and snake, raise the possibility that some sort of historical drama was being enacted on that rocky platform.

~

Von Guérard was born in 1811 in Vienna, the son of the prominent miniaturist Bernhard von Guérard with whom he travelled to Italy in his mid-teens. There he took art classes in the classical tradition and made

76

contact with the group of expatriate German painters who became known as the Nazarenes. He was among the thousands of settlers attracted to Australia by the Gold Rush, arriving in Melbourne in 1852. His short time on the goldfields was unproductive and eventually he resumed his occupation as an artist, travelling widely and painting scenery in many parts of Australia and New Zealand. He returned to Europe for the last years of his life, but his tenure in Australia lasted thirty years—and it was the period in which rampant expansion of the pastoral industry caused rapid and profound damage to the social fabric of many Aboriginal societies.

Tim Bonyhady has observed how 'European figures never seem at risk' when they appear in von Guérard's landscapes.[24] In this respect they are very different to the Aboriginal figures he depicted. Viewed as a narrative sequence, von Guérard's Australian landscapes reveal an intense interest in the changing circumstances of indigenous people. *Aborigines met on the road to the diggings* (1854), an early Australian work, depicts Aboriginal hunters in a highly active pose. Two men stride into the foreground while half a dozen others hold back so as not to disturb their quarry. *Barter*, painted the same year, takes up the subject of exchange between Aborigines and settlers. The whites—obvious visitors to the blacks' camp—are trading blankets for possum skin. In the distance, the covered wagons of pioneers are being hauled by bullocks. The

Aborigines in these images are anything but diminutive 'natives' poised against a majestic landscape. They are dynamic beings—hunters, negotiators—who clearly influence their own destinies.

A diptych called '*Bushy Park*', painted in 1861, marks a transformation from von Guérard's earlier representations of Aboriginal life. Bushy Park was a cattle station near Stratford in Victoria. Von Guérard used the expansive format of the panorama to encapsulate the sweeping vista of flat grazing land and low hill country beyond. It would be the epitome of pastoral abundance and colonial success, were it not that in one panel an Aboriginal family is positioned near a fallen tree while cattle feed in the distance. The frailty of these figures, not to mention the fact that they are camped on cleared grazing country—territory that is now someone else's—adds poignancy to the sister canvas which contains no human figures but does show two feuding bulls, white and dark, their horns interlocked. Daniel Thomas has described this painting as a 'symbolic conflict' and relates it to other motifs in von Guérard's opus such as 'a European fox stalking native kangaroos' or 'European blackberry vines invading native pastures'.[25]

Weather Board Creek Falls was among the last of von Guérard's paintings to depict an Aboriginal figure. Eventually such figures disappeared from his paintings. In this way, they reflect his pessimism about the future of Aboriginal society. This sentiment is clearly discernible within the sequence of images depicting Wentworth Falls. Each time he produced a new version of the landscape, the human presence underwent some form of transformation. In *The Weatherboard Falls*, the second, smaller painting of 1863, the Aboriginal figure is no longer a combatant. The snake is gone, the man's back is turned to the viewer. He is far more passive, a witness to the sunset scene. When, in 1866–67, von Guérard included a new rendition of the same view in his folio of coloured lithographs, the Aboriginal presence had vanished. In his stead are two pairs of European sightseers.[26] Those closest to the viewer are equipped with rifles. One crouches, the other stands, his gun pointing towards the waterfall. More distant are two other Europeans, very small, and perched on the edge of the precipice. The replacement of the Aborigine by sightseers anticipated with extraordinary foresight the rise of the tourist industry which landscape artists encouraged.

~

Von Guérard's image is part of a tradition of fine landscape paintings of Wentworth Falls that lasted throughout the nineteenth century. Augustus Earle's *Bougainville Falls, Prince Regent's Glen* (1826) was probably the earliest, depicting an episode whereby two Aboriginal guides lead the artist and his party to the waterfall. Earle depicts himself sketching while his fellow travellers clamber around a projecting rock. From Earle's sketch-book it has been established that he had met and drawn one of the 'guides' depicted, though the encounter occurred many miles west, in the Wellington Valley.[27] This transplanting of the guide made the painting a synthesis of various aspects of the artist's tour rather than the depiction of a particular moment. By the time W. C. Piguenit painted Wentworth Falls around 1876, no foreground figures were deemed necessary. As a conscious eulogist of Australian 'wilderness', Piguenit anticipates in his highly accomplished paintings the typically figureless landscapes of today that adorn the coffee shops and tourist galleries of the Blue Mountains. Few of these contemporary images depict the terrain with any spirit of originality. Landscape painting has become high street kitsch.

~

Von Guérard's depiction of snake and combatant is a fantasy, of course, but it has a peculiar, niggling kind of resonance. Having lived with a reproduction of it, my fascination increased when I saw the painting in the flesh and experienced the proportions of the scene. The 1862 canvas is 122.1 × 183.2 centimetres, a sizeable work. While immediately impressive in its totality, the painting begs closer inspection, encouraging the viewer to step forth and be immersed in the extraordinary proliferation of detail, much of it painted under a magnifying glass. Von Guérard's paintings were executed with such precision that botanists have been able to survey the flora represented in his landscapes.

The mortal players in the foreground are reduced to near-nothingness by the grandiosity of the backdrop. Perhaps it is this very insignificance that encourages the viewer to approach them and to engage. They embody, in their diminished state, a moment of encounter that emphasises both human and animal frailty positioned against the greater terror of the abyss. While symbolising the displacement that the artist witnessed as an overall condition in the colonies, it is difficult to believe that this Viennese romantic, schooled in the symbolism of Claude and Poussin, could not have been intrigued by the metaphorical associations of the mythically loaded creature that he depicted and would have personally encountered during his excursions through the Australian bush.

The snake, of course, is a symbol of evil in the Christian bestiary. In von Guérard's painting it menaces a man who, in romantic terms, could easily be thought of as inhabiting a 'state of nature'. This encounter occurs on a cliff edge, thereby intimating a fall with echoes of those key biblical descents: Lucifer's fall from heaven or Adam and Eve's from earthly paradise. Operating at this mythical level, there is also a historical dimension to the clifftop drama. A painting like Thomas Cole's *Scene from 'The Last of the Mohicans', Cora kneeling at the Feet of Tamenund* (1827) suggests that in the Americas, also, it was possible to envisage the demise of indigenous communities by depicting them on a cliff edge. In von Guérard, however, there is an added connotation not discernible in Cole's depiction of the Mohicans gathered on a ledge of overhanging rock. That the menacing creature which threatens the Aborigine might stand as a metaphor for the colonisers of his country is confirmed by the surprising array of narrative possibilities suggested in the Wentworth Falls landscapes. A man of the land stands poised with a snake. The snake vanishes. He watches the sunset. The man himself disappears. Tourists arrive. One carries a gun. . . There is the hint of a story, but its components are too open, too scattered, to plot a particular course. While the narrative might signal Aboriginal disappearance, it could also refer to the expunging of the snake.

It is this ambiguity that makes von Guérard's drawing, paintings and lithograph exciting objects of contemplation. Intriguing spectacles in their own right, they also allow one to re-approach the scene and consider its many nuances. Tempting as it is to regard the second painting, where the Aborigine gazes at the sunset, as something close to a valediction, my own wanderings around the scene have led to quite opposite imaginings. Sitting on King's Tableland, the plateau above the waterfall, I look at grooves in the rock which were caused by the sharpening of Aboriginal spears. In this plateau country, never far from a convenient expanse of sandstone bedrock, it is interesting to note how frequently such sharpening grooves are found at elevated, panoramic spots like this. Aesthetic preferences were obviously important in influencing the choice of location for the repetitious labour of sharpening spears. Viewing the sunset is a majestic moment in its own right.

Following this, one should at least attempt to consider what the view might have represented to the spear sharpeners or other Aboriginal observers. The vertiginous uncertainty that haunts *all* the figures posed along the cliff edge must be viewed in light of the reality that the valleys —the seemingly unattainable mid-ground and background of von Guerard's landscape—were the very places where the Gundungurra were most at home. The Coxs–Warragamba river system was a concentration of mammal, bird and aquatic fauna. The fertile, frequently flooded river flats provided the staples for human existence. We can imagine a pattern of occupation in which a regular life in the valleys was punctuated by seasonal excursions to the high country of the plateaus. It was the very opposite to the European practice of experiencing the landscape from the clifftops.

The resistance of the Gundungurra people who were concentrated along the rivers contributed substantially to the perception that the mountains were uncrossable by this route. Consequently, the path used by Blaxland and company, occupied on a more transitory basis by Gundungurra and other communities, became the major line of travel for the British, eventually supporting the highway, railway and ribbon of towns.

Knowing that von Guérard did not see an Aboriginal person when he drafted his initial sketch, it could be inferred that, to some degree, *all* the figures in his paintings are out of place. Situated in dangerous proximity to the chasm, these personages invoke an empathy common in many experiences of vertigo, in which the terror of the abyss is not confined to approaching it oneself; it can also take hold simply by watching someone else approach the edge.

The spread of the Blue Mountains settlement along the highway, and the development of favoured tourist haunts on dangerously exposed sections of the escarpment, are essential aspects of the way the region became a site of pilgrimage and visitation. The bones are there in von Guérard's images. A landscape of exquisite beauty, of unreachable depths and of persons vulnerable and endangered would resonate with the experiences of those who had come to occupy this land. The overwhelming sense of danger and frailty that hangs over the characters

in paintings and lithograph points not only to an endangered Aboriginal future but to the profoundly unsettled quality of the settler experience. In this way von Guérard's landscapes reflect what Ken Gelder and Jane Jacobs identify as the quality of *uncanniness* that saturates ideas of Australian nationality, especially when they attempt to negotiate or incorporate Aboriginal notions of the sacred. Drawing from Freud's 1919 essay, 'The "Uncanny"', they define the concept in the following terms: 'An "uncanny" experience may occur when one's home is rendered, somehow and in some sense, unfamiliar; one has the experience, in other words, of being in place and "out of place" simultaneously.'[28]

    More than any other, a certain curious feature convinces me of the essential truth of this proposition. When I first viewed the 1862 canvas I looked time and time again at the shadow of von Guérard's

THIS AERIAL VIEW OF KATOOMBA, COMMISSIONED BY THE LOCAL GOVERNMENT IN 1951, DRAMATICALLY REVEALS THE TOWN'S PROXIMITY TO THE ESCARPMENT. THIS CLOSENESS TO THE EDGE BRINGS A SENSE OF MORTALITY WHICH TO ME EXPRESSES THE UNSETTLED QUALITY OF THE SETTLER EXPERIENCE.

Aboriginal figure. It has disturbed me ever since. My diary from that day includes the following notes:

> Sunset. Sun hidden behind dark clouds. Aborigine posing with spears and boomerangs. His shadow is out of alignment with the sun. Indeed, judging by the shadows, there seem to be a number of light sources in the painting. Von Guérard's relationship to light deserves consideration.

This might account for the sense of tension in the painting. It is a distancing effect that actually prevents seduction. For when you know the place, and think about the pinks and reds in the western clouds, and see that incommensurate, anterior shadow reaching towards you as if the sun is setting too far to the south, you cannot feel at ease with that landscape.

I found myself wondering 'What time could this possibly be?' The answer, I concluded, was 'No time'. There is not a moment in the calendar when this combination of shadows could possibly appear. But far from being diminished, I now find von Guérard's perspicacity more pronounced. For this shadow, a chink in the timelessness of sublime nature, rendered through the unnatural conjunction of light and body, recalls with startling exactitude the phenomenal experience of an encounter with a snake. Some time back I met one as I walked up a creek to check a water pipe. Black and gleaming like wet rubber, he sunned his new skin, showing little fear as I approached, shovel in hand. With a couple of body lengths between us, his slit of yellow eye met mine. Then time froze. Bound by each other's gaze, we held our distance, watched and waited, aware that every possibility was latent in this encounter. Then it broke. I looked behind me for the merest second, returned to the snake—and it was gone. The world might have turned a few degrees in those moments when our eyes were interlocked.

On 16 October 1925, the *Blue Mountains Echo* reported that a couple had mysteriously disappeared after leaving a Katoomba guesthouse to walk one of the well-known trails:

MISSING TOURISTS
CREATE A SENSATION

On Monday morning Mr and Mrs Norman Walters walked quietly from hospitable 'Homesdale,' in Katoomba Street, casually remarking 'they were going to do the Federal Pass'.

Since then, the couple have not been seen nor heard of, and the police and trackers have been scouring the country looking for the young couple or their mangled remains.

Rumours, sombre and vermillion [*sic*], are in the air; and as the days lengthen the whisperings grow apace until the community is on tenter hooks, the occurrence being intensified owing to the strange disappearance of Mr Harry Christie a fortnight ago.

It is surmised that Walters had little money; as among his belongings was a pawn ticket showing where he had 'popped' a rug for 15/-, a few days prior to coming to the Mountains.

At 'Homesdale,' the lady had left everything neatly packed as if ready to quit, but the man's clothes were strewn carelessly about the room.

Sergeant J. R. Carter and Trooper F. Walcot, with search parties, are scouring the passes, but the rangers say the absent ones never passed by that way.[29]

Such stories appear occasionally in Blue Mountains newspapers. The emotive tone with which the journalist describes the community's anxiety is a reflection of how the plight of lost people has infused the sense of locality. Frank Hurley, the well known photographer, penned some words of warning to those who stray from the beaten track in his book *The Blue Mountains and Jenolan Caves*:

> if you do get lost, which is highly probable, don't panic. Just stay where you are until rescued. The more you plunge heedlessly through the bush, blindly striving to find your way back to civilization, the more difficult becomes the task of finding you.

This appears in a largely promotional book that celebrates the scenic diversity of the topography while simultaneously cautioning that to 'the

> *The multicursal maze is dangerous even if no minotaur is lurking, for one risks getting lost and remaining perpetually imprisoned; in such a maze one may find no solution, no center, no exit.*
>
> PENELOPE REED DOOB, *The Idea of the Labyrinth*, 1990

inexperienced eye every ridge resembles its fellow'.[30] Such statements are evidence of that pervasive metaphor repeated so often in Europeans' experiences of the Blue Mountains. George Caley used it in 1804 when he wrote of 'hills and vallies, that run in a circuitous manner in every direction' as though 'nature had formed a Labyrinth'.[31]

~

I take from my drawer a map of the Blue Mountains, smoothing its folds against the table. A paradoxical object, it both solves the labyrinth—makes it passable—and re-establishes its design in the complex, linear interplay of contours, streams, pathways and roads, occasionally intersected by my annotations or the creases in the paper.

No longer the barrier to colonial expansion, some traces of those puzzling days when the Blue Mountains were the intermediary space between reality and hope are yet discernible on my map. North of the Grose River Valley, the names of Caley and Strzelecki, colonial travellers who never knew each other, share adjacent peaks on Explorers Range. This entire area surrounding Mount Banks is known as the Carmarthen Labyrinth, and further down the chart I find other labyrinthine pockets established in nomenclature. North-west of Mount Twiss (the peak named by the astronomer William Dawes) an area is marked as the Kolonga Labyrinth. Between Glenbrook and Machins Crater lies a large area called the Blue Labyrinth; and south of Mount Solitary, Perdition Maze.[32]

I wonder at the purpose of singling out these labyrinthine remnants, of declaring labyrinths within this greater labyrinth. The ornamental mazes of parks and gardens are enclosed by walls. The wanderer enters through a gate. The distinction between the labyrinth and the rest of the world is asserted by such fixtures, but no gatekeeper or signpost warns the traveller who steps within the realm of Perdition Maze. The boundaries are elusive—or perhaps illusory—for the notion of labyrinth cannot be fixed in time or space. A question hovers around those designations of Carmarthen, Kolonga and Blue Labyrinth. Could it be that the act of nomination marks an attempt at containment?

It is not surprising that ideas of the labyrinth should appear in a colonised country. Here is a metaphor uniquely suited to that colonial conceit in which the bright light of European reason illuminates savage darkness. The labyrinth had already featured in discourses of enlightenment. When Descartes defined his 'Rules for the Direction of the Mind' he placed special emphasis on the 'ordering and arranging' of objects. In seeking knowledge, he wrote, the reader 'must follow this Rule as closely as he would the thread of Theseus if he were to enter the Labyrinth'.[33]

Descartes' use of such a metaphor seems disingenuous. The labyrinth, of course, is unique among architectural structures because it is specifically designed for getting lost. It dallies with the state of bewilderment, parodying the intricacies of reasoned argument in the over-arching complexity of its design while creating conditions for its necessity if the maze is to be decoded. That Descartes, in outlining his grandiose ground plan for rational cognition, should make such reference to the labyrinth is itself a moment of illumination within his text. It gives the pursuit of knowledge greater urgency, associating the rationalist enterprise with a sense of fear—a cosmic terror—that humanity, without the beneficial qualities of reason, is irretrievably lost. As the parody of reason and a means of defining it, the labyrinth-as-symbol embodies many contradictory properties. Conspicuous among them, given the purpose of Descartes' argument, is the mythical basis of the Theseus narrative. A fragment from the fantastic realm of Greek folklore becomes a metaphorical prop in establishing a dialectic of 'pure reason'.

~

Reflecting on his Blue Mountains discoveries, George Caley wrote:

> In speaking of the Grose as a river, we cannot with propriety consider it as such, but rather a receptacle of a great number of brooks and rills . . . [I]t does not exceed six miles before it begins to divide; and . . . subdivide till the subdivisions will become too tedious to enumerate.[34]

In this manner, with almost pleasurable irritation, Caley precisely described the ever-branching river systems of the sandstone escarpment that proved such a challenge for exploration. Although Caley's employer, Sir Joseph Banks, had botanised briefly in New South Wales when he visited with Cook in 1770, he could not believe that 'a body of land, as large as all Europe, does not produce vast rivers, capable of being

86

navigated into the heart of the interior'. He voiced concern in 1798 that a full decade of British settlement had passed and 'so much has the discovery of the interior been neglected'.[35] Using African exploration as his precedent, Banks proposed that Mungo Park, the recently returned hero of the Niger, be engaged to explore the interior of New Holland in 'a deck'd vessel of about 30 tons, under the command of a lieutenant, with orders to follow his advice in all matters of exploring'.[36] Had this recommendation been adopted, and Park come to Australia, he may have avoided the gruesome death he suffered when he mounted his second assault on the Niger in 1805. But his progress in a thirty-ton vessel would not have been extensive. When the farmer and surgeon Sir John Jamison attempted to navigate the Nepean and Warragamba rivers with a party that included 'Gilderoy, *alias* Bob, a black native', and Thomas Jones, 'my collector of natural history productions', he chose a rowboat which, though only three metres in length, was damaged in the shallow rapids. A small island near the junction of the Coxs and Wollondilly rivers marked the end point of their mission.[37] They 'suspended from a swamp-oak in its centre a well-corked bottle containing a piece of a newspaper, on which we had inscribed the names of our party and the date of our visit'.[38]

Jamison's map of the journey, where each valley rapidly branches into a network of fine capillary channels, affirms Caley's description of rivers that divide and sub-divide. To travel upstream without local knowledge was to move against the grain, as Francis Barrallier had discovered when his well-equipped expedition was forced into ignominious retreat in 1802. It was five years after the mountains had been officially crossed via the main ridge that the Jamison team sailed upstream and turned back at Bottle Island. A few months later Jamison settled on the opposite approach: following the river from the west. He ordered his botanist, Thomas Jones, to cross the range by road and follow Coxs River through the gorges until it left the mountains, not forgetting, as proof of his achievement, to collect the suspended bottle. Jones travelled with Gilderoy, the guide from the earlier expedition, and also two other Aborigines, 'Millott alias Joe' and 'Nagga alias Jack'.[39]

Unlike Barrallier, whose expedition was undermined by the fact that his guide, Gogy, was known and despised by the Gundungurra people they encountered, Jones' companions were of enormous help. Though

Courses of the Rivers Hawkesbury, Warragamba &c.

Engraved for the New South Wales Magazine.

fearful of the Mountain clan that Jamison refers to as the 'Condanora natives', the guides spoke a little Gundungurra. They helped Jones to distribute biscuits and tobacco and to arrange an exchange of tomahawks and waist belts when the Mountain people were encountered. Despite initial tension, the Condanora assisted the travellers, giving

> information of three rivers which empty into the Cox . . . they described their character, source, and country they ran through; and likewise gave them much information of the length of their journey, and the best route to the Nepean from Bottle Island.

Thomas Jones probably owed his life to his three guides, for at the end of the eleven-day journey their food was exhausted and the botanist almost crippled. By the time they reached the Jamison mansion on the Nepean 'they were greatly emaciated, Jones almost quadruped with his crutches, and a beard flowing in most patriarchal fold'.[40]

Physical fatigue notwithstanding, the Jones expedition proved to Europeans that the Blue Mountains were crossable through the valleys. White settlers began to drive their stock upriver and the disenfranchising of the Gundungurra began in earnest. That the terrain should border on the impassable in one direction, and be readily traversable from the other, conforms with an aspect of the labyrinthine imaginary as it has developed in the European experience. Much as it is associated with loss and bewilderment—maze and amazement share a common root—the existence of a key, a solution, an Ariadne thread, that will decode the labyrinth and make it passable is inextricable from the myth.

~

Thomas Jones crossed the Blue Mountains via the valleys because his mode of travelling allowed for cultural difference. He negotiated the reality that Aboriginal knowledge and experience might constitute an Ariadne thread. In the colonial context the labyrinthine confusion of cross-cultural encounter was inextricable from topographical problems. An incident that occurred during the Blaxland journey epitomises the misunderstandings that were inevitable without that cultural recognition. It happened as they climbed the range, reaching a point that offered an extensive view of the settlement to the east where:

they found a pyramidical heap of stones, the work evidently of some European, one side of which the natives had opened, probably in the expectation of finding some treasure deposited in it. This pile they concluded to be the one erected by Mr Bass, to mark the end of his journey.[41]

In attributing this cairn to the surgeon George Bass, the explorers were hopelessly wrong. His Blue Mountains journey of 1796 started many kilometres south and took him through the Burragorang Valley, the country traversed by Jamison and Jones.[42] Equally erroneously, Governor Macquarie, in describing the newly made highway in 1815, mentioned a pile of rocks near the road, 'supposed to have been placed there by Mr. Caley, as the extreme point of his tour'. The cairn became known as 'Caley's Repulse'.[43]

George Caley, however, played no part in the building of the cairn. He had made two extensive journeys into the range: one to Mount Banks in 1804, and another in the footsteps of Barrallier two years later. His path to Mount Banks followed the north side of the Grose River Valley, a line that is parallel but at least twenty kilometres away from the route of Blaxland, Lawson and Wentworth. His second journey, along Barrallier's path, was confined to the southern Blue Mountains—nowhere near the east–west ridge with its pile of rocks.

In such vein the cairn has continued to create confusion. In 1906 F. M. Bladen, an editor of historical records, contacted the Australian Historical Society and drew attention to Caley's Repulse, which had been more or less forgotten since the highway was deviated in the 1830s. 'Would it not be an appropriate spot for the placing of some permanent brass?'[45] A cairn was located—or rather rebuilt—and a plaque inserted. But as Allan Searle, a local historian, discovered when he began investigations in the 1960s, the location of the rebuilt cairn was inconsistent with that described by Blaxland, Macquarie and other journalists.[45]

Carefully sifting the area, Searle discovered no less than eighteen other cairns and arrangements of stone. The quantity of artefacts, and their similarity to others in the mountains, confirms what should always have been apparent: that the cairn was an Aboriginal construction.[46]

Searle cites the archaeologist F. D. McCarthy, whose 1970 commentary on Aboriginal stone arrangements in the Great Dividing Range observed that these artefacts are rarely isolated phenomena,

89

but tend to occur in sequences, often leading to rock engravings or initiation sites or following the mythical journey of an ancestral figure.[47] Eugene Stockton concludes from the proliferation of rock engravings in this central region of the Blue Mountains that the ridge between Linden and Woodford—the route of the 1813 expedition—was a 'specially sacred, even sacred-secret area. It was probably the favoured locale for ceremony and possibly a secluded territory for preparing candidates for initiation.'[48] Here is another reason—perhaps the most convincing—for the hesitation of Aboriginal people to reveal a path through the Blue Mountains.

All this suggests that the cairn erroneously attributed to Caley was not a 'repulse', a full stop, but part of an ongoing journey. The confusion was due to the fact that piles of rock are symbols, with their own specific connotations, in both Aboriginal and European traditions—an example of what Paul Carter evocatively describes as the 'culture of coincidence'.[49]

Of all the confusions arising from this coincidence, the most revealing is Blaxland's supposition that the Aborigines had pulled the cairn apart 'in the expectation of finding some treasure deposited in it'. The assumption here is one of illiteracy: that the Aborigines failed to recognise the cairn as a positional referent, a marker in some explanatory system (to Blaxland the closure of a journey). Instead, he interprets them as interpreting the cairn as an entity that is self-contained, its significance limited to it physical confines.

All this suggests that the greatest folly in this colonial fable was the action of dismantling the cairn. The identity of the dismantler is a mystery, but the story has interesting resonance in a little chest of treasures, the diary of Henry Antill who escorted the Macquaries across the mountains in 1815. On reaching the site of Bathurst, the party climbed a 'fine tableland about half a mile long', recently named Mount Pleasant. There they found:

> a great quantity of loose stones of a peculiar kind not seen in any part of the country we had visited. And what was still more remarkable, a number of them were thrown into heaps as if placed there by the hands of men. Supposing something might be placed under them we had one or two taken to pieces, but found nothing but the same kind of stone on the surface, of a solid and hard bed which we could not penetrate.[50]

The scenario of the governor's men unpacking cairns, searching for meaning and striking bedrock is evidence not only of confusion but of the extreme persistence with which the Australian landscape was treated as a topographical and not a cultural labyrinth. The stone cairns, likely markers of an ancestral journey, give some sense of the extent to which the Australian landscape was mythically invested before European arrival. There is undoubtedly a narrative that connects this network of cairns. But the ruptures of colonisation have obliterated many such stories. Often there is not the cultural context for their maintenance and verbal transmission over generations. In an area such as the Blue Mountains few records of these narratives, the stories of the Dreaming, have survived (at least in public discourse). And as we see later, some of the Dreaming stories that circulate are probably the construction of Europeans. But there is one story that is gradually gaining a certain prominence—a story of undoubted Aboriginal origin that crosses the Blue Mountains, explains their creation and deals with the territory of the 'Condanora' and neighbouring clans. This story decodes the labyrinth.

~

The story of Mirragan and Gurangatch concerns an era which the Gundungurra called *gun'-yung-ga'-lung* when 'all the present animals were men, or at any rate had human attributes'. These heroic personages were known as the 'Burringilling', and Mirragan and Gurangatch were among their number. The story opens with a large, deep waterhole located at what is now the junction of the Wollondilly and Wingecarribbee rivers. Gurangatch, a giant fish, was sunning himself in the shallows. Mirragan, a quoll or marsupial 'cat', 'who searched only for the largest kinds of fish' caught a glimpse of Gurangatch's eye 'which shone like a star through the water'. Mirragan tried unsuccessfully to spear the fish. He then attempted to poison him in accord with Aboriginal custom—by throwing sheets of hickory bark into the water. But the poisoned water was 'not strong enough to overcome such a large fish as he'.

When Gurangatch saw Mirragan cutting more hickory bark he 'commenced tearing up the ground along the present valley of the Wollondilly, causing the water in the lagoon to flow after him and bear him along'. Mirragan followed in pursuit and thus began the epic chase between hunter and hunted that forms the river system of the southern Blue Mountains and part of the Great Dividing Range.[51]

The story of Mirragan and Gurangatch describes the topography in intricate detail. Rock formations, waterholes, bends in the river, limestone caves are accounted for by incidents that occur during the chase. For example:

> When he [Gurangatch] reached what is now the junction of Guineacor river he turned to the left and made a few miles of the channel of that stream. Coming to a very rocky place which was hard to excavate, he changed his mind and turned back to the junction and resumed his former course. He had some difficulty in getting away from this spot and made a long, deep bend or loop in the Wollondilly which almost doubles back upon itself at that place.

The story was transcribed by R. H. Mathews, a self-taught ethnologist, who heard it at an Aboriginal reserve in the Burragorang Valley around 1900.[52] Although it could only be a fragment from a larger network of stories, some of which survive in Mathews' unpublished writings,[53] it is sufficiently detailed to form a verbal map of a considerable portion of Gundungurra territory. To use the term proposed by the ethno-musicologist Catherine Ellis (and vulgarised by Bruce Chatwin), the adventures of these Dreaming characters constitute a *song line*—a sequence of songs or stories 'which may be mapped to show their geographic location'.[54] Among their various functions, stories like this were mnemonic devices that could help the traveller navigate the terrain of the narrative. To move through the landscape is to re-enact and enliven the story; to reinforce one's connection with the ancestral creators—protagonists in the Dreaming that brings the country into being. Mathews, who published the narrative in the German journal, *Zeitschrift für Ethnologie* in 1908, was a surveyor by profession. His surveying missions brought him into contact with indigenous people from many parts of Australia. Himself a map-maker, he was cognisant of the cartographic properties of a narrative like Mirragan and Gurangatch. To use a Western metaphor, this story formed a thread of knowledge for the Gundungurra traveller.

Even today, when much of the terrain formed by the mythic chase is badly degraded or flooded by the water supply for Sydney, the story encourages an engagement with country. I first found it reprinted in *Aboriginal Legends of the Blue Mountains* (1991), a self-published collection assembled by Jim Smith, a white man, who has written bushwalking guides, local histories and various interpretations of the Blue Mountains landscape. A zoologist by training, he has studied the local ecology in considerable detail and is an expert on the history of the Blue Mountains walking tracks which sometimes follow Aboriginal routes. He relates in *Aboriginal Legends* that when he first read the Mirragan story he showed it to his mentor, the veteran bushman Ben Esgate who regarded it as 'one of the most important things he had ever been given'.[55] They went in search of some of the lesser known sites mentioned in the narrative which assisted Smith in drafting a map and 'Ecological Interpretation' of the mythic journey.

~

Around the time when R. H. Mathews was transcribing the legend of Gundungurra, Sid R. Bellingham published his account of pursuing wildlife in a publication quixotically titled *Ten Years with the Palette, Shot Gun & Rifle on the Blue Mountains* (1899). While much of it concerns his hunting expeditions through the open ranges, he was clearly preoccupied with the limestone belt of Jenolan 'which extends a distance of about six miles, [and] is honeycombed with caves and subterranean passages'.[56]

Accompanied by a friend, he would penetrate various caves. He describes an occasion when they lost their way. 'We reached about the spot where I knew we had to ascend a narrow opening, but as there were so many similar looking places, we could not find the right one.' Darkness had embraced the travellers.

> My candle, which had previously burnt too low to hold in the fingers, and which I carried on a piece of stone, expired...We were caught like rats in a cage, and had now, to take turn about, to strike matches for a light.

They escaped by a whisker, seizing a thread of twine that was left by some earlier party. 'With this for a guide, we were not long in finding our way outside, and were very thankful to see daylight again'.

Bellingham's fascination with the inner chambers of the Blue Mountains, the great cave system of Jenolan, seems a distillation of his

93

THE ARTIFICIAL HORIZON

experiences when roaming through the open bush. He describes his state of mind when walking through 'uninteresting country, where there is little or no game'. He finds himself entrapped 'by the constant dinning in my ears, of the air of some song, or a bar of music. At another time some sentence, or certain words, will keep recurring to the mind, and are very annoying—as it is impossible to eradicate them.'

Bellingham was both tantalised and overcome by the landscape he described—'rich and varied, although a blueish tinge pervades the whole scene'. In addition to his occupation as a hunter, he became a *plein air* painter—even though, by his own account, a failed one.

> The painting fits were recurrent during my whole shooting career, and although I would determine that each attempt should be the last, yet such was the beauty of the scenery, that I would again be tempted to copy it, fail, and return once more to the hunter's life.

Against his will, art would take possession of the shooter—a possessive art in every sense, for its aim, as well as the source of its failure, was to capture a topographical moment in an imitative gesture.

> I was most particular to select the same hour each day, and as nearly as possible choose the same effect. These pictures thus painted never conveyed the same feeling that the scene itself did when first observed.
>
> The result would be so unsatisfactory that it was quite a relief to give up painting and return to shooting.

Bellingham claims that among all the hardships of his shooting life, none

> oppressed me so much as painting from nature. The view at first seems beautiful. After painting for an hour it loses its charm, one's eyes fairly ache, and into the soul enters the sadness which is inherent in an Australian landscape.

~

The chase between fish and quoll, members of the Burringilling who have both animal and human characteristics, ends at a waterhole called Joolundoo, just west of the Great Divide. The story's conclusion is intriguing because the fish is never captured. Mirragan enlists the aid of his friends the water birds, who dive deep but are unable to dislodge the mighty Gurangatch from the bottom of the pool. But they do succeed in tearing from his body a strip of flesh which they cook and eat. While Mirragan's hunger is sated, the great fish lives on.

As I argue later, this story opens up a profound philosophical difference between Aboriginal and Western epistemologies. It can be seen most baldly if we compare the fate of these Aboriginal creation heroes—endowed with both animal and human characteristics—with that of the mythical occupant of the labyrinth. According to Greek legend, the hybrid Minotaur was the progeny of an 'unnatural' love between Queen Pasiphae (wife of Minos) and a handsome bull. She commissioned Daedalus, Antiquity's mythical inventor, to build the labyrinth which would imprison the Minotaur, symbol of her shame. According to legend, the labyrinth became a site of deathly transactions. A regular tribute of Athenian youths was fed to the monster until the roving hero Theseus arrived and slaughtered him, escaping the maze with the aid of a ball of thread supplied by his lover Ariadne.

In the Greek legend the labyrinth is ultimately abandoned. When the Minotaur is slaughtered he goes to the sky and becomes the star Asterion. The labyrinth becomes a domain of emptiness and endless wandering. It is the ultimate 'No Place'. This aspect of the labyrinthine imaginary has been kept alive in the narratives of modern thinkers. Jorge Luis Borges depicted the plight of the Minotaur as one of perpetual wandering and waiting. His fate is the trial of the infinite—the ultimate form of entrapment. A sense of spatial wandering is equated with the infinitude of time. A story called 'The God's Script' portrays a character—the narrator—incarcerated in a vault of stone. Next to him a caged jaguar measures 'with secret and even paces the time and space of captivity'.

> I dreamt I awoke and that on the floor there were two grains of sand. I slept again; I dreamt that the grains of sand were three. They went on multiplying in this way until they filled the prison and I lay dying beneath that vast hemisphere of sand. I realized that I was dreaming; with a vast effort I roused myself and awoke. It was useless to awake; the innumerable sand was suffocating me. Someone said to me: *You have not awakened to wakefulness, but to a previous dream. This dream is*

enclosed within another, and so on to infinity, which is the number of grains of sand. The path you must retrace is interminable and you will die before you ever really awake.[57]

The plight of this prisoner marks a constant formula in the work of Borges: death, and only death, will bring relief from the labyrinth. Thus, in the monotony of 'The House of Asterion', the Minotaur will use the bodies of his victims to 'distinguish one gallery from another' and as he treads the endless path, he eagerly awaits his slaughterer—his 'redeemer'—knowing that 'he will take me to a place with fewer galleries and fewer doors'.[58] This book considers how the Blue Mountains, perceived by Europeans as a labyrinth, reflect the anxiety and the underlying violence of the arriving culture. Within this mythological order it is the death of Aboriginal Australia that marks a place in the labyrinth.

97

CARVED INTO THE BASE OF THE THREE SISTERS, THE GIANT STAIRS CONNECT THE LOOKOUT AT ECHO POINT, KATOOMBA, WITH JAMISON VALLEY. THIS SECTION OF THE PATH WAS PHOTOGRAPHED BEFORE ITS OFFICIAL OPENING IN 1932. WIRE SAFETY NETTING HAD YET TO BE FITTED.

Passage Three

INTO THE LABYRINTH

...it is seldom that any article so dropped, escapes the quick-sighted natives, to whom the surface of the earth is, in fact, as legible as a newspaper, so accustomed are they to read in any traces left thereon, the events of the day.

THOMAS MITCHELL, *Three Expeditions into the Interior of Australia*, 1838

OVERTURE   I'M ON THE road to Wombeyan Caves. A perilous, unsealed track just wide enough for a car, it runs west from the highland town of Mittagong. The terrain drops steeply on the left. A truck carting marble from the quarry near the caves comes careering round a bend and forces me to reverse. By my definition this is the southern boundary of the Blue Mountains. I'm driving to Wombeyan with a cluster of narratives drawing me on. Among them is the knowledge that these extensive limestone caverns were among the first attractions when tourism began in this part of the world. The same is true of Jenolan Caves to the north, which a settler called Whalan explored in 1838. The proliferation of visitors and souvenir hunters was so great that in 1866 one Jeremiah Wilson was appointed Keeper of Jenolan Caves on a salary of £35 a year. Visitors would arrive by foot or by horse and sleep in the enormous caverns known as Devil's Coachouse and Grand Arch where a dancing platform was erected in 1869.

Why the desire to enter the darkness with a candle and tentatively find a path? And what of earlier perceptions of the caves, their mention in the story of Mirragan and Gurangatch? As R. H. Mathews recorded in the Gundungurra legend, Wombeyan Caves were formed when Gurangatch, the mighty fish, burrowed underground from the Wollondilly River. His quarry, the native cat, Mirragan,

> did not care to go into any of the subterranaean passages, therefore he went on top of the rocks and dug a hole as deep as he could go and then prodded a long pole down it as far as it would reach. . . . There are several weather worn pot holes on top of the Whambeyan caves still, which are said to be those made by Mirragan on that occasion.[1]

There are other narratives fresh in my mind. Every so often an access road to a private property veers off to the right. At one of these Ivan Milat, the man convicted of murdering seven backpacking hitchhikers, was said to have done his gun practice. Hundreds of spent cartridges were collected by police.

The narratives that draw me further into the country, the associations suggested by the land itself, often have little obvious connection. Ivan Milat and Gurangatch do not sit comfortably together. It's this sense of discontinuity that makes colonised territory so curious and difficult to grasp. There is such an abundance of routes, tales,

overgrown pathways—disparate but co-existent. They twist with the contours, sometimes intersecting, but always create an incomplete picture. So how might one appreciate and inhabit this deeply scored landscape? The Gundungurra story, in which map and narrative are fused, shows how land is inherently textual, always inviting us to read and interpret. But instead of Mitchell's newspaper, with its typographic clarity, it suggests to me some vast library that Borges might have conjured in his stories—a library captured by storm and dispersed across a continent, its contents seeping and mulching into a soil where fragments of phrase and fable, snatches of languages lost and remembered, are always being uncovered.

At the caves there was a little party—just four of us. We were met by a guide who ushered us through a doorway in the rock. He carried a torch on his belt like a policeman's baton, and manipulated the electric lighting with the adroitness of a magician. We entered a cavity and stood in blackest darkness as he unleashed his well-worn spiel explaining the formation of limestone caves, activating the hidden bulbs at appropriate moments, illustrating his pedagogic enterprise with examples 'from the field'.

Stuck there, with the guide's voice resounding in the darkness, we had nothing to do but wait and listen. The story was familiar. When

A photograph showing the mysterious formations known as helectites in Jenolan Caves.

precipitation strikes the ground above, it penetrates the soil, collecting the acidity of rotting vegetation and slowly penetrating the underlying limestone—itself the remnant of a vast coral reef. Collecting iron and minerals that will later serve as pigmentation, the solution seeps through cracks and fissures, trickling ever downwards, until it enters the subterranean cavity by way of a suspended stalactite, a calcified remnant of all the drips preceding it. He illuminates a single icicle of rock which casts a long shadow from its spotlight. Then, clicking the switches, an entire suspended forest opens up above our heads. This cave has teeth.

From the topmost stalactite, the columns and stalagmites, right down to the creek in the bowel of the cave—*snap*, and we glimpse it below us through a crack—everything is determined by the downward movement of water. The regime is one of verticality: the perfect expression of gravitational force. The chamber now glows with a soft yellow hue, like a tastefully lit drawing room, the reality of which is betrayed not so much by our hushed awe, but by the presence of a random, indisputable plop.

Then, lovingly—he would stroke it if touching were permitted—he brings to our attention the one element that refutes the logic of everything he's said. The fragile helectite, subject of a thousand theories, starts life as a stalactite, but decides at some point to resist the downward plunge, and sends out a lateral shoot, an aberrant tentacle parallel to the floor, the existence of which has never been adequately explained. It provides a metaphor for the pages that follow.

IMAGES OF SHADOW, images of light: two paintings by von Guérard suggest an entry to the maze. Compare the 1862 composition, *Weather Board Creek Falls, Jamiesons Valley, New South Wales*, with his *Mount Kosciusko, from the Victorian Border (Mount Hope Ranges)*, painted four years later.[2] They are both romantic depictions of Australian scenery, grappling with the prospect of nature in its rawness. For a contemporary critic, an earlier von Guérard painting of the mountain categorically debunked 'the theory, if such a theory be now held by anyone, that Australian scenery possesses no elements of the sublime'.[3]

In common usage, both the Blue Mountains and Kosciuszko landscapes would probably pass as examples of the sublime. And yet they are such vastly different scenes. The 1866 painting of the mountain sits far more securely in conventions of the picturesque. Diminutive human figures, an encampment of white settlers, are placed among the lower trees, suggesting scale and grandeur. As we have seen, the foreground of *Weather Board Creek Falls* is a scene of ambiguous drama. Instead of those tranquil colonists camping respectfully beneath the mountain, there is the Aboriginal figure poised in combat with the serpent. The dilemma of the Aborigine, in danger of being forced over the precipice, reinforces an uncertainty about whether the eye is being led outwards or downwards. Perhaps the trajectory is one of flight towards the blurry horizon of early evening. Or perhaps the eye, like the figure in the foreground, is set to tumble into darkness.

Strictly speaking, *Weather Board Creek Falls* is a more convincing rendition of the sublime, a term defined by Edmund Burke in the mid-eighteenth century. His *Philosophical Enquiry into the Origin of our Ideas of the Sublime and the Beautiful* (1759) emphasised that, in the human imagination, 'the most extensive province of pleasure and pain', it is from the latter that we derive our sense of the sublime. As he described it:

> Whatever is fitted in any sort to excite the ideas of pain, and danger, that is to say, whatever is in any sort terrible, or is conversant about terrible objects, or operates in a manner analogous to terror, is a source of the sublime; that is, it is productive of the strongest emotion which the mind is capable of feeling.

Among the numerous examples that constitute the bulk of Burke's treatise is the case of a tower or mountain, 'a powerful cause of the

I A MOUNTAIN IS NOT A PLATEAU

And leave a light where all before was dark

W. C. WENTWORTH, *Australasia*, 1823

sublime', and much more affective than a 'hundred yards of even ground'. In a moment of conjecture that provides insight into the peculiar dynamics of von Guérard's painting and the subsequent development of the Blue Mountains as a tourist spectacle viewed from above, Burke proposed that 'height is less grand than depth; and that we are more struck at looking down a precipice, than at looking up at an object of equal height'.[4]

Burke's preoccupation with the terror, the awfulness, of nature, offers insights into the ways in which Europeans negotiated the labyrinthine qualities of Australian landscape. Natural elements, sometimes familiar though often rendered strange by the colonial context, would infiltrate perceptions of land, society and culture. Speculation about the contrast between height and depth is particularly pertinent when considering the Blue Mountains as a cultural landscape. There is the reality that development is clustered near the tops of cliffs and the curiosity that the name for the range is a misnomer. So annoyed was Griffith Taylor, doyen of Australian geographers, that 'Visitors to the Blue "Mountains" find no mountains at all!' that he attempted—without success—to re-name them 'the Blue Plateau'.[5]

Leaving for a moment the plateaus known as mountains, consider *Mount Kosciusko, seen from the Victorian Border*, an unambiguous and almost idyllic image of ascension. The dead tree in the foreground specifically emphasises the upward transition. Its lower bole shares the shadow of the campsite; the upper branches capture the light that bathes the mountains. The gaze of the viewer, transported from the human figures to the lofty peak, seems to emulate the passage of a mountaineer. Von Guérard himself had climbed the mount in 1862. One of his most celebrated paintings, *North-east view from the northern top of Mount Kosciusko* (1863), depicts the play of light on snow around the summit.[6] Von Guérard climbed the mountain in the company of the German scientist Georg Neumayer, who at the summit performed barometric observations to calculate its height. As art historian Tim Bonyhady describes it, several contradictory imperatives helped shape the 1863 painting. The scientific purpose of the journey and the expectation that the artist render a topographical likeness run counter to his sense of 'national significance' in depicting the loftiest mountain in Australia.[7] In contemplating the paintings, and the fact that the Kosciuszko he depicts has a more

104

mountainous aspect than what is discerned in the field, it is worth recalling that the geologist Paul Strzelecki, an expatriate Pole who ascended it in 1839 and named it after the great democratic leader of his homeland, is recorded as saying that it reminded him of the mound above Tadeusz Kosciuszko's tomb in Kraków.[8]

In Strzelecki's mind, as much as in von Guérard's, the mound became a mountain. In describing it to his former lover, Adyna Turno, Strzelecki wrote lyrically of 'discovering' the peak:

> The highest of the Australian Alps—it towers over the entire continent—whose summit, before my coming had not been reached by anyone, with its everlasting snows, the silence and dignity surrounding it, I have reserved and consecrated as a reminder...of a name dear and hallowed to every Pole, to every human being, to every friend of freedom and honour—Kosciuszko.[9]

He sent her a native blossom, plucked from the summit. 'I believe that you will be the first Polish woman to have a flower from that mountain. Let it remind you ever of freedom, patriotism and love'.[10]

Strzelecki's adventures on Mount Kosciuszko were preceded by a less congenial mission. In August 1839, he surveyed the northern Blue Mountains, discovering that between the ranges 'lie yawning chasms, deep winding gorges, and frightful precipices'.

> Narrow, gloomy, and profound, these stupendous rents in the bosom of the earth are inclosed between gigantic walls of a sandstone rock, sometimes receding from, sometimes frightfully overhanging the dark bed of the ravine, and its black silent eddies, or its foaming torrents of water.[11]

The botanist George Caley had travelled a similar path in 1804, naming part of the area 'Devil's Wilderness' in deference to the 'dreary appearance, abruptness, intricate, and dangerous route we experienced'.[12] Strzelecki, journeying in a wintry September thirty-five years later, made no acknowledgment of the earlier traveller—he may not have known of his existence—but their perceptions of the tortuous terrain, riddled with canyons, were remarkably similar. The geologist considered it an 'endless labyrinth of almost subterranean gullies'[13] and the botanist, as I have mentioned, wrote of 'hills and vallies [sic], that run in a circuitous manner in every direction' as though 'nature had formed a Labyrinth'.

Strzelecki travelled with scientific instruments for determining altitude—'two Gay-Lussac mountain barometers, and Dr. Wollaston's apparatus for ascertaining the boiling point of water'. His wide-ranging explorations were part of a vast geological survey of south-east Australia which plotted the chain of plateaus that meanders up the coast. He memorialised this 7000-mile journey by creating a map that was twenty-five feet long, five feet wide and scaled at a quarter inch to the mile. Strzelecki was a map-maker of monumental proportions.

In 1845 he published a lengthy account of his work in Australia. In accord with its geological purpose, Strzelecki's *Physical Description of New South Wales and Van Diemens Land* is a highly stratified book. The main body of the work consists of solid topographical data, but layered beneath it are numerous overblown footnotes containing extracts from his traveller's journal. This practice was common enough in the nineteenth century, reflecting a desire that the book might retain credibility as a scientific document while still appealing to the broad public interest in literature of exotic places. It is through this rigid dichotomy between scientific and anecdotal modes of expression that I would like to examine an event that provides a fascinating contrast to the ascent of the mountain he named. Perhaps it is not surprising that his most labyrinthine tribulation—the experience, to use a phrase of Conrad's, of losing himself 'in all the glories of exploration'—should be recorded thus in one of these overgrown footnotes:

> The current of the river Grose and its precipitous banks frustrated all my efforts to regain Mount King George, on the side of Mount Hay, and obliged me to go round by the source of the river, crossing on the way all its tributary torrents, and plunging anew into those savage solitary defiles which remain in the same state as when the black men first surrendered them to the white.
>
> Some days spent in toilsome climbing and scrambling brought me at length to Mount King George. Mount Tomah appeared quite close to it; but immense ravines lay between and torrents of rain in a great measure concealed the view. To proceed onwards was, however, my only alternative. I therefore redoubled my pace; ascended and de-

scended; climbing, sliding, and clinging, until at length I found myself in the midst of a forest of high and thick fern, bending beneath the weight of the still falling rain, and my progress through which resembled the act of swimming rather than of walking. The temperature, however, had hitherto rendered that progress bearable; but on approaching the summit of the mountain it changed; showers of hail began to fall, and were soon succeeded by a frost. My clothes stiffened on my limbs; the latter began to feel numb, and I soon felt it would be necessary to abandon the prosecution of the observations I had wished to make. I therefore began to descend the mountain, anxiously seeking, right and left, for some friendly cavern where I might be able to kindle a fire and dry my clothes. Three hours were vainly spent in search of one—night approached—the heavens lowered—the rain and hail continued to pour. The nearest habitation, as I had been informed, lay eighteen miles off, in the direction of the river Hawkesbury: fortunately for me, one, of which I had heard nothing, presented itself suddenly before my eyes. To perceive it—to utter a cry of joy—to encourage my exhausted and helpless servant, and to fly towards it, was the act of the same moment. To recognise our state of distress and to relieve it, was a part the owner of the dwelling performed with equal promptitude.

He took off my wet clothes, wrapped me in others from his own wardrobe, placed me before a blazing fire, brought me food, and surrounded me with every comfort, without once asking who I was, whence I came, or what might be my business!! My memory furnishes me with the recollection of few transitions so sudden and so agreeable; few states of discomfort transformed within the space of a few minutes into one of comfort so complete, and still fewer traits of hospitality so truly primitive.[14]

This flowery reminiscence, embedded in the footnote strata of Strzelecki's text, offers an amusing parable on the cartographic enterprise. The narrator sets out on a quest of discovery. His ambition is to interpret territory by climbing a mountain and performing scientific observations. But the weather turns and forces his retreat. This circumstance transforms the mission into a more elemental quest, the object of which is survival, not knowledge. He fruitlessly seeks shelter from the Earth itself, a

THE ARTIFICIAL HORIZON

'friendly cavern where I might be able to kindle a fire'. Yet none presents itself. He is saved by a surrogate cave, a farmer's dwelling, where the warmth of a contained fire disperses the effect of the untamed, exterior elements. Perhaps it is the substitution where hut meets the requirements of cave that motivates the reference to hospitality 'so truly primitive'.

This document details a moment of collapse in the cartographic mission—an occasion on which the desire to measure and quantify the physical environment folds back upon itself, forcing the cartographer to stumble blindly and unknowingly. For this reason, it is an apposite text for carrying us into the labyrinth, for considering the ethics and poetics of those extreme situations where, in attempting to locate themselves, people get lost.

Like many narratives of being lost, Strzelecki's is intimately connected with the depletion of light. The sense that his journey extends into darkness, while constantly apparent, is dramatically conveyed by his romantic phrase, 'the heavens lowered'. Implicit here is the notion that the proper distance between the sky and the traveller has been corrupted. There is plenty of bathos in this footnote, which gives it an operatic dimension. A man struggling on a hillside becomes a tableau of cosmic proportions.

This is made all the more remarkable by the transformation that occurs at the end of the ordeal. We learn that it is not just an 'I' but a 'we' who *shared* the experience. Throughout the episode it was not just Strzelecki swimming through fern, searching for a cave, but also 'my exhausted and helpless servant'. A particular problem in his use of language—hinged on the inability to position himself in relation to others—is revealed with this quixotic use of the personal pronoun. Of course, there are many factors at work here, including codes of etiquette about the degree to which a traveller who presented himself as a 'count' during his Australian sojourn would acknowledge his servant as a companion. Yet, accepting this, I would add that another, quite different, tradition comes into play in this narrative: a tradition that encompasses, and indeed makes inextricable, the dual phenomena of solitude in language and solitude in space. Ariadne might provide the thread, but at some level it is always a lone man who wanders the labyrinth.

Solitude, the lurking phantom that haunts the European imagination, is doubly activated by the alien properties of the Australian

OPPOSITE: In 1839 when Paul Strzelecki was lost in the area around Mount King George (now Mount Banks), his progress thorough 'a forest of high and thick fern…resembled the act of swimming rather than of walking.' By the late nineteenth century, however, the fern-filled gullies of Australian rainforests had become objects of beauty. This illustration appeared in a popular tourist guide.

bush. Strzelecki's footnote, with its belated acknowledgment of the servant and its dubious account of Aboriginal capitulation, is haunted by the fear of solitude. The text builds a labyrinth, but it does so only in order that it might be dismantled. This occurs when the hut is sighted and its unnamed occupant plies them with the contents of his larder and wardrobe. It is surely the greatest sign of hope in Strzelecki's footnote that, when the labyrinth is broken, the solitary wanderer is joined in ensemble; the 'I' becomes 'we'. Then, and only then, does the figure of the servant come into being in Strzelecki's text.

In the annals of colonial exploration, this type of conceit is the norm rather than the exception. The very notion of exploration necessitated strategies of exclusion which negated the presence of both indigenous inhabitants and previous travellers. The multiplicity of a team or party was reduced to the singular, roving ego of the leader. Even when the explorer was being led by a guide (as was common), the leader alone was credited with the honour and glory of the 'discovery'. In this respect, the practice of exploration was codified by military notions of hierarchy and depended on skills in writing, cartography and alignments with systems of authority, which were usually limited to travellers of the officer class.

Given these conventions, it is interesting that the figure of the servant should appear at all in Strzelecki's footnote. To some extent, it is explained by the return to the social world which occurs when they enter the house. But quite beyond this, the unexpected appearance of the servant provides some insight into the way hierarchies were both upheld and broken down by the practice of exploration.

No less than Europe itself, the society that developed in colonial Australia was stratified to the most extraordinary degree. Social differences were probably even heightened by the overt presence of convicts, who in the home countries had been confined, out of sight, in hulks and prisons but in the colony were everywhere apparent. The stigma attached to felonry was considerable, but the entire colony was nonetheless dependent on convict labour and enterprise. Strzelecki, like many gentleman travellers, accepted a convict servant as his companion for his journey into the Blue Mountains.[15]

It is often observed that societies that make the most emphatic distinctions between classes or castes of people nevertheless create extraordinary opportunities for their interaction. This was certainly true in Australia, where settlers, soldiers and officers found labourers, companions and frequently sexual partners from among the convict ranks. It is this phenomenon, whereby social hierarchies were on one level being defined and enforced and on another being broken down in unpredictable ways, that gave a certain volatility to the colonial culture.

Unlikely partnerships occurred constantly during the early colonial years. Convicthood, as both social symbol and life experience, was allowed to surface and infiltrate the cultural pattern in a manner that would have been impossible in Europe. In trying to unravel the significance of the labyrinth-as-symbol, the scenario of the aristocratic Pole struggling for life with the exiled Briton provides a poignant insight. The notion of a labyrinth in the Blue Mountains and its proximity to the penal colony are deeply connected. The lone figure in the labyrinth, the spectre that inhabits Strzelecki's footnote, closely resembles the figure of a prisoner—trapped in darkness—enclosed in space. The themes of captivity and confinement had special resonance in this society: a resonance that extended beyond the convicts themselves, that could touch anyone in the colonial community.

Strzelecki does not say enough about his servant for the influence of convicthood to be taken much further in this particular case. But if we go back a few years, to the journey of 1804 when George Caley travelled through and named the Devil's Wilderness, we get a stronger impression. A man of humble origin, the son of a stable hand, Caley was self-educated in botany and fortunate enough to win the valuable support of Sir Joseph Banks. From 1800 to 1810 he was the direct employee of Banks, serving as his collector of natural specimens in New South Wales.

Caley was accompanied by three emancipated convicts when he set off on this journey, the first of his two journeys into the Blue Mountains.[16] To understand the inspiration for Caley's excursion requires an appreciation of the Blue Mountains skyline as seen from certain parts of the Cumberland Plain and complete abandonment of the oft-repeated story that early explorers failed to cross the mountains because they followed valleys instead of ridges. From places such as Rouse Hill and Windsor, the overall uniformity of the blue and distant high country is punctuated by a series of helmet-like domes. The writer Nancy Phelan likens them to the backs of so many whales.[17] Like Mount Jellore, the summits known as Hay, Banks, Tomah and Wilson are formed of basalt. They are igneous extrusions that appeared millions of years after the surrounding sandstone had taken something like its present form.

Caley's mission was directed towards one of these protrusions. He had sighted it from the plains and, like Strzelecki, named it after his personal hero. Once again, it was the mountainous feature, the eminence bathed in light, that exerted a magnetic influence on the European traveller. 'I found myself elevated in a manner I knew not why,'[18] wrote Caley, when he finally reached the summit of Mount Banks.

But that brief moment of elevation was preceded by a tedious trajectory which at times seemed a self-conscious mimicry of those endless packages of seeds, preserved flowers and animals both stuffed and bottled that he was constantly despatching to Banks (the great Enlightenment figure in England). The westerly path to Mount Banks was crowded with the obstacles of darkness. He narrates their descent into a valley which 'put one in mind of looking down a Coal pit. From its great depth, darkness, dampness, and the hideous noise some frogs or toads made, caused me to call it *Dismal Dingle*.'[19]

Caley's place names frequently emphasise the theme of darkness: Devil's Wilderness, Dark Valley, Skeleton Rocks, Gurglepot, Gaping Gill, Mistake Point and, in contradistinction, Luminous Valley, a cavern of glow-worms which, on waking in the night, he thinks are stars. Few of these names have survived on current maps, and in circumstances that would have infuriated Caley, Mount Banks was again 'discovered' by the brothers Hamilton and Rawdon Hume in 1827 and re-named King George's Mount.[20] The name was adopted on the official survey maps, which explains the designation that appears in Strzelecki's footnote. It has since returned to Mount Banks.

Where Strzelecki attempted to dispel darkness, lodging his experience in the 'sub-strata' of those elaborate footnotes, Caley used place names to give it a playful emphasis. But unlike the Polish nobleman, the botanist had a very different attitude to his convict companions. They have a real presence in his journal, and on occasions we can sense quite clearly how their perceptions were influencing his own account. On the return passage from Mount Banks, he notes that the 'men would not stop any in Dismal Dingle, even to take of [*sic*] their loads . . . They said they would sooner prefer the worst cell they had ever seen in a prison before it.'[21]

This darkness in the Earth seemed to infiltrate every aspect of the range. Governor King, on interviewing the returned travellers, recorded that

> the rocks to the west of that range wear the most barren and forbidding aspect, which men, animals, birds, and vegetation has [sic] ever been strangers to, a better proof of which may not be adduced than the remark of one of Cayley's party . . . who exclaimed on Seeing Two Solitary Crows, 'that they had lost their way'.[22]

Darkness below, darkness above: a community whose experience of forced migration involved a passage through British prisons, dockside hulks, the containment of convict transports. Those who have studied the conditions of transportation have emphasised the claustrophobic conditions of the hulks and convict ships. 'The fact is that the prison quarters were always dark and gloomy, and utterly foul,' writes one historian. Convicts were often kept in chains, and those who transgressed during the voyage were placed in 'confinement boxes' which were so small that they held only one person at a time.[23] The colony was itself modelled for the containment of these exiles and, as we shall see, the landscape was a convenient adjunct to a prison without walls. Those who were not of their class would often marvel at this newfound proximity to the former underground denizens of militant Ireland or the industrial slums. They 'resembled more a party of banditti, such as I have read of, than anything else', wrote Elizabeth Hawkins, as she recalled the glare of firelight on the faces of her convict labourers.[24]

A division both internal and external—psychological and social— is exposed by a gap in the landscape, the threat of the abyss, the fear of the lone wanderer in the labyrinth. If we compare these experiences of darkness to the sense of light and elevation that von Guérard captured in his painting of Mount Kosciuszko or that Caley experienced briefly on the summit of Mount Banks, certain features of the discourse of Enlightenment, and their peculiar inflections in the Australian context, might be discerned.

113

2 LINE WITHOUT LIMIT

IF CONVICTS WERE regarded as inhabitants or agents of darkness, the officers who commanded ships and administered the colony had a special investment in the specificity of light. Consider the case of Lieutenant William Dawes, the First Fleet astronomer and cartographer. He was responsible for winding the maritime chronometers on the voyage from England—they were necessary for the calculation of longitude—and he produced an early map of the New South Wales colony.

Dawes' friend Watkin Tench reveals in another memorable footnote that William Dawes was very good at counting. During their surveying expeditions they would 'steer by compass' and calculate distance by

> counting the number of paces, of which two thousand two hundred on good ground were allowed to be a mile...This arduous task was always allotted to Mr Dawes, who, from habit and superior skill, performed it almost without a stop or an interruption of conversation.[25]

The desire to calculate, the need to quantify movement like grains of corn or money—what to make of this compulsion? It is an action both linear and circular, necessitating the return to a point of origin, a 'home' number, once the 2200 has been reached. At one level this type of measuring is material in the extreme. Yet it has an ethereal subtext. With his numerical ordering of footsteps, Dawes was creating a trajectory. So where on Earth might it stop? Theoretically there is no end to such counting. It is a system that permits no horizon.

Since the context for his idiosyncratic style of walking was a period of colonisation, its cultural specificity—its alien character—must be doubly emphasised. The prosaic business of measuring and counting can be analysed in terms of both the material benefits it brought to its practitioners and the deeper assumptions about the cosmos that it reveals. Dawes' system of numbering, like the hypothetical arrow that its passage traces, is pure artifice. It was brought to the Australian coast by men who had enclosed the world with numbers—their system of longitude and latitude—which assisted movement across the oceans and facilitated a return to remote points of discovery. Thus, the arrival of the First Fleet in 1788 was itself a form of re-enactment, an echo of Cook's arrival eighteen years earlier.

The use of a numerical system to determine spatial position can challenge the evidence of the bodily senses. Watkin Tench was allotted the unfortunate task of surveying the shores of Botany Bay, which Cook had described as 'some of the finest meadows in the world'. Hauling himself through slush and bog, he was unable to find two hundred acres that might be cultivated.

> We were unanimously of the opinion, that had not the nautical part of Mr. Cook's description, in which we include the latitude and longitude of the bay, been so accurately laid down, there would exist the utmost reason to believe, that those who have described the contiguous country, had never seen it.[26]

Despite such differing impressions of the country, the veracity of Cook's co-ordinates is never queried. Cartographic logic is prioritised over bodily experience.

The records of Tench and Dawes are valuable for a nuts-and-bolts understanding of how the colonists dealt with unknown land. Dawes' map of Sydney and environs, dated March 1791, demonstrates clearly how habitual it was for the British officers to bring geometrical designs to the physical terrain.[27] A series of angulated trajectories, journeys both accomplished and anticipated, zig-zag through the whiteness. 'Track intended in the course of the Winter of the year one Thousand Seven Hundred and Ninety one', reads one of these captions, the words written along the course of the route, carving territory.

As a student of mathematics quickly learns, triangles, lines, circles, squares and all the forms that make up the science of geometry do not exist in the experienced world. Geometric space is fantastic, and in the sense that it functions by hypothesis—assuming an ideal space—a space that exists nowhere—it is also utopic.[28]

The fact that these officers invoked a utopian space while grappling with actual places immediately complicates any assumption about the unproblematic alignment between cartography and topography. Now, in referring to their use of space as utopian, I am not suggesting for a moment that these men were absent-minded abstractionists, ill-equipped to deal with the physical world. This was certainly not the case. Tench, Dawes and their colleagues were practical men, charged with the enormous responsibility of conducting a fleet of ships to the other side

115

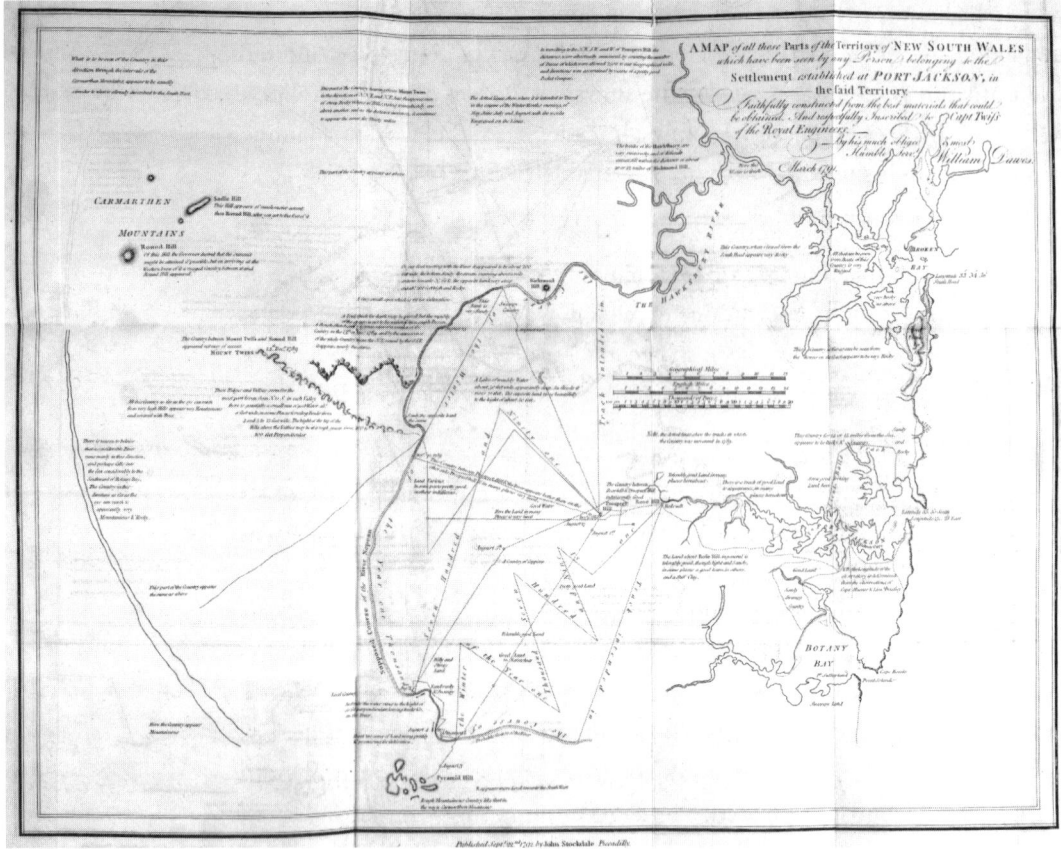

of the world. They were practitioners before they were theorists, but their practice was highly distinctive because their regime was governed by the ocean rather than the land. Any attempt to explicate the world view of these early colonial cartographers must emphasise the significance of this maritime experience. Only then can the curious relationship between hypothetical and topographical space be understood.

For the reader familiar with naval charts, Dawes' map of Sydney and environs will no doubt be a thoroughly comprehensible object. In crossing the oceans, ships travel in the same segmented fashion as Dawes did, casting a bearing with their compass, following it for a time, and then adjusting to a new angle. The convict transports were powered by wind; tacking was often essential. The zig-zag paths inscribed on Dawes' map can be likened to a ship travelling against the breeze. This is not some academic imposition. It is reflected in the map itself, for vessels were used to explore the waterways, patterning the coast in a design remarkably similar to that on present-day charts. Seafaring was the common language among these travellers; they invoked it when waterways narrowed and they were forced to walk the land. Tench writes of this when he describes their inland expeditions.

> At night, when we halted, all these courses were separately cast up, and worked by a traverse table in the manner a ship's reckoning is kept; so that by observing this precaution we always knew exactly where we were . . .; an unspeakable advantage in a new country, where one hill, and one tree, is so like another that fatal wanderings would ensue without it.[29]

The implications of treating land as ocean are worthy of scrutiny. The ocean is the one element of the earthly sphere that consistently mimics the expansive neutrality of geometric space. To the Europeans, this neutrality was embodied not only in the homogeneity and expansive qualities of the ocean but also in its legal status. Unlike the land, the ocean is devoid of human occupants. Consequently, the transfer of a maritime imaginary to the Australian continent had social consequences of considerable gravity. I will say more about this shortly. For the moment, I wish to connect this elemental transpositioning—the treatment of land as sea—with some observations about the role of fantasy in the perception of space.

Bernard Smith, in an essay on Coleridge's *The Rime of the Ancient Mariner*, has provided an elegant case study of the manner in which actual journeys (in this case Cook's second voyage) provided fuel for imaginative ventures. He suggests, in a brief aside, that Cook's tour of discovery is comparable to our contemporary space missions in exciting the artistic imagination.[30] If we regard the nineteenth century as the age of the seafaring novel, and the twentieth as the age of science fiction, Smith's analogy is most appropriate. As the oceanic void was filled by knowledge, the even more endless heavens were opened as the new site of scientific and imaginative speculation.

This is all very well for writers and film-makers, but for Dawes and company, their peculiar method of negotiating terrain was ultimately unworkable. The land is too rich in nuance and complexity to be treated as ocean. The lesson was forced on Dawes when, in December 1789, he led the first official British exploration into the Blue Mountains. Apart

OPPOSITE: THE ASTRONOMER WILLIAM DAWES DRAFTED THIS EARLY MAP OF THE COLONY IN 1791. THE ZIG-ZAG MANNER OF HIS JOURNEYING MIRRORS THE MOVEMENT OF A SHIP TACKING AGAINST THE BREEZE. DAWES CALCULATED DISTANCES BY COUNTING HIS FOOTSTEPS AND COULD MAINTAIN A CONVERSATION WHILE HE DID SO. HIS FORAY INTO THE BLUE MOUNTAINS DID NOT GET VERY FAR BECAUSE HE WAS RIGIDLY DETERMINED TO REACH THE PROTUBERANCE HE CALLED ROUND HILL (NOW MOUNT HAY). IT IS RARELY POSSIBLE TO FOLLOW A STRAIGHT LINE THROUGH THIS DEEPLY DISSECTED COUNTRY.

from a brief testimony written in 1827—a peculiar document in which Dawes, aged, impoverished, and living in the West Indies, wrote to Lord Bathurst claiming back pay of 5s. a day for that westward journey made 38 years earlier[31]—the map of 1791 is the only extant account in his own hand. But the difficulties he encountered are clear enough. Marked on the western side of his chart is a protuberance called Round Hill. Like Caley, Dawes was drawn by the basalt caps, setting as his objective the peak that is now known as Mount Hay. Its depiction on the map is accompanied by an inscription which reads: 'Of this Hill the Governor decreed that the summit might be attained if possible.'

This direction was executed with military precision. Accompanied by two other officers, Dawes forded the Nepean River and followed his compass without deviation. There was no hope of success. He was entering steeply contoured country where sandstone is intersected by a succession of deeply furrowed ravines. The 'line of march', as described by his contemporary, Judge-Advocate David Collins, 'happened to lie, nearly from his setting out, across a line of high and steep rocky precipices, which required much caution in descending, as well as labour in ascending'.[32] George Caley would later liken this type of topography to 'travelling over the tops of the houses in a town'.[33] Tench did not participate in the journey but he reports that 'they found the country so rugged, and the difficulty of walking so excessive, that in three days they were able to penetrate only fifteen miles: and were therefore obliged to relinquish their object'.[34] They had come to a minor crest—Dawes' name of Mount Twiss was a tribute to a friend in the Royal Engineers—where, as he mildly put it, the country 'appeared not easy of access'. Taking a back-bearing, they retraced their steps, having reached a point, by pedemetric computation, fifty-four miles from the coast: further inland, according to Tench, who published his *Account of Settlement* in 1793, 'than any persons ever were before or since'.

Dawes' journey and the map he produced are modest footnotes in Australian history. Yet the case is worthy of interest for several reasons. The map refers not to the 'Blue' but to the 'Carmarthen' Mountains, the name chosen by Governor Phillip in 1788.[35] In official correspondence they remained, for many years, the Carmarthen Mountains and Lansdowne Hills (named after places in Britain), despite being rapidly known as the Blue Mountains in the vernacular. The conflicting

118

1. Major (later Sir) Thomas Mitchell (1792–1855) was deputy surveyor-general of New South Wales when he climbed Mount Jellore in 1828. Convict labourers cleared the summit of all but seven trees and with the aid of a theodolite Mitchell drafted this northward view of the Blue Mountains and surrounding ranges. He met local Gundungurra people during his survey but, according to his journal, none accompanied him to the summit—the Aboriginal man depicted in the foreground is probably a retrospective insertion.

2. THOMAS MITCHELL SKETCHED THE GUNDUNGURRA LEADER MOYENGULLY DURING HIS SURVEY OF 1828.
THE 'OLD KING' REJECTED THE CONVICT TROUSERS HE WAS OFFERED IN RECOMPENSE FOR SITTING.
MITCHELL WAS FORCED TO SURRENDER A FINE GREY PAIR FROM HIS OWN WARDROBE.

3. A GLIMPSE OF SUNRISE AT NARROW NECK. WHILE SCENES LIKE THIS MIGHT SUGGEST WILDERNESS, HUMAN INFLUENCE IS STILL APPARENT. THE ARTIFICIAL LAKE BURRAGORANG (WATER SUPPLY FOR SYDNEY) IS VISIBLE FROM THE PLATEAU AND ELECTRICITY TRANSMISSION LINES CUT ACROSS THE VALLEY.

4. At The Edge Maxvision cinema in Katoomba you can have the 'ultimate Blue Mountains wilderness experience'. Making extensive use of aerial photography, the movie *The Edge* toys with the sense of vertigo that has helped shape perceptions of this colonised landscape.

5. The novelist David Foster is among various observers who discern a fundamental dichotomy between the mountains and the sea in Australian culture. The two aspects are succinctly compressed in this graphic dating from 1914.

6. 'A reflection of the object or view was seen by half of the eye and the pencil point by the other half. As the images fused on the retina it was possible to trace the outline of the reflection.' This was how John Hammond described the operation of a camera lucida, the drafting instrument used by Major James Wallis in creating his watercolour Hawkesbury and Blue Mountains, from Windsor, in 1815.

7. Two Aboriginal figures inhabit the foreground of this early painting of Sydney Harbour with the Blue Mountains in the distance. Although unsigned, it is attributed to the surveyor George Evans. In late 1813 Evans transcended the horizon he had previously painted. Following the blazes of Blaxland and his party, he led the team that established the route for a road to Bathurst.

8. The western skyline—visible almost daily—took fourteen years to find its way into pictorial representation, despite much artistic activity in the colony. William Westall's sketch is thought to be the first view of the Blue Mountains from Sydney. It was drawn in 1802, the year he sailed with Matthew Flinders to circumnavigate Australia. Westall evoked the 'noble savage' when he added Aborigines to the foreground of the watercolour version.

9. Bradley's watercolour shows the limited visual field in the early days of settlement.

10. Thomas Watling focused on a moment of departure when he depicted a ship leaving Sydney Harbour.

11. Eugène von Guérard's sunset vista of Weatherboard (now Wentworth) Falls provides one of the most splendid and intriguing colonial depictions of Jamison Valley. It was painted in Melbourne three years after the artist's Blue Mountains tour in 1859. While von Guérard developed this work from a detailed sketch that was drawn in the field, aspects of the painting, including the human figure in the foreground, were imagined.

12. ANTICIPATING THE EMERGENCE OF A TOURIST INDUSTRY, THE ABORIGINAL FIGURE WAS REPLACED BY SIGHTSEERS IN THE LITHOGRAPH VERSION OF VON GUÉRARD'S VIEW OF WEATHERBOARD FALLS.

13. Eugène von Guérard painted this view in 1866. Australia's highest peak, located in the Snowy Mountains of New South Wales, was named after the Polish patriot Tadeusz Kosciuszko. (The Polish spelling has been restored to the landmark, but not to the painting.) The peak appears on this canvas as a gracious mountain, although Paul Strzelecki, who named it, once claimed that it reminded him of Tadeusz Kosciuszko's burial mound in Kraków.

14. FRANK HURLEY PHOTOGRAPHED BILL DAVIS WHILE HE PAINTED THE THREE SISTERS AT KATOOMBA.

PUBLISHED IN 1952, THE PHOTO PROBABLY DATES FROM THE 1940S.

15. The base of Katoomba Falls photographed from the Scenic Skyway cable car.
In 1907 when the waterfall was frozen, a 13-year-old boy and a young woman fell to their deaths in separate incidents on the same day. The accessibility of the escarpment lends itself to occasional accidents and more frequent suicides.

16. Mel Ward as he appeared on the cover of Reader's Digest in 1957. The magazine pointed out that Ward's museum contained '7,000 native curios collected all over the world.'

17. In his writing as well as his painting, the surveyor William Govett displayed a fascination with the modality of falling. In this watercolour he shows a wagon toppling over the precipice. His diary records that some 'Black fellows who were loitering by' (visible on the road) upset the bullocks and caused the accident.

18. Marjorie Maitland Howard sketched Vere Gordon Childe as he gave his final lecture at London's Institute of Archaeology in 1956. He wore Central Asian dress and held an Australian Aboriginal spear.

19. Aboriginal people drew charcoal images of escaped cattle during the early years of British settlement.

In 1993 vandals attacked the site, using red automotive paint to scrawl drawings and obscenities.

20. In the nineteenth century Captain Starlight and his gang of bushrangers stole a prize stallion called the Duke of Athol. Partially covering Aboriginal markings, they drew images of this and other horses on the walls of the cave called Livery Stable in the Gardens of Stone National Park.

21. The metal grille across Bull Cave was built in 1982. It did not stop graffitists, who carried equipment to cut it open. The cage has since been mended and the cattle drawn on its walls are locked and double-locked within a violated pictorial surface.

nomenclature expressed in Dawes' document intimates the dispute between convicts and their masters about what lay within and beyond the mountains. The premature termination of the expedition is also highly significant, for it demonstrates how the attempt to impose European spatial principles would be thwarted by the specificity of place. To read the country, to be able to move, the colonists must learn to decipher the meandering and idiosyncratic lines of the land itself, rather than impose the uniform radiants of the compass.

Furthermore, the curious phenomenon of Dawes counting his paces, locating himself on a trajectory that is ultimately transfinite, raises the question of how a journey founded on such principles might ever find a genuine point of termination. For a sense of the cosmic aspirations of the cartographic enterprise, we need look no further than the colonists' ethnographic enquiries. It so often happens that the encounter with a strange society immediately highlights the interrogator's concerns. After learning that the Sydney Aborigines did not count above the number four, Tench immediately asked how they might conceive notions that are *beyond number.*

> The question of, whether they believe in the immortality of the soul, will take up very little time to answer. They are universally fearful of spirits. They call a spirit, *Mawn:* they often scruple to approach a corpse, saying that the *mawn* will seize them, and that it fastens upon them in the night when asleep. When asked where their deceased friends are, they always point to the skies. To believe in after existence is to confess the immortality of some part of being. To enquire whether they assign a *limited* period to such future state would be superfluous: this is one of the subtleties of speculation, which a savage may be supposed not to have considered, without impeachment either of his sagacity or happiness.[36]

Concepts of eternity, infinitude and timelessness, it seems, are never far from a mind consumed by numerical pedantry. Tench's encounter with the 'savage', where the prospect of eternity is projected but ultimately denied, runs counterpoint to his description of Dawes counting footsteps, numbering them like the years of life's journey.

For what is he reaching towards as hundreds become thousands and numbers grow? Sympathise with his predicament. He is walking towards the Infinite, towards—where? This is the paradox of infinitude: every number brings it closer but dispels it further. Unless it invokes some exterior category, some notion of transcendence, the system is one of perpetual displacement.

The cartographic logic Europeans brought to the Australian coast was cosmological as much as it was rational. William Dawes, who approached the southern skies with a commission from the Board of Longitude to observe a comet last seen in 1661 (it never arrived), was more than measurer and scientist. Certainly, his eye might be glued to the lens, or his brain minding the footsteps. His friend Elizabeth Macarthur described him as 'so much engaged with the stars that to mortal eyes he is not always visible'.[37] Yet in each of his empirical projects—gazing towards heaven or walking the infinite line—there exists the imminent possibility of a state beyond measure.

In writing about the fantasies associated with topographical experience, I am trying to acknowledge the desire for transcendence: the manifold ways in which it was expressed, used, commodified and abused. This much is essential if even the textbook events of colonial history are to be understood. The desire for transcendence encompasses but goes well beyond debates that are purely 'philosophical', for it concerns the actions and lives of the people who lived here. As Graeme Davison has pointed out, the colonial settlement was expressly designed to monitor and regulate a population that was 'doing time'.[38] Basic needs and desires—of movement, assembly, work, self-expression, self-location, worship, even diet—were subject to the most rigid supervision. Functioning within this regime of control was the economy of rum, that agent of obliteration which for so many people substituted the numerical abstraction of financial currency. Drunkenness among convicts and soldiers, and also among the Aborigines displaced by settlement, occurred on a scale that is scarcely conceivable. The tangled and conflicting narratives of escape, suicide or the desire to 'make good', to forge a new life from the old, become far more understandable when we acknowledge that extremities of repression were inextricably connected with the promise of vectors without limit.

Perhaps William Dawes understood this best of all. Although there is a comic aspect to his counting of footsteps, he should ultimately be remembered as perhaps the most interesting mind and the most outspoken humanitarian in the early colony. Dawes had developed a friendship with an Aboriginal woman called Patyegarang, and they met on a regular basis to teach each other their respective languages. The glossary he devised constitutes the most thorough colonial record of the tongue we now call Darug.[39] This attempt to reconcile the profound cultural differences exposed by colonisation gives context to an incident that occurred at the end of 1790, when Dawes fell irretrievably foul of Governor Phillip and was threatened with court martial for insubordination.

The dispute concerned a punitive mission against the Aborigines of Botany Bay, one of whom, probably the celebrated warrior Pemulwuy, had killed the governor's 'gamekeeper', a man called M'entire, who had long been suspected of 'having shot and injured' the blacks.[40] Tench led the party; Dawes was ordered to accompany. Their command was to

> proceed to the head of Botany Bay; and thence. . . if practicable, to bring away two natives as prisoners: and to put to death ten.. . . That we were to cut off, and bring in the heads of the slain, for which purpose, hatchets and bags would be furnished.[41]

Dawes objected, and sought counsel from the parson, Richard Johnson. Tench chose to bargain, and the governor consented to reduce the number of victims. Despite two separate missions, the inhabitants of Botany Bay avoided the British and none was killed or captured. But the rift between governor and officer was never healed, and Dawes left the colony in late 1791. At the request of William Wilberforce, he took up residence in Freetown and became governor of the Sierra Leone Company—that flawed but extraordinary enterprise which sought to provide a home in north-west Africa for liberated slaves.[42]

In one way or another, the remainder of Dawes' life was an attempt to mitigate the damage of colonisation. It is worth considering what role his experience with Patyegarang and other Sydney Aborigines might have had in directing his eventual path. While it is difficult to believe that these encounters were not extremely formative, it is also salutary to realise that in making an attempt at cross-cultural under-standing, Dawes signalled a possible departure from forms of knowledge based on transcendence and positioned Aboriginal experience as a possible thread.

3 A Chimerical Establishment

Consider a moment in colonial administration that points to a different form of mapping. In October 1802, Philip Gidley King, who was governor of New South Wales from 1800 to 1806, was forced by rebellious sentiments among the convicts—the Irish in particular—to issue this most unusual General Order:

> The Governor has for some time been informed of a Report, as wicked as it is false, and calculated to bring the believers of it to Destruction, that a Settlement of White People exists on the other side of the Mountains, &c., And that several of the Prisoners were so far deluded as to concert means for reaching that Settlement, in consequence of which, several have lately absconded from their Labour, Nine of whom have been apprehended, and on the Examination before the Magistrates, it appeared that some of them, instead of taking the course to the Mountains, had gone to the Sea-side, others had reached near the Nepean, whilst those less instructed than the latter, had wandered about near the place they had left, after being absent Ten Days, most of them nearly starved, and living on Grass. . . . [From] the folly of the late Land adventurers, joined to the punishment they have already received in being nearly starved, and the Corporeal Punishment awarded by the Magistrates as an example, it is hoped that what has occurred to those ignorant and infatuated People may have its effect upon others, and prevent such Schemes, as wild as they proved unsuccessful and destructive to those concerned in them.[43]

It was not the first occasion on which convicts had escaped for imagined communities. In 1791, twenty men and a pregnant woman absconded from Rose Hill on the Parramatta River, taking clothes and provisions, seeking a passage to China or a settlement where they might live without work. One died of fatigue, another was killed by Aborigines. Tench interviewed some of the survivors at the Rose Hill hospital.

> I asked these men if they really supposed it possible to reach China: they answered, that they were certainly made to believe (they knew not how) that at a considerable distance to the northward existed a large river, which separated this country from the back part of China; and that when it should be crossed (which was practicable) they would find themselves among a copper-coloured people, who would receive and treat them kindly. . .[44]

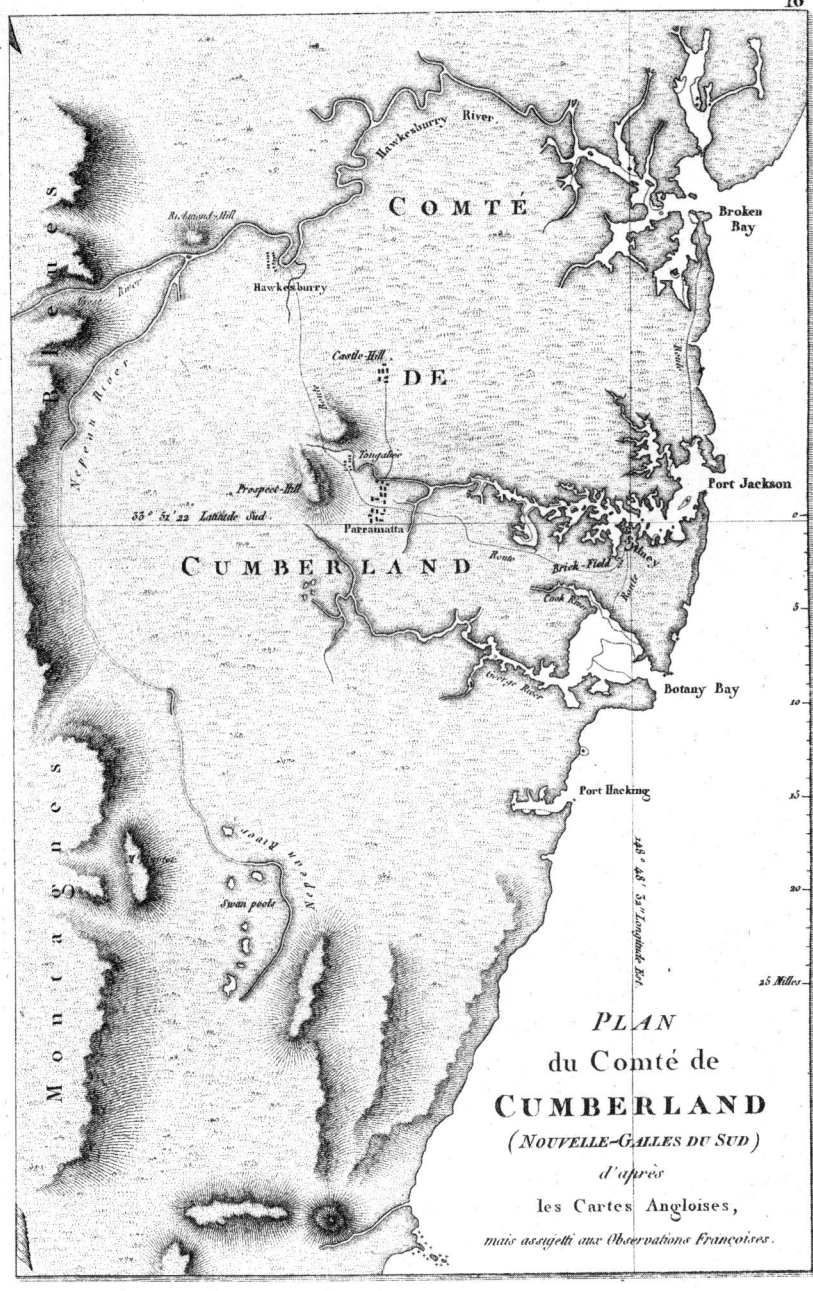

16

COMTÉ

DE

CUMBERLAND

Hawkesbury River

Broken
Bay

Hawkesbury

Richmond-Hill

Castle-Hill

Prospect-Hill

Parramatta

Port Jackson

Brick-Field

Botany Bay

Port Hacking

Swan pools

Montagnes Bleues

Nepean River

PLAN
du Comté de
CUMBERLAND
(NOUVELLE-GALLES DU SUD)
d'après
les Cartes Angloises,
mais assujetti aux Observations Françoises.

THIS ELEGANT MAP OF
THE SYDNEY BASIN WAS
DRAFTED BY THE
FRENCH SCIENTIFIC
EXPEDITION LED BY
NICOLAS BAUDIN THAT
REACHED SYDNEY IN
1802. IT DEPICTS THE
MAJOR FEATURES AND
LOCALITIES MENTIONED
IN THE TALES OF
CONVICT ESCAPE AND
INSURRECTION DURING
THAT EARLY COLONIAL
PERIOD: PARRAMATTA,
CASTLE HILL, THE
HAWKESBURY RIVER
AND OF COURSE *les
Montagnes Bleues*.

These escapes for illusory settlements indicate the extent of the
convicts' dislocation. They offer a salient reminder that the cartographic
exercises being carried out by Dawes and his contemporaries were
confined to the executive strata of the colony. Convicts, travelling in
darkened ships towards a destination that they might know only as

Botany Bay or *New South Wales*, had plenty of time to construct their imaginary geographies, if little hard data on which to improvise. Information circulated through a predominantly verbal economy, subject to the hyperbole of rumour. So the stories of nearby China or the imaginary settlement across the mountains multiplied with an abundance that infuriated their mostly English masters.

In February 1803, King reported to Lord Hobart that fifteen 'mutinous Irish', recently arrived on the *Hercules*, had 'left their labour at Castle Hill' and while at large, committed 'every possible enormity except murder'.[45] The newly formed *Sydney Gazette*, the colony's first newspaper, reported on their escapades. They had left the agricultural settlement of Castle Hill (north of Parramatta) and embarked on a rampage of robbery and violence. Guns, ammunition, clothes, razors, and even silver spoons were stolen from various households, and a manservant was shot in the face, to be rendered a 'ghastly spectacle'. Two of the escapees were arrested on the second day after their flight, and the majority were captured a week later in the country between the Hawkesbury River and the mountains. At the ensuing trial,

> one of the unhappy men declared, that he had embarked in this fatal expedition with no other view, than that of crossing the mountains, which the judicious and well-equipped have found impassable, and thereby returning to his family![46]

Three of the escapees, Patrick Gannan, Francis Simpson and Patrick Macdermot, were sentenced to death for these exploits. On 22 March they were conveyed by boat from Sydney to Parramatta, and the following morning conducted in 'solemn procession' the eight miles to Castle Hill.

> The fatal tree, which had been purposely erected near to the spot on which they had committed the offence for which they were about to atone, was half-surrounded by the Parramatta Detachment, formed semi-circularly. At a proper distance stood a concourse of spectators, composed chiefly of the prisoners employed at Castle Hill and places adjacent, orderly assembled, with their overseers.

After the Reverend Samuel Marsden prayed for the condemned men 'with his usual fervour', news arrived that Macdermot had been reprieved. As the *Sydney Gazette* reported it, Gannan and Simpson were left to mount the scaffold—a cart that was drawn away—and were swiftly 'launched into eternity'. Gannan showed penitence before the hanging, but Simpson 'died truly impenitent and hardened'.[47]

The execution of Gannan and Simpson was typical of the corporal punishments administered under the colonial regime. Hangings, floggings, the donning of humiliating apparel created public spectacles, theatrical in design, which referred to the sufferer's transgression in their choice of environmental location. Thus, the journey upriver of the three escapees, where the state symbolically returned them to their point of departure, forced the enactment of a new narrative that would ameliorate the one they created of their own volition. Castle Hill, which adjoins the high ridge of Pennant Hills, offers a clear prospect of the Blue Mountains; perhaps the men could see them from the scaffold. Convicts and soldiers had left their morning duties to attend the hanging. This moral instruction, it was hoped, would counter the rash fantasies promulgated in speech and thought. The public execution, as Michel Foucault demonstrated so persuasively, is a form of writing: the transgressor's body becomes a surface for the inscription of law.[48] After execution, the corpse would often be sent to a surgeon for dissection, ostensibly for the purpose of medical research. It was a clear demonstration of the power of the state over life and limb. For some victims, the thought of being dissected was more terrifying than the prospect of hanging itself.

The public hanging ended life through the confluence of two opposing elements: the fall into flight and its immediate arrest by the restriction of the rope. The leap outwards, the freedom from containment—indeed everything suggested by flight of bird—was implied as quickly as it was denied. That was the situation at Castle Hill as Macdermot was spared and the others tumbled, their corpses a forbidding rebuttal to anyone so wicked or deluded as to countenance flight, to entertain the notion of what the governor referred to as 'a chimerical establishment'.[49]

It didn't work. Four months later, Governor King was again forced to warn his subjects of the 'dismal consequences' of the 'rash project of crossing the Mountains'. A lack of data that would refute the convict claims tested his own creative abilities and forced the adoption of an official fantasy that might combat the story he was trying to dismiss. The governor warned of 'the numerous and large Lagoons by which these Mountains are intersected' and assured his reader that adventurers would be rewarded with 'death under accumulated miseries'.[50]

125

4

FORGOTTEN

JOURNEYS

THE FANTASY OF a settlement beyond the mountains is a continuing theme in the early colonial records, appearing in 1791 and continuing even after Blaxland, Lawson and Wentworth's 'first crossing' of 1813. Governor John Hunter had been as exasperated as King when, in 1798, he tried a practical experiment—a forced exploration that would convince the colony of the impassability of the mountains.

The mission was provoked by a series of escapes, some involving theft of valuable property, and the familiar troubles with the Irish. A party had recently fled in government boats; two breeding mares were stolen by other escapees; and then came intelligence of a plan involving sixty convicts who would cross the mountains to reach a 'fancied paradise'. In a despatch to the Duke of Portland, Hunter writes of the conspirators possessing 'a figure of a compass drawn upon paper', accompanied by written directions. ('The ignorance of these deluded people, my Lord, would scarcely be credited.') Acting from 'a strong desire to save these men, worthless as they are', Hunter ordered that the convicts select four of their own number who would 'prepare for a journey of discovery... in order that they might have an opportunity of relating, upon their return, whatever they saw and met with'.[51]

As an attempt to instruct the convicts by example, the expedition had little value. News reached Hunter that the chosen four intended to meet with a band of escapees, kill the guides intended to accompany them, then proceed to the settlement across the mountains. So extra soldiers were assigned to the party when it left Parramatta in January 1798. In the company of the governor's agents, the mission quickly lost its shine, and before they had even entered the foothills the convicts tired of the journey and insisted that the soldiers return them to the settlement. The 'guides', who numbered three men, continued on regardless.

The names of these travellers are not mentioned in Hunter's despatches. But he refers to their leader as a man who had lived 'many months among the mountain savages'. Contemporary records, which include a journal kept by another of the three, indicate that this was John Wilson, a former convict who frequently appears in the annals of early settlement. David Collins described him as a man whose 'term of transportation being expired, preferred living among the natives in the vicinity of the [Hawkesbury] river, to earning the wages of honest industry by working for settlers'. He developed 'an intermediate language between his own and theirs' and was given the name Bun-bo-è.

Wilson was an unorthodox and highly ambiguous figure in the penal colony: a man who established close relations with the Aborigines at a time of deep suspicion and frequent hostility. In 1791, a little more than three years after the arrival of the First Fleet, Wilson briefly returned from his Aboriginal companions with shoulders and breast 'scarified after their custom . . . He made his appearance with no other covering than an apron of a kangaroo's skin.' This reference to ritualistic scarification, again from the record of David Collins, reveals that Wilson had experienced the formalities of some sort of Aboriginal initiation. Collins also describes an occasion when, on meeting some settlers, Wilson declared himself an Aborigine 'and pointed out a very old woman as his mother, who was weak and credulous enough to acknowledge him as her son'.[52] The joke, however, was probably on Collins. He was evidently unaware that for Wilson to be accepted into an Aboriginal community it was almost inevitable that relations of kinship would have to be established by adoption. So the idea of him having an Aboriginal 'mother' is not far-fetched.

From 1791 he lived, at various times, as both whitefellow and Aborigine. Some writers—the most memorable being Eric Willmot in his historical novel *Pemulwuy* (1987)—have depicted the Bun-bo-è/ Wilson personage as an underworld hero who resisted the English colony and supported the guerilla warfare being conducted against settlers. There is some worth in this portrayal, although Wilson's motives were not entirely altruistic. His penchant was for female flesh, and young flesh at that. There is mention of him trying to abduct a girl from the settlement 'whose age could not have been beyond nine or ten years', and his death in 1800 came from an Aboriginal spear. Collins claims that after many indulgences with 'their young females', he took one 'against her inclinations'.[53] For this he paid with his life.

The passion for young girls does not sit happily with political hagiography. But it is a reminder that colonial men, frustrated by the gender imbalance within the colony, had a special interest in Aboriginal women. Whatever the motivation—and quite possibly Bun-bo-è did 'go native' to secure sexual partners—his support of the Aboriginal cause when relations turned violent is beyond dispute. This would have been invaluable given his inside knowledge of the enemy. In 1797 he was mentioned in a list of absconders who were assisting 'numerous bodys of the natives' in depriving settlers of their livestock, 'burning their houses, and destroying in a few minutes the whole fruits of their former industry, as well as wounding and some-times murdering them'. By this time an unofficial war was raging. The General Order which names Wilson and the other former convicts warned them to surrender within fourteen days or risk immediate execution without trial.[54]

Extraordinary as it might seem, just eight months later Wilson was leading the government expedition into the Blue Mountains, ostensibly proving the fallaciousness of the utopian settlement. He had surrendered to the governor who, 'well knowing, from his former habits, that if he punished and sent him to hard labour, he would quickly rejoin his late companions', decided to take advantage of his skills, influenced no doubt by Wilson's claim that he had been over a hundred miles in every direction of the settlement.[55] To accompany him, Hunter appointed one of his own servants, 'an intelligent lad', selected for his enthusiasm and ability to write.[56] As scribe, he would keep an account of the journey: a written record from a trusted servant seemed preferable to the oral testimony of Wilson who was presumably illiterate. The journal survived intact, but not the name of its author.[57] Historians for many years erroneously referred to the boy-servant as Barracks. The investigations of Alec Chisholm in the 1960s have shown that his real name was John Price.[58] The journal indicates that their third companion was a man called Roe, about whom nothing more is known.

The Price journal opens on 24 January 1798. They crossed the Nepean River south-west of Sydney and headed in a south-sou'westerly direction into the mountains. Later comments suggest that Wilson had some familiarity with the area, but this particular route was new to all the party. The convicts and their sentries had returned, yet the travellers were still under the impression that the fabled white settlement might be found. If Wilson considered it a fiction, he did nothing to dispel it from the mind of his secretary who wrote on the second day of their journey:

> We saw a great many kangaroos and emews, and we fell in with a party of natives which gave a very good account of the place we were in search of; that there was a great deal of corn and potatoes,

and that the people were very friendly. We hearkened to their advice; we altered our course according to their directions.[59]

A man promised to meet them later—'he would take us to a party of natives who had been there; but he did not come according to his promise'. They continued and later that day found a cave on the Nepean River which contained 'a great deal of salt'. The discovery was significant because the colony was suffering a dearth of salt at this time. That cave became the impetus for a second, far more extensive, journey two months later.

On 28 January the travellers met with more Aborigines. 'Wilson ran and caught one of them, a girl, thinking to learn something from them, but her language was so different from that one which we had with us that we could not understand her.' They had crossed a territorial boundary, departing the land of the Darug language—'the one which we had with us'—to enter the domain of the Gundungurra.

The journal states that the girl was kept overnight—'she cried and fretted'—then released in the morning with the gift of a small tomahawk. Surely this action put the travellers at risk? They had firearms, of course, but the girl's people would have been favoured by their familiarity with the terrain, competence with spears and superiority of numbers. Reprisal would have been easy. No doubt the party had a sleepless night, leaning on their muskets. Since the linguistic barrier and the girl's terror made the gleaning of information impossible, the reason for the abduction, if not for sexual purposes, remains a matter for speculation. So often in these documents, the unsaid speaks louder than words.

The journey continued until 30 January, proceeding west past the site of the town of Mittagong until they reached a river, the Wollondilly, having travelled through the mountains a distance of ninety kilometres. On sighting the river, Wilson proposed making a canoe and continuing further but he was held back by the weariness of the scribe and Roe. Supplies were exhausted and the men were now entirely dependent for their survival on the bush knowledge that Wilson had acquired from the Darug. Sometimes they ate grubs and roots. '[T]he other man and myself were very faint and tired,' writes the scribe. 'Wilson was well and hearty.' Looking down at the Wollondilly, having eaten nothing 'but two small birds each we were afraid to venture on the other side of the river . . .

[O]ur shoes was gone and our feet were very much bruised with the rocks, so we asked Wilson to return.' The cost of sending Roe and the boy, thereby acquiring a written record, was the premature termination of the expedition. They returned to settlement by a different route.

Like many of the Blue Mountains journals, the Price document vastly overstates the distances travelled. (Unlike Dawes, they were not great counters of footsteps.) But in other respects, the diary gives a convincing account of the journey that is sufficiently descriptive to allow a later generation of travellers—rucksack-bearing historians—to trace its minutiae on foot, draft maps and speculate on the particularities of the route. The predilection for re-enactment, such a staple in the production of Australian history, took hold among Blue Mountains scholars in the early years of the twentieth century. The journeys mentioned so far, and nearly every expedition of which a record exists, have been the subject of some form of re-enactment.

Perhaps this conscious re-tracing of someone else's footsteps, so common in the preparation of historical narratives, echoes the unfolding of history itself. On hearing about the discovery of salt, Governor Hunter decreed that immediate re-enactment was necessary, this time with more reliable company. Henry Hacking, the quarter-master of the *Sirius*, who had led a short expedition into the Blue Mountains in 1794, joined Wilson, the boy-servant and a man called Collins (not the judge-advocate) on a return visit to the Nepean River which departed from Prospect Hill on 9 March 1798.

They returned to the cliff where the salt had been found and collected samples which were sent to Sir Joseph Banks in London. On the fourteenth, the party split. (The salt was not a vein as they had hoped, but a thin layer caused by condensation.) Hacking returned to Sydney, while Wilson, Collins and the scribe, having adequate provisions, set off through 'nasty, scrubby, stony country' on a further tour of discovery that took them almost twice as far as the last.

This time they encountered no Aborigines whatsoever, having taken a route parallel but slightly west of the one used in January. This allowed them to ascend Jellore, with its wonderful view to the north. From there, instead of turning inland to their previous terminus above the Wollondilly, they continued south-west, reaching, on 19 March, 'a most beautifull country . . . It is not in my power to lay it down fine enough'. They continued west-sou'west, terminating their journey on the twenty-third when they reached a summit that R. H. Cambage identified as Mount Towrang, just a few miles east of the present city of Goulburn. Once more they looked towards a river—unknown to them, it was still the Wollondilly—'that seemed to run to the W'd'.

When the Price journal was first considered by Australian historians, its significance was not entirely overlooked. 'I submit that the evidence justifies the conclusion that "the reputed passage of the Blue Mountains in 1798," becomes a matter of historical fact,' declared Thomas Whitley in 1904.[60] For the standard historiography, this was quite a shocker. Whitley's judgement was never popularly accepted. It is curious that Blaxland, Lawson and Wentworth's 'first crossing' was being disputed around the time of Federation—an era in which the myth of their discovery was being energetically affirmed by other historians. But then the practice of debunking the Blaxland discovery has itself become part of the mythologising of the journey, instilling a flavour of distinctly Australian irony: a 'first crossing' that was not the first. A latter-day example of this approach is Chris Cunningham's 1996 book *The Blue Mountains Rediscovered: Beyond the Myths of Early Australian Exploration.*

R. H. Cambage, who wrote about Wilson in 1920, was more moderate in his appraisal of the Wilson journey. Whitley had taken too literally the journal's distances and the comments about a westerly flowing watercourse. Perhaps they only reached the upper Wollondilly. But Whitley, it must be remembered, is talking about a *passage*, whereas Cambage thinks in terms of a *crossing*. He emphasises that Blaxland, Lawson and Wentworth were the first to make it through the Blue Mountains, though concludes his paper by lavishly praising the intrepid John Price—that

> plucky, intelligent lad, who eagerly volunteered for this most hazardous adventure . . . [W]e are moved to admire the great services rendered by many Australian pioneers in plunging into the mountain fastnesses, and opening up ways for the future progress and development of our great country.[61]

My intention is not to prove that Wilson/Bun-bo-è, Price and Collins made a first crossing or passage over the Blue Mountains. That idea is a conceit—as people have realised all along. Aborigines have been moving in, through, and around the Blue Mountains for tens of thousands of years. The important point to me is the way in which an actual journey, designed to dispel the notion of a mythical settlement, was itself relegated to the realm of myth.

With a few notable exceptions, like Paul Carter's analysis of the mythical China in *The Road to Botany Bay* (1987),[62] the historiographic record has suffered badly by ignoring the role of fantasy in the shaping of human destiny. We have seen how Bun-bo-è's travels, motivated by the fictional settlement and informed in matters of practicality by his transgressive decision to enter an Aboriginal community, were far more extensive than the rational enterprise of William Dawes. They also problematise the common claim that the arrival of cartography in a colonial context will inevitably enhance the power of the empire state.[63]

Such a view is very deceptive because it makes no allowance for the considerable role played by the fictional, the fantastic, the imagined, in propelling or thwarting movement. Furthermore, it tends to discourage a genuine appraisal of cartography, which is actually a complex and ambiguous process. The discipline of measuring angles and distances, of reading the representation rather than the land itself, often hindered rather than facilitated movement. The widespread reluctance to accept this indicates how easy it is to succumb to the spell of the cartographer, who does not make the world real but simply imposes a realist fantasy upon it. To understand why people moved in the way they did—to appreciate the occupation of this country in its particularity—the mythology we bring to places must be studied with the utmost attention. There is a virtual journey, an Orphean trajectory, that guides and shadows the overlander.

The tendency in historical writing to negate the significance of the imagination cannot be isolated from the discourses of reason and responsibility which saturate colonial documents and still exert considerable influence on understandings of historical 'truth'. Consider the moralistic tone with which the imagination is described in the following extract—a report on the hanging of three Tasmanian Aborigines at Port Phillip in 1842. When the time is set for the execution,

> all their castle-building was knocked to pieces, the fairy fabrics constructed by the imagination dissolved like mist, and the dark blank of impending death stunned them.[64]

Andrew Lattas, in studying the language of colonial authority, has described the frequency with which imagination was cast in these highly pejorative terms. Criminality was 'seen to have its roots in irrationality'—the exertions of an active mind were a profound threat to what the *Sydney Gazette* described as 'the mild government of Reason'.[65] According to this world-view, crime and social fragmentation showed blatant disregard for structure and hierarchy and were often associated with the vanity of attempting to step beyond one's 'station'. Lattas writes:

> Vice and Foible were seen to 'both originate in the romantic meanderings of the imagination unguided by the torch of reason'. . . Imagination was thus that realm within which man risked losing himself.[66]

This was the ethical landscape in which became manifest those elaborate mental topographies of adjacent Chinas, white utopias, families one might return to beyond the mountains. They produced labyrinthine images on the part of colonial authorities who viewed the Australian landscape as an extension of their prison without walls. Yet, as the economy of the imagination floated into stranger realms, images were produced that provoked all sorts of action. They sparked escapes, expeditions, attacks on life. They bridged the convict chasm between fixity and the desire for transcendence.

133

5

REFLECTION

AND

PROJECTION

I beheld, this day,

for the first time,

a distant blue

horizon, exactly

resembling that of

the ocean.

THOMAS MITCHELL,
Three Expeditions
into the Interior
of Australia, 1838.

THE TALES OF imagined communities on the western side of the Blue Mountains could be described as helectites: those strange limestone growths that shoot laterally from stalactites and challenge the drift of a prevailing logic. They emerge from that logic—precipitated by actual places, people and events. But they defy that logic, tipping it into parody and exposing the space of poetic journeying that is so frequently opened up by the schematisation of physical terrain.

Comparing these helectite structures with the official, cartographic ordering of space being attempted by British officers reveals a basic duality in the perception of terrain. Spatial concepts were influenced by the presence or absence of light. Dawes and Tench sought direction from the heavenly constellations; the convicts in their hulls had no such guidance. The distinction between those who were with the light and those without was central to the language of authority at the end of the eighteenth century. 'The moral condition of by far the greater part of our population is that of tenfold darkness,' declared the Wesley Mission House in describing the lower orders of New South Wales.[67] Convict projections of utopian spaces—emanations of the 'darkened' intellect—were clearly transgressive. Governors described them as 'wicked', 'ignorant', 'deluded'. The enlightened ones considered it their privilege and duty to impose assumptions about how the darkened mind should be properly directed towards the light.

Assertions about the proper course of the mind and the actual constitution of physical space were dependent on a state-endorsed understanding of what was 'real'. To this end, scientific proofs—such as cartographic ordering of space—were important weapons in the battle against the excesses of the imagination. It pays to remember that this language of authority was emerging at a unique time in the intellectual history of Europe. Across a broad range of human endeavours, including the exploration and colonisation of the Pacific, the practical benefits of science were being impressed upon monarchs and governments of the West. But science was still an emerging discipline, very different from the secularised practice that arose in the wake of Darwin. The majority of scientists would have shared Descartes' position that rational cognition was an admirable demonstration of the power of God. The late eighteenth and early nineteenth centuries gave rise to a unique and unrepeatable alignment of science, divinity and the State. Yet it was a fleeting transit: divested of divinity, science would eventually come to Earth from the heavens and the godhead would be sacrificially hurled into the abyss.

The suspicion attached to the power of imagination at the end of the eighteenth century was considerable. Imagination was intrinsically disruptive, rebellious or perverse, and many of the disciplinary procedures invoked by the State were directed at curtailing its excesses. The consequences of this degrading of the imaginative faculty have been analysed by the Italian scholar Giorgio Agamben. He argues that for the Ancients imagination had been the 'supreme medium of knowledge' because it functioned as an intermediary between the senses and the intellect. Since it is 'the imagination which forms dream images, this explains the particular relationship to truth which dreams have in the ancient world'. Imagination, writes Agamben,

> was not a 'subjective' thing, but was rather the coincidence of subjective and objective, of internal and external . . . [N]ow it is its combinatory and hallucinatory character, to which Antiquity gave secondary importance, that is given primacy. From having been the subject of experience the phantasm becomes the subject of mental alienation, visions and magical phenomena—in other words, everything that is excluded by real experience.[68]

Agamben associates the expropriation of imagination as a legitimate aspect of experience with Descartes and the arrival of modern science. Descartes' formulation of the *ego cogito* proposed a direct relationship between 'the new *ego* and the corporeal world'. There was no longer the 'need for any mediation'. The result of this was not to dispel the imagination from the human psyche—that is surely impossible—but to cast a shadow over the realm of experience. 'This shadow is desire, the idea of experience as fugitive and inexhaustible.'[69]

To examine the denigration of imagination and its influence upon notions of 'the real', consider a story about another place of blueness—not the Blue Mountains, but a 'Blue Island', supposedly visited by French explorers and described in the 64-page pamphlet *Fragmens* [sic] *du Dernier Voyage de La Pérouse* that was published anonymously in France in 1797. La Pérouse was the renowned navigator whose frigates, the *Boussole* and the *Astrolabe,* arrived at Botany Bay just a few days after the

British in 1788. The French anchored there for about six weeks, botanising along the shore and fraternising with the British officers. Departing on 10 March, the two ships were reputedly destined for Mauritius. But they never arrived. Their fate was the subject of considerable anxiety and conjecture in France for many years. Not until 1826 was it firmly ascertained that both vessels had been wrecked off Vanikoro in the Santa Cruz group of islands.[70]

The Blue Island described in *Fragmens* was purportedly located in the Pacific and visited by the French explorers before they reached the Australian coast. The text opens with an unsigned foreword, the author of which claims to be a British seaman of the First Fleet, a friend of 'Captain Watkin-Tenck [*sic*]', who befriended the French mariners and visited them frequently during their sojourn in Botany Bay. On one of these occasions he 'could not resist the temptation of removing a hand-written notebook' from a French officer's cabin. In later life, the seaman was shipwrecked off the coast of France and held prisoner. He tells of being lent money by a French citizen, to whom, in gratitude, he gave the French officer's manuscript which forms the basis of the publication. He insisted that his own identity be permanently concealed. Of course, there is no such place as the 'Blue Island' and the *Fragmens* is a literary hoax the success of which can be measured by the fact that, as recently as 1941, a La Pérouse scholar was still treating it as a genuine artefact.

As an example of the helectite narrative, *Fragmens* is an extremely valuable document. With its reference to Watkin Tench, whose French translation of *A Narrative of the Expedition to Botany Bay* had appeared in 1791, and an appendix listing botanical specimens discovered on the island, the text exploits the generic conventions of travel literature to create an extraordinary projection of colonial influence on the Pacific.

The journal of the lost French officer describes the visit to the imagined isle as an experience of unqualified happiness. They discover fantastic animals; the seamen join the artists and naturalists in painting and theorising; and the natives live in harmonious union, presided over by a kindly oligarchy of twenty-four male elders. To the great surprise of the visitors, some of the older natives know a few words of French, and in a peculiar echo of their impending disappearance—a reflection in the reflection—it is revealed that a previous lost ship has visited the island and introduced various refinements, including the art of wood turning and cabinet making. The visit concludes when the French witness a great festival that 'unveiled for us all the mysteries of this island'.

The ensuing pageant maps out the civilising of the Blue Islanders, starting near the shore where groups walk about with clubs, their 'hair unkempt', performing dances 'as wild as those of the natives of New Zealand'. They eat raw meat and enact a bloody battle.

> Suddenly all this agitation ceased. A longboat in the European style appeared in the distance; curiosity broke up the groups of savages; the object grew larger. Imagine our surprise: we saw four individuals in European clothes. There was a woman among them: she was holding her arms out towards the boat. . . . The insults and the angry gestures ceased when the natives saw the woman; a few chiefs stepped forward onto the shoreline and forbade any hostile action.

Peace and happiness are heralded by the notes of an oboe aboard the boat. 'Although it was absurdly distorted we could nevertheless make out a certain passage which resembled our old music, Rameau's march of the natives'.

The identity of the journal's author is not known, although John Dunmore has proposed that his familiarity with botany and abundance of classical allusions would make him 'an educated man, probably of the minor nobility, or at least of the professional classes'. In lionising the island's government, with its hereditary circle of elders, he makes his disdain for the French Revolution clearly felt.

There was nothing new about situating a political critique on an imaginary island; Thomas More had founded the tradition in 1516 with the publication of the original *Utopia,* literally a 'no-place' or 'not-place' situated between Europe and the Americas, and a multitude of writers followed in his footsteps, often finding the imaginary location a useful device in circumventing the restrictions of censorship. The influence of Francis Bacon's *Nova Atlantis* (1617) and Defoe's *Robinson Crusoe* (1719), the latter arguably the most influential novel of the eighteenth century, can also be discerned in *Fragmens*.[71]

Where the anonymous work differs is in the author's attempt to pass off his fantasy as a bona fide account. Readers of *Robinson Crusoe* or *Gulliver's Travels* were hardly under the illusion that these novels were anything but pretence. Dunmore suggests that, at the time of the

Fragmens, utopias set in the Pacific were increasingly common. 'Growing sophistication among readers and a better knowledge of geography made it necessary for authors to provide credible explanations.' For the writers of these fictions, it became an era of verisimilitude.[72]

One has only to consider the most resounding cultural developments that appeared under nineteenth-century capitalism to realise that the interest in verisimilitude was not confined to creators of literary utopia. Whether we turn to the rise of realism and naturalism in the novel, the transformations in print technology or the advent of photography, the interest in representational practices that emulate the appearance of 'real life' are constantly apparent. The cultural fixation with making likenesses can, as Marx observed, be related to the standardisation of commodities under mass production. But it also bears heavily on Agamben's discussion about the diminution of the imaginative faculty since the Enlightenment.

It is here that an object such as *Fragmens du Dernier Voyage de La Pérouse* becomes really interesting, as it tends to undermine the authority of likenesses of 'the real'. As life becomes more crowded with semblances of 'the real', the distinction between reality and fantasy becomes more obtuse and the opportunities for simulating 'the real' are more abundant. It was this context of confusion that the anonymous French writer exploited with such success.

The impact of this phenomenon on colonial history was profound. Forgery was a common crime for which prisoners were transported to New South Wales and, in a curious twist that art historians could probe more deeply, the majority of convict artists—Thomas Watling, Francis Greenway, James Grove, Joseph Lycett, to name a few—were indicted for this very transgression. If it were possible to enumerate other crimes of verisimilitude, like the common offence of robbery by impersonation, we would doubtless discover that the imitation of things and people was presenting a real threat to social order. The lack of hard currency in the colony and the tendency for economic exchange to be based on letters of credit and I.O.U.s—easily reproducible and legally transferable—go some way towards explaining the popularity of transactions based on that less forgeable commodity, rum.

These occurrences are a good reminder of what the anthropologist Michael Taussig describes as the propensity of an 'artefact that portrays something' to give its creator 'power over that which is portrayed'. For Taussig, working from ethnographic sources, the art of mimesis is a cross-cultural phenomenon. He gives memorable examples of how the Cuna shamans of Colombia devised healing rituals that used carved wooden figures garbed in European clothes. The salient point here is that the Cuna employed an image of the Other in order to be healed or derive other magical benefits. In the wake of Walter Benjamin, Taussig argues that the ability of mimesis to transport us into someone else's conceptual or philosophical space has radical potential. 'Benjamin affirms that the mimetic faculty is the rudiment of a former compulsion of persons to "become and behave like something else."'[73]

Accepting that objects of verisimilitude hover around this possibility of becoming Other, a reading of *Fragmens* inevitably alerts us to a related but very different desire that becomes manifest under colonialism. In the last episode of the story, where the Blue Islanders, dressed as Europeans, are heard playing a distorted version of Rameau's 'Chaconne des Sauvages', the synthesis between reflection and projection is accomplished with horrifying finality. For at this moment the anonymous anti-revolutionary, having cast the savage Other in a likeness of his own idealised state, limits the voice of that Other to the ineffectual mimicry of its own caricature. Far from permitting an epistemic crossover, this contorted strategy of reflection is specifically concerned with rendering the Other a likeness—but always an inferior, diminished likeness—of the Western self. Perhaps 'reflection' is the key term in this scenario, which involves a particularly arrogant form of narcissism. Reflection, in a European context, has very specific connotations with the mirror.

Western concern with verisimilitude and the extremity of its influence on pictorial conventions has been associated with Christianity's break from its Judaic origins. The discarding of Moses' dictum 'You shall make no idols' marks one of the great distinctions between Old and New Testament thinking. Martin Jay in *Downcast Eyes*, a study of attitudes to the visual, has dated this from as early as the first century when Philo of Alexandria, a converted Jew, in order to make Christian doctrine more palatable to pagans, ensured that 'biblical references to hearing were systematically transformed into ones referring to sight'. For theologians the idea of mirroring, highlighted by the development of silver-backed looking glasses in sixteenth-century Venice, provided an explanation for God's presence on Earth.[74] In the words of the critic and educator Paul Zweig, 'God came down into the world as into a mirror. He came down to possess an image of His own divinity.'[75] Implicit here, as Martin Jay suggests, is a very extreme emphasis on St John's claim that God is light, and life 'the light of men'.

In this cultural context, the mirrored reflection has been pivotal in 'completing' the European sense of the world. This preoccupation with mirroring and the idea that the cosmos, or more recently the individual, requires a reflection of itself in order to be made whole, have special pertinence given that from 1524, with Giovanni Da Verranzo's exploration of the North American coast, looking glasses were used as objects of exchange between Europeans and indigenous people.[76]

The symbolism of dispersing mirrors at times of cross-cultural encounter has fascinated writers such as Michael Taussig, Gerald Sider and Paul Carter. The explorer, by distributing this alien technology, reinforces the conceit that reflection in the Western gaze is the necessary precondition for the uncivilised indigene to be brought into being.

Yet despite its symbolic resonance, the mirror, with its undiscriminating power of reflection, remains an ambiguous object. Paul Carter has been particularly fascinated by the way John Batman, a Tasmanian speculator, attempted in 1835 to buy land on the banks of the Yarra River—the future site of Melbourne—with a package of commodities that included thirty looking glasses.[77] In another essay, Carter speculates on the meaning of mirrors for traditional Aborigines. How would they compare with reflections found in the natural environment?[78]

Central to Carter's argument is the intimation that the mirror image is bizarre or uncanny. The mirror flattens the world, severs face from body and places the subject in a virtual environment that is unattainable. Far from providing certainty or comfort—a divine reflection of God's purpose—the mirror image, under conditions of modernity, seems to highlight the deceptive qualities of reflection. At no time are these more clearly demonstrated than when we hold a piece of writing to the looking glass and see the clear characters of our text converted into unreadable nonsense. The great symbol of verisimilitude becomes the agent of reversal and distortion.

In the journal of John Hunter, we find a humorous response to Carter's question about how Aborigines experienced mirrors. Travelling the waters near Sydney, he writes of meeting

> a few natives, who came off to us in their boats with much
> chearfulness [*sic*] and good humour; I thought I had seen them
> before: they received a few presents, among which was a looking
> glass, which we took much trouble to shew them the use of: they
> were some time before they observed their own figure in the glass,
> but when they did, they turned it up and looked behind it; then
> pointed to the water, signifying that they could see their figure
> reflected as well from that.[79]

There is a humorous sense of anticlimax in the way Hunter relates this anecdote. The gift is no more than an encumbrance.

The natives dismiss the gift of reflection because they have it already. Despite much evidence to the contrary, the colonists failed to realise that the Aborigines, who dealt with the physics of refraction every time they speared a fish, were savvy in manipulating the politics of distortion and reflection. Here we return to that helectite narrative, the tale of the white settlement on the western side of the Blue Mountains. How was it that this evocation of inverted symmetry—a settlement corresponding to Sydney on the coast, but where people are happy—became fixed in the minds of the fledgling colony?

Commenting on the occasion where Wilson, Price and Roe were told during their first expedition of 1798 about the illusory settlement by a group of Aborigines, Cambage wrote dismissively that 'the natives . . . were, as usual, ready to reply in the affirmative to any leading questions'.[80] Here is the figure of the child-savage who idiotically affirms everything that the white man says, a familiar stereotype in the annals of Australian history.

Putting clichés aside, there is no doubt about their adeptness in mimicry. But it was not a mindless mirroring of European preconceptions, as Tench makes abundantly clear when he describes a journey with two Darug men in 1791.

> We had no sooner halted, and given them something to eat, than they
> began to play ten thousand tricks and gambols. They imitated the
> leaping of the kanguroo; sang; danced; poized the spear; and met in
> mock encounter. But their principal source of merriment was again
> derived from our misfortunes, in tumbling amidst nettles, and sliding
> down precipices, which they mimicked with inimitable drollery.[81]

141

From this we can ascertain that mimicry was an established feature in Aboriginal performance practices—it remains so to this day—and that much of its attraction was due to the joy of parody. It is, I suspect, through recognition of this parodic tendency in the art of making likenesses that the most fruitful means of interpreting the myth of the imagined settlement might be devised.

Whether the myth originated with the Aborigines or the convicts, or whether they arrived at it independently, is impossible to establish. Certainly, the willingness of the Aborigines to convey the myth would have verified its authenticity among the convict population. The fact that the western settlement was sometimes referred to as China—a shipping destination and therefore a possible route of escape—would suggest the particular influence of convict experience. Significantly, both groups developed the myth for their own purposes. Given that it was told by the two categories of people most powerless under colonial law, I cannot help but recall Michael Taussig's proposition that making a likeness of something is a way of gaining 'power over that which is portrayed'.

We have already considered how the mythical settlement empowered convicts in their movement across space. In contrast, the Aboriginal deployment of the myth during the early colonial years had the opposite effect of restraining the advancement of British authority. It was used strategically when questions were asked about what lay beyond the mountains and how to get there. Such questions *were* asked and their presumptuousness made them unanswerable. Like the British themselves, and like every other culture on the planet, the Australian Aborigines have protocols about travelling on other people's land. Between the coast and the Blue Mountains lay a linguistic boundary that divided two dialects of Darug. This was known by at least some of the British—Watkin Tench even recorded a comparative glossary of words on the coast and those on the Hawkesbury. The two would certainly have travelled on each other's land—ceremonial business, hunting, marriage and intercommunal negotiation would have made it inevitable—but it did not give one clan the right to lead strangers, whose motives were not beyond suspicion, onto neighbouring ground.

143

Dramatic evidence of this can be found in Barrallier's journal of 1802 expedition up the Nepean River, where the Aboriginal Gogy, exiled by his people and living as a fringe dweller in Sydney, accompanied the explorer into Gundungurra territory, evoking the formidable fury of a leader called Mootik who, after snubbing him in every possible way, offered him a woman as wife if he agreed to abandon Barrallier's expedition. Fearful for his life, Gogy parted company with Barrallier who battled onwards, finally deterred by 'a multitude of pyramids or cones, standing like as many detached sugar-loaves placed on top of one another'.[82]

Later, by the 1830s, when the Aborigines around Sydney and many along the eastern coast had been dispossessed of their land, the guiding and assistance of explorers became more common. But these were desperate times. The twenty-five years when the mountains remained 'uncrossable' are testimony to the success of a deliberate policy of obstruction. The myth of the utopian settlement as part of that strategy allowed Aborigines, when responding to questions about the Blue Mountains, simply to forge a likeness, raise a mirror and give the whites an image of themselves.

So was it a case of pure deceit or did the Aborigines in some way also believe in the western settlement? It is likely that they both believed and disbelieved. The question of belief, when it comes to myth, is very difficult because the great quality of myth is its ability to resolve, in narrative, anxieties that cannot be alleviated in daily life. Myths are delicately situated between the acknowledgment of what is and the desire for something different.

Certainly, the western settlement may have had resonances in Aboriginal culture that are now difficult if not impossible to grasp. If these narratives are read in relation to the longstanding tradition, described by the critic and film-maker Ross Gibson, whereby Arcadian ideals have been persistently projected onto the Australian interior,[83] we find evidence of a hybrid dreaming, rooted in Aboriginal as well as European culture. The number of recorded cases in which Aborigines, on first encounter, thought white people were ghosts are sufficient to suggest that, throughout much of Aboriginal Australia, white was considered the colour of death. Whether the white settlement that Aborigines enthusiastically affirmed was developed from their own suppositions about the afterlife, whether it reflected a desire to make the colonists dead, or whether it was an eschatological projection in the wake of the devastating smallpox epidemic of 1789 are all within the realm of possibility.

We have only snippets of evidence, but what there is suggests that the myth survived and evolved through the early decades of British settlement. By 1802, when Péron told the story, the harbourside qualities of Sydney had been mythologically incorporated: the white people of the inland, 'like the English', resided by an immense lake. Twenty-five years later, with the road over the mountains well established, the vision of a great body of water was still being perpetuated, although significantly it had been divested of people. In 1827, William John Dumaresq, a brother-in-law of Governor Sir Ralf Darling, rode to Bathurst where the first 'real' white settlement in the west had been established. He continued to the outlying Wellington Valley where he received Aboriginal testimony

> that there exists in the western country, many days off, a vast interior sea, where the water is salt, and where *whales* are seen to spout! The manner in which they imitated the whale throwing up water was so

completely satisfactory as to leave little doubt of the fact, and it is not likely these inland blacks could have known it but from actual observation.[84]

Again we can sense how myth reverberates through the landscape, and how another narrative, which mirrored the maritime experience of those people who had come across the oceans, would orientate explorers over the ensuing decades as they searched for the inland sea.

Far from discounting these myths of place as convict oddities or the verifications of head-nodding 'natives', we should acknowledge that they are, despite their indeterminacy, among the most important fragments that survive from the colonial period. The essence of their poignancy is that they voice the plight of people wrenched from their own place in the world; people thrust into a labyrinth. This occurred within a unique historical framework—a period of extraordinary attempts to suppress the play of imagination, a time when the logic of verisimilitude would cast its reflecting projection from the coast to the horizon. This labyrinth is a mirror maze, its fluid boundaries bewildering the wanderer, wavering between object and reflection.

145

JOHN PAINE'S HAND-COLOURED ALBUMEN PRINT (C. 1890) IS TITLED *Shady Nook, Katoomba*. THE LUSH FOLIAGE OF THE VALLEY
AND THE QUIET INTIMACY OF THE HUMAN SUBJECTS SEEM MORE IMPORTANT THAN THE MONOLITH ON THE HORIZON.
EVENTUALLY, HOWEVER, TRI SAXA OR THE THREE SISTERS WOULD BECOME THE DEFINING LANDMARK OF THE BLUE MOUNTAINS.

Passage Four

THE ECHO AND THE
SOUND ITSELF

And in fact a good deal of what they were after he could not have told, even if he had wanted to, for the simple reason that there were no words for it in their tongue; yet when, as sometimes happened, he fell back on the native word, the only one that could express it, their eyes went hard, as if the mere existence of a language they did not know was a provocation, a way of making them helpless.

DAVID MALOUF, *Remembering Babylon*, 1993

What shall I say

about the quest

for petrified

meaning?

CHRIS WALLACE-
CRABBE, 'STONES',
1994

AN UNDATED POSTCARD shows a stump of tree beside a road. The caption, inscribed on the image itself, identifies the stump as the 'Explorer's [*sic*] Tree, Katoomba', which was reputedly initialled by one or all three of the Blaxland party as they journeyed through the Blue Mountains in 1813. This undated photograph evidently originates from the years after 1904 when the top of the tree was removed. Sitting on its stone plinth and framed by surrounding fence, it suggests those special graves where a border is erected to emphasise their importance and discourage disturbance of the deceased.

There is no evidence that Blaxland, Lawson or Wentworth ever signed the tree in question. (Their journals record that their route was marked with nothing more than the blaze of an axe.) The placement of the fence and identifying plaque in the 1880s seems to be associated with the development of Katoomba's Carrington Hotel and the commercial imperative to have a 'historical' attraction close by.[1] That the signature, even if it were genuine, would be impossible to authenticate is unwittingly revealed by a Blue Mountains guide book of 1904, which cautioned that the 'letters notched on that great day are not now traceable, save by a pre-conceived imagination'. It says of William Lawson that he would probably regret the signing, 'and curse the woeful precedent he made, for the autographs of Billy Smith and Tommy Snobkin (subsequent explorers who have reached this tree), are only too visible in hideous plenitude'.[2]

This did nothing to upset the veneration poured upon the tree which had quickly died in its tomb of masonry. Its condition was so poor in 1929 that a local newspaper suggested the council remove the existing stump,

> take a careful cast, and mould it in concrete, exercising care to display the famous initials. . . . The grim inroads of time and neglect have sealed the fate of the original remembrancer. The sole alternative is to create a lasting simulacrum, to usurp the place of the rapidly vanishing original.[3]

This proposal was not adopted in its entirety, though the stump has been filled with concrete to hold in place what little timber remains.

The petrification of the stump and its association with the myth of a 'First Crossing' as well as the reality that explorers followed an Abori-

ginal route encapsulate many of the themes addressed in this passage. It is composed of two sister essays, the first a speculation on the names and narratives of the great sandstone monoliths that have become the most renowned features of the Blue Mountains landscape. Treating these landmarks as conspicuous objects in the 'dreamwork' of imperialism, the focus is on the rocky pinnacles of Orphan Rock and the Three Sisters, both of which are described in 'Aboriginal' legends of doubtful provenance as indigenous women who were turned to stone. The second essay, 'Homage to Catalina', works against the drift of such narratives, which, in the culture of tourism, position the petrified women as the sentinels of a dying race. I developed the latter essay by making contact with some Aboriginal descendants—people who, far from vanishing, have remained within their traditional territory. I was seeking narratives about the area of hanging swamp below my house, the headwaters of Katoomba Falls Creek and home to the town's fringe dwellers, who lived in rough, improvised dwellings until their eviction in 1957 when an ill-fated motor racing circuit was built on the site. Moving between dreams of country and social history, this passage concerns the visions that have been projected onto the Blue Mountains landscape, the myths that developed in their wake and the material effect of these fantasies upon those who live in their midst.

I

MORPHIC
ECHOES,
STONY
SILENCES

There was
something stirring
about the
association of
women and
vertigo and death.
With a trembling
voice he had
asked them to
keep still. He
arranged the view
and locked them
in his frame. He
depressed the
shutter and
extinguished time.

DELIA FALCONER,
The Service of
Clouds, 1997

THE FRONTISPIECE OF Frank Hurley's camera study *The Blue Mountains and Jenolan Caves* offers moment for reflection.[4] Here is an iconic landmark, the sandstone formation known as the Three Sisters, and in the foreground, perched on edge of cliff, a painter smokes and dabbles, and re-creates the view.

As the first photograph in this 1952 publication and one of the handful reproduced in colour, the image has special prominence. This is concordant with Hurley's personal commitment to promoting the Blue Mountains and the overwhelming fascination of the Three Sisters as a tourist spectacle that presently attracts three million visitors each year. In actuality, as in imagery, the Three Sisters are awesome: sheer yet crumbling, they rise a thousand feet above the forest floor. The Jamison Valley in which they are situated is fed by scores of waterfalls and cascades. The view alternates between the damp luxuriance of rainforest and the stark yellow of weathered cliff. It was just a few miles eastward that von Guérard did the drawing for his memorable paintings. This was the landscape that suggested to the young Charles Darwin a 'grand bay or gulf . . . showing headland behind headland, as on a bold sea coast'.

Hurley's photograph was taken from Echo Point, the most popular Blue Mountains lookout. With its frame within the frame, the photo is literally resonant, suggesting the interplay between object and image which has distinguished the cultural history of this site. That play is often visual (usually involving photography) but extends to other sorts of image. As its name suggests, Echo Point is a place for listening as well as looking. And its prime attraction, the Three Sisters, is the subject of a legend that raises the troubling issue of how Aboriginal occupation has been encoded as both a presence and an absence in the colonial imagination.

The Three Sisters legend is disseminated by tour guides, tourist literature and, most memorably, a fountain sculpture west of Echo Point. Fashioned from chicken wire and concrete—I once heard it described as 'papier mâché gone wrong'—the fountain depicts the rocky pinnacles of the Three Sisters as nymph-like figures, frozen in ballerinic poses. The fountain is a rather spectacular example of Blue Mountains kitsch, built in the latter half of the 1960s by Lyall Randolph, a trained sculptor and a minor, probably marginal, figure in Sydney art circles whose other

SCULPTED FROM CHICKEN WIRE AND CEMENT RENDER, THE THREE SISTERS FOUNTAIN IS LOCATED OUTSIDE THE SCENIC WORLD PAVILION, THE LAUNCHING POINT FOR THE SCENIC RAILWAY AND THE SCENIC SKYWAY. A COIN-ACTIVATED RECORDING TELLS THE STORY OF THE SISTERS BEING TURNED TO STONE DURING A BATTLE BETWEEN FEUDING ABORIGINAL TRIBES.

known credit was the production and installation at personal expense of the well-known mermaid statues at Bondi Beach.

Randolph's fountain is located on the edge of the escarpment outside the pavilion known as Scenic World, which, after Echo Point, is probably the most visited tourist spot in the Blue Mountains. It was Harry Hammon (1911–2000), the proprietor of the highly successful Scenic Railway Company, who commissioned the fountain as part of an expanding cluster of attractions. In 1945 Hammon, then the owner of a transport business, acquired the old coal hoist, a remnant from Jamison Valley's mining era that dates from the late 1870s. Since the 1920s, hikers had saved themselves the climb up the escarpment by taking a ride on this little train. The movement of people rather than coal had come to represent a more bankable future, and the railway was renamed the 'Mountain Devil' (a reference to the indigenous shrub *Lambertia formosa*, the fruit of which resembles a devil's head). When Hammon acquired the ride after the war it became known as the Scenic Railway, supposedly the 'world's steepest'. It was augmented in 1957 when, with the assistance of an engineer, Hammon transformed some old shale mining equipment into a cable-car ride called the Scenic Skyway. In the 1980s he built his most ambitious project, the Orphan Rocker—a roller coaster ride with an 876-metre track. To Hammon's fury, the ride was not compliant with Australian safety standards; it still sits lifeless along the clifftop, never having carried a commercial passenger.[5] More successful is

a new 'gondola'-type ride which also links clifftop and valley. Known as
the Sceniscender Cable Car, it opened for business in 2000, the year of
Hammon's death.

~

The Three Sisters Fountain is positioned outside the jostling den of
souvenir shops, movie theatre and pinball arcade from which the various
rides launch into the valley. The fountain is equipped with a coin-
activated device that tells the following tale:

This fountain represents the legend of the turning into stone of the three Aboriginal sisters of the local Kedumba Tribe. Back in the Dreamtime, in the time of the legend, the three exceptionally beautiful Aboriginal maidens were in love with three warriors of the rival Nepean tribe. One day the three warriors came to claim the sisters. A horrific battle was waged, and to prevent the girls from being spirited away the witch-doctor cast a spell on them and turned the maidens into stone for their protection. . . . In the closing stages of the battle, the witch-doctor himself was killed and is now unable to release them from his spell.

Although peddled as an ancient Aboriginal belief—and just possibly it is—the provenance of this story is reminiscent of the Blue Mountains themselves: the more light you shine, the hazier it gets. When Jim Smith researched its origins for his collection *Aboriginal Legends of the Blue Mountains*, he could find no record of a Three Sisters legend until 1949. In that year it appeared in a popular magazine, *Outdoors and Fishing*, under the authorship of the Blue Mountains identity Melbourne 'Mel' Ward, an amateur zoologist and proprietor of a natural history museum, widely noted for its collection of crabs. Here is Ward's version of the story:

A land mark familiar to thousands of visitors today is the beautiful rock formation known as the Three Sisters at Katoomba. Few who look upon them realise that these indeed are three giant women known to the tribes as Weemala, Meenie and Gunedoo. In this panoply of stone they have stood for thousands of years ever since the fatal day of the great battle.

Very beautiful were the three giant maidens and proud was the Katoomba tribe to whom they belonged. Other tribes were envious and wanted to have them but permission could not be obtained from their tribe, so at last one tribe bolder and more resolute attacked the Katoomba tribe in force and a terrible battle ranged across the mountains. Blood flowed and stained the ground more red than the sunset colours on the great cliffs along the valley.

Tide of battle was going against the Katoomba tribe so Weemala, Meenie and Gunedoo ran to the edge and stood in the valley. Side by side they stood and watched the fight. The Sorcerer of the Katoomba tribe, realising that the fight was strongly against his people, ran to where the giantesses stood and with a magic spell turned them to stone. Then he rushed back into the battle only to be struck down and killed.

With the battle over, the victorious tribe rushed to where the beautiful great maidens had been standing to find only three great pinnacles of rock standing mute and immovable, gazing with stony stare along the beautiful valley. No one has discovered the chant which will set them free of the enchantment.[6]

The dubious legacy of this story, published by a white man who never identified his informants, has done nothing to dampen its popularity. For many visitors, including the thousands who hear it in Japanese translation, the petrification of the sisters is their one foray into a long and complex history of Aboriginal occupation.

While we cannot entirely discount the possibility that the Three Sisters legend had an Aboriginal source, it is more than possible, as the circumstances of its circulation tend to suggest, that the story is the creation of a white man, intended to bestow upon the landmark some added 'colour'. Smith relates that Ward reputedly claimed that Aborigines in the Burragorang Valley told him the story in 1928. But his informants

remain unnamed and there is even doubt about whether he was in the Blue Mountains at that time. Ward's record as an ethnographer is certainly patchy. He did not honour scholarly conventions and on various occasions published under his own name legends that were collected by others.[7]

The ambiguity surrounding the story makes it an especially revealing text in the dreamwork of imperialism. For surely it is the hallmark of colonisation with its deletions, its denials, its gaping losses and absences, that our sense of the past is perpetually unstable, always liable to crack or shatter or fold back upon itself. Under these conditions, the Three Sisters legend should not be dismissed as a 'bogus' myth. Rather, precisely *because* of its ambiguous meaning and origin, it qualifies as myth in the deepest sense. As Roberto Calasso writes of myths in general, 'No sooner have you grabbed hold of it than myth opens out into a fan of a thousand segments.' He likens the web-like structure of myth to language: 'There is no such thing as the isolated mythical event, just as there is no such thing as the isolated word.'[8] The Three Sisters legend is a fragment from an extensive mythological order, emerging from a region that has a limited economy beyond that of spectatorship but which always, it seems, has been a privileged place for marvel and speculation.

Aspects of the legend invite comparison with that other threesome so dominant in national mythology: Blaxland, Wentworth and Lawson. Wentworth celebrated their crossing in his poem *Australasia*, an orgy of pastoral imagery in which Australia's 'inmost plains' become 'A new Arcadia' to 'teem with simple swains'.[9] The Arcadian reference anticipated a chain of classical imaginings—Wentworth would write reverently of the 'pure models of Greece and Rome'—which remains entrenched in Blue Mountains taxonomy and is blatantly evident in a name like Echo Point.

Hence the appropriateness of Echo Point in launching an investigation of how meaning bounces back and forth between cultures or—to be more specific—between mythological orders. There are many ways in which this mythological heritage might be read. In terms of local history, the classical myth of Echo and Narcissus, in which the besotted nymph pines away until reduced to a repetitious voice while the youth she adores is drowned in his own self-image, could be read as an oblique subtext on a lookout which, renowned for its scenic beauty, is also the favoured suicide spot in the Blue Mountains. It seems to me that the youth's fall and the nymph's disembodiment do hammer out a rather eerie echo that reflects more generally on connections between grandiosity and mortality—connections previously alluded to in discussing Edmund Burke's idea of the sublime.

Hopefully, this will advance the case for a more sympathetic treatment of myth in historical practice. Myth, after all, represents a pattern of enunciation and provides a reservoir of metaphors when experience is metamorphosed into cultural memory. In the case at hand, myth provides an analogical tool for interpreting collective experience, for linking Echo's compulsive mimicry—a speechlessness within speech itself—with a greater history. How is it that a mythology can emerge in someone's name without apparent consultation? What is it about the make-up of a community that allows certain acts of speech to become mute at the moment of enunciation? Why is it a longstanding principle in the Blue Mountains—a trait common to much of Australia—that Aboriginal presence, schematised in European imaginings, is so easily converted to absence?

~

Here we return to the story of Mirragan and Gurangatch, arguably the most powerful narrative of Blue Mountains travel—a story from a verified Aboriginal source. It was told around 1900 to the surveyor, coroner and amateur anthropologist R. H. Mathews, a pioneer in the field of cross-cultural research who lived from 1841 until 1918. The story concerns the southern Blue Mountains, the country you look towards from Echo Point. Far from being a tale of petrification—the transmogrification of women into mute sentinels—it is a fleet-footed current of dynamism and detail, a rapturous celebration of the chase. Mirragan, the greatest of hunters, spies Gurangatch, the greatest of fish, who, to evade capture, tears up 'the ground along the present valley of the Wollondilly [River], causing the water in the lagoon to flow after him and bear him along'.[10]

Thus begins the process that creates the river system of the southern Blue Mountains, a chase that constitutes the oldest map of this part of the world. It is reasonable to assume that, as well as serving as a navigational aid, its recitation to R. H. Mathews, who transcribed and published it in the German journal *Zeitschrift für Ethnologie*, also established a territorial claim on the part of its narrators, members of the Gundungurra language group who resided in 1900 on a few acres known as 'Aboriginal Reserve No. 26' in the Burragorang Valley.[11] As Mathews would have come to realise, the Mirragan and Gurangatch story was part of a vast network of narratives that spread across Aboriginal Australia. Jim Smith proposes that the powerful Gurangatch was a Murray cod (*Maccullochella peeli*), the largest of Australia's freshwater fish. In 1903 when Mathews documented the Aboriginal fish traps of Brewarrina, 700 kilometres from the Blue Mountains, he revealed that a section of these traps (used for catching Murray cod and other species), was known by the name *Mirragan*. Evidently, the distant Ngemba people of the Barwon River were also familiar with the protagonists of the Gundungurra creation story.[12]

Mathews' interest in indigenous culture and his friendships with many Aboriginal people were integral to his research and documentation. Self-taught in ethnology, yet the author of more than 170 papers in learned journals and the recipient of the Godard silver medal from the Anthropological Society of Paris, Mathews can be numbered among those unusual Australians, like those identified by Henry Reynolds in *This Whispering in our Hearts* (1998), who sympathised with and respected Aboriginal people in an era when this was anything but the norm. Janet Mathews, the wife of his grandson, was told by several elderly

Aborigines whose parents had known him that R. H. Mathews 'had been given an Aboriginal name, Miranen, meaning "well-liked man"'.[13] An interesting insight into his approach appears in a tribute by the anthropologist A. P. Elkin. Observing the traditional protocol for approaching an Aboriginal camp, Elkin wrote, Mathews 'usually lit a small fire and sat at it until invited to join the group'.[14] This ability to adopt Aboriginal customs and enact basic gestures of respect provides a pointed contrast to some of the attempts to procure or display Aboriginal knowledge that are described below.

~

The widely disseminated legend of the Three Sisters, its origin dubious, and the lesser known story of Mirragan and Gurangatch are founded on opposite principles. In Mirragan, the land is created through a process of movement, while the Three Sisters are testament to a condition of stasis.

It is quite appropriate to regard this as a *philosophical* difference— a difference emerging from the encounter of an agrarian and a nomadic epistemology. Yet, importantly, it is also a dichotomy (hinting at the possibility of rapprochement) that appears within European thought itself. When Nietzsche gave vent to his aphorism 'Only ideas *won by walking* have any value', he was not only responding to Flaubert's proposition 'One can think and write only when sitting down'[15] but challenging a root-bound tradition that attained its apotheosis in the pages of Kant. In *The Conflict of the Faculties* (1798), Kant had warned of 'Pathological Feelings that Come from Thinking at Unsuitable Times'. If a scholar:

> taxes his energy by occupying himself with a specific thought when he is eating or walking, he inflicts two tasks on himself at the same time—on the head and the stomach or on the head and the feet; and in the first case this brings on hypochondria, in the second, vertigo.

The pedestrian, he emphasised, must observe 'a firm resolution to go on a *diet with regard to thinking*'.[16]

When negotiating the topos of Echo Point, the desire for movement is replete with a danger that recalls Kant's severe prediction that thinking while walking will result in vertigo. Here is a landscape both natural and constructed—a 'holiday playground' as Frank Hurley called it—in which the visitor is constantly poised on clifftop ledges that make a stopping point of every view and toy endlessly with the fear, so precariously manifest in Hurley's photograph, where the artist's impression, propped in paintbox lid, hovers on the edge of the abyss.

THROUGH A STRANGE LENS

The project of charting the Three Sisters' place in colonial imaginings could start with Ernest Brougham Docker. A judge by profession but a photographer by passion, Docker is reputed to have kept his court sitting until the small hours of the morning to allow a free day for taking photographs.[17] Considered the most accomplished amateur of his milieu, he was a particular aficionado of the stereographic camera. With this device he took two young girls and a Mrs Vivian to the Blue Mountains township of Katoomba where they made an image of a name then new. The resulting stereograph, *The Three Sisters, Katoomba*, dated 1898, launched a much-repeated gag: the photographic depiction of three women before the Three Sisters.[18]

The sense of melancholy common to many old photographs has a poignancy bordering on freakishness in Docker's image. In part, this is due to the technology itself. The mode of looking is obsolete, as are the subjects. You slide the doubled card into metal clasps, peer through the lens of a wooden mask. And, as the illusion takes form, the two becoming one, the eyes can roam within this virtual zone, a keyhole world, with sisters at the safety rail, Sisters on the horizon; a scene of foliage, pleated cotton, flowing tress: femininity, somehow unbridled, to be watched by both women and men.

In his noted study *Techniques of the Observer*, the art historian Jonathan Crary remarked that the stereographic image, with its simulated three-dimensionality, is literally *obscene*. This is due to more than the association of pornography and stereoscopy that is sometimes attributed to the latter's demise. Crary describes stereographic representation as perpetrating 'a derangement of the conventional functioning of optical cues'.[19] Far from replicating a visible reality, the stereograph processes appearances to create its own symbolic order: a vivid example of what Benjamin described as modernity's need 'to take possession of the object—from the closest proximity—in an image and the reproduction of an image'.[20]

The still image, more than the moving image, records an absence.

SAM ROHDIE, *The Passion of Pier Paolo Pasolini*, 1995

ERNEST BROUGHAM
DOCKER (1839–1923)
WAS A JUDGE AND
AMATEUR
PHOTOGRAPHER. HIS
1898 STEREOGRAPH, *The
Three Sisters, Katoomba,*
HELPED POPULARISE THE
IDEA OF THE ROCK
FORMATION BEING THE
THREE SISTERS.
PREVIOUSLY IT WAS
KNOWN AS TRI SAXA.
THE ABORIGINAL NAME
WAS APPARENTLY NEVER
RECORDED.

At a purely polemical level, this is explicit in the Docker stereograph where the conjunction of trinities becomes a means of assimilating the landscape into a European schema, rendering it feminine and thereby more easily subordinate to possession. But what is most interesting about this image is that the terms of that possessiveness are themselves imbued with a deep uncertainty which seems connected with its limitation as a mimetic object. As Crary suggests, there is something disturbingly unreal about the stereographic image. In his 2000 book *The Colonial Earth*, a study of Australian art and environment, Tim Bonyhady describes the sort of trickery used by stereographers in documenting landscapes. Trees or foliage were often cleared and plants sometimes repositioned in order to heighten the three-dimensional illusion.[21] This rearrangement of scenery seems to echo the perceptual reordering that occurs. While the stereographic depth of field is almost palpable, the human figures, like the tree and the distant formation in Docker's image, are completely lacking in volume. Floating like cardboard cut-outs in a diorama, each pictorial element seems isolated from its surrounding elements. With such a sense of disconnectedness it could easily be inferred that the real object of Docker's view is not the women, the formation, the likeness between the two, but, on the contrary, the gulf that separates them and appears to infiltrate every aspect of the picture. In this respect, Jonathan Crary's observation that the stereoscopic illusion is one of 'vertiginous uncertainty about the distance separating forms' is relevant indeed.[22] The emphasis on the abyss and the spectral quality of the women dampens any suspicion that their position on the precipice is at all secure.

Docker's image, circulated and discussed in the *Australian Photographic Journal* of 1900,[23] was symptomatic of a wider shift in perceptions of the Blue Mountains. The change is evident if we compare his stereo with a hand-coloured albumen print by John Paine, a professional photographer, which dates from about 1890.[24] In this romantic view, three adult figures cross a footbridge in a ferny glade. They occupy the lower half of the picture and correspond to the horizonal feature of the Three Sisters, distant and roughly the same size. For Paine, the association between rock and human subjects was not particularly feminine. The threesome consisted of two women and a man, and the title, 'Shady Nook, Katoomba', emphasised the personal space of the valley over the dramatic edifice of the pinnacles.

At the time when Paine took this photo, the Three Sisters were known as Tri Saxa (from the Latin *saxum*, meaning stone or rock). It was not until the late 1890s—with no apparent mention of an Aboriginal belief—that the rocks were personified as sisters and Tri Saxa Point became Echo Point. Even then, it attracted few visitors because access was restricted by a private property—the substantial grounds of Sir Frederick Darley's 'Lilianfels' estate. With the subdivision of his garden in 1908 a public reserve was established opposite the Three Sisters. Later, in the 1930s, municipal authorities further emphasised the vertiginous qualities of Echo Point by extending the lookout onto a projecting platform.

~

On the Prince Henry Cliff Walk, which connects Echo Point with Katoomba Falls and numerous other lookouts around Jamison Valley, the splendour and drama of the abyss are constantly apparent. Accidents and intentional jumps are an inevitable reality. I have spoken to police whose job it is to collect human remains from the bottom of Echo Point. And sometimes as I pace the trail, savouring the sensuous views to Mount Solitary and beyond, I recall accidents I have read about in the local papers. All these tragedies have their own peculiarities, their own odd

HARRY PHILLIPS
(1873–1944) WAS A
POSTCARD AND
LANDSCAPE
PHOTOGRAPHER BASED
FOR MANY YEARS IN
KATOOMBA. HE
PROVIDED INSPIRATION
FOR DELIA FALCONER'S
NOVEL *The Service of
Clouds* (1997). IN THIS
PHOTOGRAPH FROM THE
1930S, PHILLIPS
DEPICTED THE
CANTILEVERED VIEWING
PLATFORM AT ECHO
POINT. THIS PROJECTING
LOOKOUT DID NOT
IMPROVE VISIBILITY BUT
IT DID HEIGHTEN THE
SENSATION OF STANDING
AT THE EDGE OF AN
ENORMOUS DROP.

THE ARTIFICIAL HORIZON

details that stick in the mind. But the strangest to my knowledge occurred in July 1907—a bizarre double fatality. 'A MOUNTAIN SENSATION', the headline read, and the story explained how William T. J. Lannon, a thirteen-year-old resident of Sydney, had stood with his sister at Katoomba Falls. The winter was cold, the waterfall frozen. 'He was trying to get icicles,' the newspaper explained, 'which were hanging in great length, and slipped on to the rocks at the top of the second fall.' He fell some 200 feet, and when he was found, his head was 'jammed between two rocks and scarcely a bone left sound'. Later that afternoon, two sisters, visiting from Bathurst, inspected the scene of the accident. One of them, Henriette M'Aviney, aged twenty-three, stepped on the same place as the boy and also fell. She was 'literally smashed to pieces'. Her sister was 'out of her mind with the shock'. The newspaper solemnly reported that, 'The trustees have now fenced the dangerous spot'.[25]

In contemplating these freak fatalities, I cannot help but draw a connection between the stereoscopic illusion—the 'vertiginous' quality of its scenic order—and the re-ordering of scenery itself which began on a grand scale at the close of the nineteenth century. The history of the extensive and often elaborately designed walking tracks through the Blue Mountains has been a subject of particular interest to Jim Smith. He has charted a particular pattern of development, the prototype for which can be found in the landscape modifications of Sir Henry Parkes, the so-called 'father' of Australian Federation, who privately built a network of tracks around Faulconbridge, his Blue Mountains retreat. Parkes later became a trustee of the Wentworth Falls reserve, gazetted in 1870, where his vision of bushland made accessible by interconnecting pathways was further developed, this time on public land.[26] The pathways around Wentworth Falls, typical of the upper Blue Mountains tracks in the way they negotiate the cliffs with ladders and stairs carved directly into rock, were started around 1890 when a former sea captain, James Murray, lowered a labourer down the cliff face to mark a route for steps.[27]

The cliffs of the Jamison, Megalong and Grose valleys are lined with monumental staircases, lookouts and walking tracks, most dating from around the turn of the century. Smith has shown how a variety of routes—some Aboriginal and others of convict or settler origin—were incorporated into the network of recreational tracks. They were part of an ideology that upheld the clean air and recuperative virtues of the high country. Smith describes them with a sense of celebration, arguing that they allowed walkers to develop a meaningful connection with the Australian environment. He takes umbrage at scholars such as Anne Burke who see the tracks as 'indicative of the desire to slice-up and overcome "nature"'.[28]

Smith mounts a compelling argument for recognising the ingenuity, creativity, craftsmanship and environmental sensitivity of those who designed and built the walking tracks of the Blue Mountains. That is beyond dispute. And while there is no lack of evidence that walkers for many generations have found relaxation, communion with nature and a sense of spiritual nourishment, through their engagement with this cultural landscape, there is also an aspect to these environmental modifications that touches upon John Low's 'dark side of the Mountains'.

Delia Falconer's novel *The Service of Clouds* (1997) evokes this quality of the Blue Mountains landscape, often using the lookout as the scene for impending crisis. The final chapters of the book, developed from documentary research, extend the sense of a landscape of sadness by detailing the Blue Mountains' role as a treatment centre for patients with tuberculosis. While its pure air and proximity to Sydney have given the area the reputation as a place of retreat and recovery, the precipitous terrain, made accessible by walking tracks and lookouts, sometimes proved too much for people in the grip of depression. Deaths by falling or the simple temptation to jump are the corollary to the life-giving virtue of nature-made-accessible. The penchant for lookout points, cliff walks and contrivances like the cantilevered platform at Echo Point exceeds any straightforward desire to enhance the view, encouraging an experience of spectatorship that viscerally affects the bodily senses by toying with the edge of the abyss.

In this respect, Jamison Valley (described as an 'amphitheatre' since the days of Macquarie) became a place of performance in which the experiences and anxieties of a community, and especially the tensions concerning its relationship to country, could be enacted, remembered, inscribed. Hence the significance of those recurrent references to endangered childhood: Docker's photo, the memory of William Lannon, the provocative allure of the stony sisters. Among place names in the Jamison and Megalong—Ruined Castle, Mount Solitary, Devil's Hole, Sublime

ORPHAN ROCK IS
LOCATED IN JAMISON
VALLEY NEAR
KATOOMBA FALLS.
IN 1909 A
PREPOSTEROUS
'ABORIGINAL' LEGEND
WAS PUBLISHED
WHICH CLAIMED
THAT THE ROCK WAS
ONCE 'A LITTLE
BLACK GIRL CALLED
MOOBRA' WHO WAS
TURNED TO STONE BY
FAIRIES TO PROTECT
HER FROM TRIBAL
WARFARE. THOUGH
OBVIOUS FANTASIES,
SUCH STORIES
REFLECT DEEPLY ON
THE DREAMWORK OF
IMPERIALISM.
LANDMARKS LIKE
THIS WOULD
SYMBOLISE THE
PUTATIVE
DISAPPEARANCE OF
ABORIGINAL
COMMUNITIES. THIS
ILLUSTRATION FROM
THE 1880S SHOWS
THE COAL HOIST
THAT BECAME THE
SCENIC RAILWAY
AND THE MINERS
ENCAMPMENT AT ITS
BASE. IRONICALLY,
NUMEROUS
ABORIGINAL
WORKERS FOUND
EMPLOYMENT IN
THE MINES.

MORPHIC ECHOES, STONY SILENCES

Point, Inspiration Point, Dog Face, Point Repulse—the dual theme of childhood and loss reverberates in its own quiet way to find a stopping point of sorts at a concealed pinnacle, not far from the Three Sisters, and immediately opposite the site of William Lannon's death, called Orphan Rock.

Two years after William died, the *Blue Mountains Echo* published an 'Aboriginal' legend (again devoid of attribution) concerning Orphan Rock. Given generic similarities, it is possible that the story or an echo of it was an inspiration for Melbourne Ward when he turned his gaze to the Three Sisters. This time it concerns the tribe of 'a little black girl called Moobra', again embroiled in conflict with its neighbours. Her people are killed and she is adopted by the tribe of her enemies. Despite 'the kindness of the blacks' she pines for her loved ones, and one evening she escapes the camp and sleeps beside a stream.

> After some time she woke, hearing sweet singing near her, and she beheld a most beautiful scene. Dancing on the green moss, and sporting round the small pools made by the stream, were innumerable fairies. Some were gaily dressed in silken web costumes of all colours. The little men wore small caps, with feathers stuck in the sides, short jackets, and pretty knickerbockers . . . The ladies were clothed in silken robes of varied hue, and their beautiful hair streamed in the breeze.[29]

These unlikely inhabitants of the Australian forest cared for the girl, protecting her with their magic. But the tribe was angry at her absconding. They searched and found her, the men gathering to attack. On discovering:

> that their weapons always missed their mark, the angry savages attempted to surround the little girl, intending to capture her and put her to death. Scarcely had they begun to carry this plan into effect when the fairies, designing their motive, showed themselves, and fearing that Moobra would be taken and ill-treated, they lifted her up the steep mountain pass, and setting her upon a high rock, changed her into a figure of stone. Seeing this the Dumbras became terrified, and, turning away, fled with all speed and were never seen again near the spot.

The aboriginal tribes which had been led by Kario and Kurrong are now extinct, but the remains of the black girl, Moobra, are still to be seen standing majestically alone on a dark stone pedestal towering above the valley near the famous Katoomba Falls.[30]

As grim in style as it is in content, the 1910 story of Orphan Rock is a compelling example of how the lost child and indeed the lost world of childhood have figured in colonial imaginings of the Australian bush.

The story, generically framed as a European fairy tale, gestures at the host of European children, lost in the bush, who haunt the colonial imagination. Turning the leaves of this enduring family album, one could shift from the solitary girl obscured by foliage of Frederick McCubbin's painting *Lost* to Joan Lindsay's tale of the schoolgirls disappearing at Hanging Rock. It is a numerous family: the *Little Boy Lost* of Rolf Harris fame; John Heyer's outback film, *The Back of Beyond*, in which two sisters disappear in an 'ocean of sand'. Peter Pierce, in his study of this recurring theme in Australian culture, has suggested that the 'figure of the child stands in part for the apprehensions of adults about having to settle in a place where they might never be at peace'.[31] This is certainly true of the nomenclature in Jamison Valley, though it is distinctive for its process of transference: the white boy who fell, the white woman who followed, the Docker daughters of the stereo-graphic view—converted in narrative to Aboriginal youth, a youth that is frozen in stone.

This gives the tale of Orphan Rock a decidedly sinister aspect, reflecting a social policy that would make the dismantling of Aboriginal families the corollary to terrestrial conquest. Peter Pierce also discerns a connection between white children lost in the Australian bush and what has become known as the 'stolen generations' of Aborigines.[32] The bizarre legend of benevolent fairies who rescue a distraught Aboriginal child from the perils of both the bush and her own family does resonate with wel-fare practices whereby children were forcibly apprenticed, placed in foster care or sent to institutional homes. These were policies that deliberately separated Aboriginal children from their families, that made them orphans and launched them into the world as lost ones in their own country.

167

What is the connection between myths of petrified Aborigines and the widely held belief that they were representatives of a 'stone-age' culture? A connection is tellingly personified in the figure of Mel Ward, who first published the Three Sisters legend. In 1957, eight years after that publication, a photograph of Ward appeared on the cover of *Reader's Digest*. He is depicted in his strange, echoic monument—the Museum of Natural History and Native Art, located in the grounds of the Hydro Majestic, a grand hotel perched on the clifftop at the Blue Mountains town of Medlow Bath. He appears as a white-haired, reflective custodian of his collection, solemnly holding and staring at an elaborately carved drum. Arrayed around him is a host of wooden masks and carvings, pickings from Pacific islands, cluttered among ornamental poles and carvings. Other photos from the same period suggest some fanciful cornucopia to 'the Primitive'. Spears radiate from walls as artificial rafters, their labels of identification dangling like pennants. Woven mats and fish traps, carved motifs and musical instruments are crammed along walls and shelves. A stuffed kangaroo surveys it all. Positioned along a chest of drawers (would you dare to open them?) half a dozen skulls provide the focal point at the termination of a corridor, literally a dead-end.[33]

Ward's letters, held by the Australian Museum, elucidate his collecting process. They can make for startling reading. In 1947 he received correspondence from one M. D. McPaul in Theodore, Queensland, announcing an expedition 'to collect some aboriginal mummies. . . . from an area about 50 or 60 miles from here and would be pleased to know if you are interested in these to the extent of making it a paying proposition for me to get some'. He also offered 'some fragmentary specimens of the meal grinding stones in this area' and, on a different note, asked whether Ward had received a scorpion, fearful it was damaged in the post.[34]

Ward's archive contains many such letters. He had contacts throughout the country, many of them white officials—police officers or mission superintendents—who, with a little financial lubrication, assisted with the collection of objects. Many of these were zoological or mineral specimens, yet others involved the plunder of graves. A correspondent in the Northern Territory made an excited offer of nine baby skeletons wrapped in bark. Ethically, there appeared to be no distinction between the gathering of Aboriginal remains and the purchase of 'natural' specimens. A Queensland correspondent could proffer Aboriginal carvings and sketches of beetles.

Ward's biography reveals a combined passion for showmanship and collecting. He lived from 1903 to 1966, son of the vaudeville performers Hugh and Grace Ward. He left school at age sixteen, made his stage debut as a dancer in *The Bing Boys on Broadway*, then trod the boards for another eight years before retiring youthfully on a private income. He devoted time and fortune to his childhood fascination for crabs. Although he had virtually no formal training, he appears to have made a genuine contribution to carcinology, becoming an honorary zoologist with the Australian Museum and identifying more than one hundred varieties of crustacea.

Ward's collecting, which started in the 1920s, was initially confined to crabs. He gathered thousands of them, from tiny creatures scooped perilously from the surface of Cuban quicksand to gnarly monsters a metre wide. Travelling widely throughout Australia, the Pacific and South America, he gradually broadened his interests to include all sorts of natural and what was euphemistically known as 'ethnological' paraphernalia.[35]

In 1943 Ward opened the Museum of Natural History and Native Art at the Hydro Majestic. Its motto was 'Man, know thyself' and the curatorial policy was as eclectic as it was frequently grotesque. The display included stuffed animals and birds, a brass cannon with an Arabic inscription, the bushranger Thunderbolt's pistol, a 'hideous' stonefish, Queen Victoria's signature, a Tibetan double-toned bell, embroidered maps by Captain Cook's wife. At the time when he appeared on its cover, the *Reader's Digest* would report that the collection contained 40 000 shells, 30 000 crabs, 20 000 insects and reptiles and '7000 native curios collected all over the world . . . Experts rate this priceless collection as second only to that in the Vatican City.'[36] Even young children were co-opted into Mel Ward's regime of collection. He purchased snakes at the rate of sixpence per foot.

As a collector of objects and a disseminator of stories, Mel Ward was full of contradictions. The encyclopaedic scope of his collection conformed to a nineteenth-century model of museology in which

169

geological and biological specimens shared company with human artefacts and bodily remains. The racial assumptions manifest in the display were, perhaps, typical of the era. Bones and artefacts were usually obtained from cultures that were anything but extinct. Yet placed in this funereal context, surrounded by stones, fossils, stuffed animals and colonial bric-a-brac, it would be difficult to interpret them as anything other than vestiges of an ancient past. Ward confirmed his adherence to racial hierarchy when describing the museum.

> The anthropological collection is arranged in a natural sequence from the simplest stone age culture of the Tasmanian natives . . . then to New Guinea and the South Sea Islands, progressing from one culture to another and showing the gradual improvement.[37]

In placing cultural artefacts alongside Aboriginal crania, Ward's project was inevitably linked with what the historian Tom Griffiths has pithily described as that 'arithmetic of arrogance'—the phrenological discourse that afforded European scientists an invariable 'index to their own racial superiority'.[38]

Griffiths' study, *Hunters and Collectors*, provides illuminating background to the Museum of Natural History and Native Art. He links the gentile passion for a 'cabinet of curiosities' and broader practices of museology and collecting with a history of European discovery and expansion. He also provides vivid portraiture of earlier, equally driven keepers of the private museum such as R. E. Johns, a court clerk in Victoria who, from the 1850s, amassed a collection of bones and artefacts no less diverse and bizarre than Melbourne Ward's. Griffiths' book is particularly useful for the way in which it opens up the debates and tensions concerning museum practices. Ward's taxidermic exhibition, opening in the wake of World War II, must have seemed a dated concept for many of his contemporaries. Griffiths argues that the period after 1900 brought a vital interest in the Australian bush and increasing scepticism about the value of placing specimens behind glass. He quotes Charles Barrett who claimed that 'the best work of the taxidermist bears but a faint resemblance to Nature'. For Barrett, 'the only way to study bird-life is to dwell among the feathered folk themselves'.[39]

Despite, or perhaps in light of, such criticisms, Ward worked strenuously at making his museum a place that was both lively and entertaining. Certainly, he did not eschew the world about him, as seems to have been the case with some of Griffiths' case studies. Ever the Thespian, he guided visitors through the museum, gave numerous public lectures and broadcasts and appeared regularly on television. In his own writings, Ward emphasised the need to impart information, tell stories and create dialogue to do with his collection. This desire to give voice to the exhibits attained its perverse zenith when a branch of the museum was opened at the La Plaza building at Echo Point in 1959. Around the ethnological collection he installed 'life sized figures of aboriginals'. A system of loud speakers gave 'the impression of the native talking about their own relics'.[40]

Curiously, considering these activities, Ward professed a great admiration for Aboriginal people. He had had some contact with remote Aboriginal communities in northern Australia and was eventually admitted to the New South Wales Anthropological Society, frequently corresponding with A. P. Elkin, who represented the public face of anthropology in Australia. But, like many people of his time, Ward focused on the re-creation of a 'traditional model of Aboriginal culture as it was prior to contact with European "civilization"'.[41] The publication of the Three Sisters story, one of a series of legends in *Outdoors and Fishing*, was part of this re-creation. He reproduced them in *Legends of the Mountains* and *Legend Walk*, self-published booklets on the bushwalks he guided from the Hydro Majestic hotel.

Despite his evident familiarity with anthropological conventions, Ward never credited an Aboriginal informant or provided such basic data as the place or date of transcription. Jim Smith regards this failure as deeply suspect, contrasting it with Ward's rigour in labelling every crab he collected. The vague, retrospective claim that the story came from Aborigines in the Burragorang was the closest he came to attribution.[42]

~

Unlike the story of Mirragan and Gurangatch, and the vast bulk of Aboriginal mythology, Ward's 'Aboriginal' stories were not usually place-specific. (The Three Sisters legend is an exception in this regard.) Rather, they took the form of children's tales, based on such themes as 'why Australian trees have shiny bark', 'why the evening sky is red' and 'why pollen from wattle makes us sneeze'. Referencing a world of fairy tale or the moral certainty of Aesop's *Fables*, Ward's re-writing of Aboriginal culture used a contemporary frame of science and modernity to evoke

171

nostalgia for a folkloric past. In the opening of *Legend Walk*—presumably recited along bush trails—he offered to 'take you out of the atomic world of the white man and give you a different outlook on the world you are looking at'.[43] Ward, it seems, could produce only a fossilised rendition of Aboriginal culture.

In the end Mel Ward, like anyone else, was unable to circumvent the exigencies of time's process. His museum dated badly and when he died in 1966 a fraction of his collection was admitted to the Australian Museum. Years later, when the auctioneers came in to clear his widow's estate, much of what remained was thrown away. Zoological specimens were decaying in their bottles, a rotten, spirituous soup.

THE RETURN OF THE 'NATIVE'

Let us visit, if only briefly, the grimmest of Blue Mountains narratives—a macabre shadow to those stories of lost children. The time is daybreak. A bloody trail has led us to this point. They wait in the bushes: Kibble of Windsor, his mate Tom Coolan, and Gratten of Nepean. With these white men are two unnamed black trackers who take 'great delight in killing wild blackfellow'. Watching, stalking. Before them lies the 'ferocious tribe' that killed a British soldier on the western road. When they had reached the campsite they saw figures lit by firelight. 'Two of the black gins, wearing soldiers' coats, were sitting on a log, each having a hand of the murdered soldier and pulling the sinews together at the same time singing, "Soldier make a do-boy, a do-boy, a do-boy," thus making a song of this cruel and bloody deed.'

Spilled blood begets more blood, according to the story. As dawn lightens the valley, they creep towards the camp, and

> coming stealthily in, they got close up to it when a little dog gave the alarm, and one of the blacks got up, but was shot down almost immediately. The gins and piccaninnies set up a scream, but many were shot before they could rise, others running here and there trying to escape their pursuers. One of the gins, who climbed up a short bushy tree with her child . . . was shot by Kibble, who also took the piccaninny and dashed its brains out against a tree near where its mother lay, saying as he did so, 'Nits would come to lice'. About one-half (numbering about 20) were slaughtered on that memorable morning by the three bloodthirsty wretches.[44]

James T. Ryan's 1894 memoir, from which this narrative is extracted, bears the title *Reminiscences of Australia*. The author literally assumes the voice of the nation, and the Blue Mountains massacre, temporally located around the time of his birth and positioned at the beginning of the book, is presented as a founding event. It is an incident of which he nominally disapproves; yet, like some ancient mariner, he finds perverse pleasure in gripping his audience with this tale of terror. Intimations of such titillation have already appeared in the terrain of this journey. In *Outdoors and Fishing*, Ward's Three Sisters legend had described a battle in which 'Blood flowed and stained the ground more red than the sunset colours on the great cliffs along the valley.' The tale of Orphan Rock sententiously and erroneously declared that the 'aboriginal tribes' of the Blue Mountains 'are now extinct'.

It is appropriate to regard all these narratives in similar light, for their concerns have a way of overlapping. There's the connection between landscape and violent conflict; the brutalisation of femininity and childhood; the link between trinities and moments of foundation. Sharing these mythic (if historically influenced) premises, it turns out that Ryan's narrative is itself a myth of place. Local historians have scoured the story, checked its abundant details—names of perpetrators; the incident of the murdered soldier, which could hardly have escaped the detailed journal of William Cox—to find that not a skerrick fits with recorded data.[45] In the way of myth, the story is both true and untrue. As blood begets blood, this epiphany of violence reflects the process of colonisation, enumerating horrific moments all of which could correlate with events that happened elsewhere, across the country. And yet it perpetrates its own peculiar horror—a secondary terror—by projecting violence onto part of the country where, quite possibly, no such event ever occurred. Perhaps it is this type of deathly invocation that inspired Michael Taussig's observation that,

> In the making of modern nations, the dead do double duty. Out of nowhere it seems, people conjure up a slice of deadness and borrow from it their names, battle cries, and costumes, in order to present the new scene of world history in dazzling form.[46]

~

173

The path of this narrative has been tortuous as well as vertiginous—a cliff-bound trek, resonant with stony echoes, which bounce between the hard places of rock and culture to affect their own strange metamorphosis. A journey along weathered steps, chiselled from sandstone; odd views through murky lenses. Story of a fallen child. Landscape is always a space of memory. Looking at photos from Mel Ward's museum, I find an entry to a cluttered corridor, leading to a shelf of bones. Death, I look you in the face.

What is the museum if not a failed attempt to harness nature's process; the sanctioned means, in an age of science, of approaching death, boxed in a cabinet, and gazing at its bland sublimity? This is the cultic basis that underlies those lofty concerns of ordering, knowing, making real. Hence the connection of museums with archaeology—the ceaseless salvaging of the dead, the past. Hence also the museum's special fascination with ancient Egypt, 'a society which devoted most of its wealth, and apparently all of its imagination to death and the afterlife...' In the visceral phrase of the curator and historian Susan M. Pearce, writing of the trade in withered hands and feet, mummified cats and crocodiles, the Egypt of the museum will 'help to fill our mouths with the taste of mortality'.[47]

Our journey so far suggests that the border between Mel Ward's museum and the wider world was never fixed. Again, the concerns overlap. The broad themes painted on the land itself—the mortification of formations, the absences of colonisation—are merely distilled, synthesised, in that little world of taxidermic excess. If we acknowledge, in the words of the poet James Fenton, that museum visitors 'find the landscape of their childhood marked out/Here in the chaotic piles of souvenirs'[48]—the collector's cabinet stemming from and indulging a childish fascination—then the dark space of the museum and the elusive valley of the lost child share another deep connection.

In this vein, the cultural studies scholar Chris Healy has remarked on the frequency with which Aboriginal narratives have 'been seized as antipodean fairy tales'. While, as Healy claims, this has involved a transformation that turns Aboriginal lore into 'harmless, local and simple stories for white children', it is something more.[49] The museum operates as a theatre for the scrutiny of death—a rare outlet in a culture where death, especially for children, is obscured, suppressed and denied. But it is also a way of *framing* death; a theatre of curatorial choice about who, or what cultures, will symbolise death's process. In the way of the fairy tale, such theatre involves an act of enchantment, an invocation. In Ward's museum, it was the figure of a universalised 'native'—disinterred from Australia and the Pacific Islands—that became the deathly embodiment.

Thus summoned from the deepest spiral of the Styx, such visions of the 'native' would perpetuate the inscription of allochronism—that process described by Johannes Fabian where the construction of a putatively authentic past 'serves to denounce an inauthentic present'.[50] This is certainly reflected in constructions of the childish savage, examples of which are legion. And once again, it involves a making dead and a doubling of the dead, confining the 'native' to a life of childhood, confining that childhood to a distant land of the past.

~

There is a philosophical difference between, on the one hand, the bookish enclave of Kant and Flaubert and, on the other, Nietzsche's assertion that only ideas won by walking have any value. This difference, pointing to a tension between dynamism and stasis, is mapped by the mythic construction of the Blue Mountains. In the popular imagination, this mapping has involved the deployment of that religiously loaded symbol, the trinity. We have a contrast between Blaxland's dynamic trio, travelling west and bringing the nation into being, and that of the static, stony sisters. The connection between them was grandiloquently expressed in 1966 when Lyall Randolph, the sculptor of Harry Hammon's fountain, announced a plan 'to make three huge heads' of the explorers Blaxland, Lawson and Wentworth in the vicinity of the Three Sisters. From the side of a 1000-foot cliff, they would 'stare out to the symbolic west'.[51] A similar idea had been mooted previously when the publisher Oswald L. Ziegler proposed a Mount Rushmore style monument that would overlook the Grose River Valley.[52] But neither project got off the ground. Unlike the Three Sisters, the three explorers have been more successful in avoiding the perils of petrification.

For all its emphasis on rootedness and possession, the West, with its history of transport, communication and colonisation, has embraced movement with an enthusiasm that has seen no parallel. It would appear that the cultural construction of the Blue Mountains, which articulates

175

the possibility of movement within rigid projections of race and gender, has in the process established patterns of movement that toy with the abyss, reminding pedestrians of their mortality and dallying with vertigo as both a physiological and cultural condition.

Despite various attempts to confine and displace them, Aboriginal people have never been expunged from the Blue Mountains. As we will see, a discrete Aboriginal community lived in Katoomba until the 1950s, within a few hundred metres of where I write. This community, within walking distance of the Echo Point museum, is the great absence in Mel Ward's story. In contrast to the ragged but nonetheless indisputable presence of these fringe dwellers, Ward preferred his skulls and simulacra, mouthing platitudes about the past.

Ward's case is not exceptional. It is one of the great complexities of post-colonialism that the distinction between genuine survivors of the colonial process and the simulacra thrown up in its wake is so blurred. This bowdlerised topography, where constructions of 'the native' are coined as the figure of death, becomes the junk yard in which we all, to some extent, are forced to scavenge.

OSWALD L. ZIEGLER WAS A NATIONALIST AND PROLIFIC PUBLISHER OF AUSTRALIANA. HE ONCE PROPOSED A MOUNT RUSHMORE STYLE MONUMENT TO BLAXLAND, WENTWORTH AND LAWSON, AN IDEA THAT ALSO OCCURRED TO LYALL RANDOLPH, CREATOR OF THE THREE SISTERS FOUNTAIN, IN THE 1960S. NO ONE ACTED ON THESE PROPOSALS. UNLIKE THE THREE SISTERS, THE THREE EXPLORERS HAVE EVADED THE PERILS OF PETRIFICATION.

IN 1999 I met June Barker (nee Ferguson) who lives in the town of Lightning Ridge in north-west New South Wales. The daughter of the Aboriginal preacher Duncan Ferguson and grand-daughter of William Ferguson, the famous activist for Aboriginal rights, June spent much of her childhood at the Brewarrina Aboriginal Station or 'Mission' as it was commonly known. As a teenager in the late 1940s, she was sent to work at a guesthouse in Katoomba. Her father had used his influence to ensure she was placed with Christian proprietors who would treat her kindly and pay a decent wage. It was one of the house guests, a worker for the Aborigines Inland Mission, who introduced June to some of the Aboriginal residents of the town. This is how she had described her reception:

> She'd already told the people down there about me coming and they were looking forward to meeting me and this old lady, I always re-member her: as we were walking up she came out with her arms outstretched to me and said, 'Oh our country cousin, they tell me you come from where there's no hills and mountains, you come there from the flat country'. And I always remembered her. [. . .] She was Granny Lock. She said we've been here a long time. She could talk in the language too. [. . .] She said your people been out there a long time, our people been here a long time. The mountains. She said our

THE CATALINA RACING CIRCUIT WAS BUILT IN 1957 AS A VENUE FOR MOTOR SPORTS. THE TRACK DISPLACED A SMALL, UNOFFICAL SETTLEMENT KNOWN AS THE GULLY WHICH INCLUDED MANY OF KATOOMBA'S ABORIGINAL FAMILIES.

people, our people, they even took those 'explorers', they call them, she said, you know those white fellows, they took them over the mountains, and she said, she sort of got angry, and she said: 'They never thought of them, they never *mention* them'. [. . .] She sort of shut her fist and, 'Ahhhhhh, ahhhhhh', she went, like that. 'They never found their way over the mountains, our people took them over the mountains. Our men took 'em over the mountains'. And I don't think the missionary lady I was with liked her saying that.[53]

June Barker regrets that she didn't get to know Granny Lock and her community better. Her employers at the guesthouse strongly disapproved of her associating with the local Aborigines. But this brief encounter offers a revealing starting point in considering the history of the Katoomba fringe dwellers who lived in what is called 'the Gully'. It indicates how enduring Aboriginal attachment to country has been and it reveals the persistence of a localised culture, grounded in oral testimony, that disputes the legend of a 'First Crossing'. In that brief encounter there is a clear indication of the way Granny Lock schematised all of Australia as Aboriginal, and how each region contains people who have 'been here a long time'.

Contrast the confidence with which Granny Lock welcomed June Barker to her country with the sentiments contained in *The Jumbly history of Parramatta* (1915), a publication written by the journalist Frank Walford, who would serve three terms as mayor of the Blue Mountains. Walford published a poem articulating what was then a very common view—that the 'Aboriginal race' was on the brink of extinction:

> King Billy Long has passed, and, in his shoes
> Another stands, while out at La Perouse
> His lineal descendants, yielding way
> To tougher fibre, near the close of day.
> And there the tourist sees the native spend
> That twilight gloom, which spells a racial end.
> Rack'd with disease, and quite degenerate,
> The Aborigine awaits his fate.[54]

As June Barker's encounter makes clear, the fate of Katoomba's Aboriginal population had little in common with the vision of impending extinction articulated by Walford (or 'Double-Yew' as he styled himself on this occasion). But through his support for a car racing circuit which runs through the area of forested and sometimes swampy parkland that bears his name, Frank Walford is associated with a different kind of extinction: the break-up of the community that June visited, an unofficial encampment of people with longstanding attachment to a particular piece of ground.

Built in 1957, the Catalina Park Racing Circuit forced the eviction of a community of fringe dwellers who, from the late nineteenth century, had lived in rough, improvised dwellings. Located within traditional Gundungurra territory, the area was inhabited by people of direct Gundungurra lineage. Others were Darug descendants, and a few came from other Aboriginal communities. There were also a number of people of entirely European descent. It was one of those heterogeneous, makeshift encampments, unofficial but recognised to some degree by local authorities, that were once reasonably common in rural Australia. A broad mix of inhabitants, united to some degree by experiences of poverty or displacement, would make a base, build a shelter and eke out an existence on the edge of town. The existence of this community provides a context for the mythology of petrified women previously discussed. Pitted against the presumed disappearance of the Aboriginal population was the reality of its endurance (albeit in greatly diminished numbers) on a fragment of ancestral ground.

One might ask how an Aboriginal person would have felt among the skulls, spears and evolutionary displays of Mel Ward's museum. Interestingly, it is possible to answer this question, for one day, during her Katoomba residency, June Barker was taken to the Hydro Majestic hotel.

They showed you through everything. And then there was a little museum thing next door. I didn't know anything about these museums then, that people collected things. [. . .] Never heard of a museum, didn't know that these collectors were around. And so we went in there and there was this guy there [. . .] He was there telling everybody about all these Aborigines and all this and that. There was a big group there. I must have been standing in the group, and all of a sudden he spotted me in the group. And he said: 'Oh, and we've got one girl here today, an Australian Aboriginal girl'. And everyone sort

179

of all looked around and I was sort of standing there looking stupid and so, no one sort of said anything, a couple of them might have said hullo to me, a couple of them clapped. I don't know what the clappin' was for. [. . .] So I was just standin' there lookin' stupid.

When asked how she felt to be singled out in that way June said: 'it made me feel a bit uneasy because, you know, I knew that everyone knew that I was different'.[55]

Feeling awkward was probably the inevitable reaction for someone in June's position. For Ward, delivering his discourse, the Aboriginal girl could only serve as an example, a spectacle, or a prop. She provided a real-life illustration that supported *his* form of knowledge. Just as Ward failed to liaise with the Aboriginal community of Katoomba when designing his displays and peddling his Dreamtime stories, he refused to acknowledge that the Australian Aboriginal girl might herself have something to say.

In turning away from the projected visions of Aboriginal life and culture, I have attended to the minutiae of a patch of parkland and its people. Researching it became possible in 1997 when I moved to the Blue Mountains and settled in a house on the edge of Frank Walford Park. Living within the landscape that had long exerted such fascination brought gradual membership of the community and the opportunity to record some of the stories of those who live here.

The experience of researching the community, of attempting a kind of ethnography from within, was influenced by the anthropologist Michael Jackson, who wrote so poignantly of the twentieth century as one of 'uprootedness'. 'All over the world, fewer and fewer people live out their lives in the place where they were born.' At no other time, he proposes, 'has the question of belonging seemed so urgent'.[56] Jackson, who has studied re-location and dislocation within remote Aboriginal communities, is a significant voice in a growing 'literature of belonging'. The historian Peter Read is also a key figure in this movement. In books such as *Returning to Nothing: The meaning of lost places* (1996) and more recently *Belonging: Australians, Place and Aboriginal Ownership* (2000), Read has laid out methodological tools for enquiring into the relationships between people and places. Informed by his studies of Aboriginal history, Read sees the need for home and country as axiomatic to people

180

of all cultures. Through extended interviews and group discussions, he taps the feelings and memories evoked by the relationship to place. Like Jackson, he has come to see a fractured relationship to home as emblematic in the experience of modernity. His work is significant for its treatment of subjective and often emotional testimony, establishing its legitimacy as a source in historical discussion.

My oral history recordings about Frank Walford Park were made in 1999. They were gathered on the understanding that the testimony would contribute both to this book and to a radio documentary commissioned by the Australian Broadcasting Corporation.[57] A surprising aspect of the project was the immediacy with which historical issues were firmly brought into the present. The events in the Gully are consistent with the broad postwar trend noted by Heather Goodall, in which it seemed desirable among welfare bodies and other 'experts' to dissolve self-contained Aboriginal communities so they might be assimilated into the wider social mix.[58] Here was a story of forced eviction—an event only forty years distant. Far from relegating the seizure of territory to some safely remote colonial past, this had occurred within living memory.

To the extent that I could, I gathered stories about what had happened in my own back yard. The process was curious. The enquiry became my own means of making home. To consider issues as apparently mundane as what it means to live in a particular house, on a street, on this hill or that, within a particular ecology, can, in their minutiae, provide nuanced responses to historical questions that for all of us are common ground.

OUR TOWN

Looking back from Mount Solitary or Narrow Neck, the cliff-bound plateaus that border Jamison Valley, the Carrington smokestack marks the town. A brick obelisk protruding from the pile of white hotel buildings gathered about the hilltop, the landmark chimney is a reminder of the dual origins of Katoomba. Among Europeans, the locality was first known as The Crushers, an unadorned train stop on the main western line which had opened in the late 1860s. The village proper rustled into being in 1879 when John Britty North, sometimes referred to as the 'father' of the town, sunk the first coal and shale mines in the valley and hoisted his booty up the cliff face on the steep, cable-pulled railway that was eventually acquired by the Hammon family and operated as the Scenic Railway.

Just a few years later the Great Western Hotel, which became the Carrington upon the visit of the English lord, opened its doors. Cottages spread around the base and commercial premises were established along the steep, downhill sweep of Katoomba Street, also visible from across the valley. The name *Katoomba*, a derivation of *Kedumba* and reputedly an Aboriginal word meaning 'plenty water tumble down here', had by now firmly taken hold.[59] The Carrington's octagonal smokestack was actually an afterthought, appearing in 1913 with the construction of a powerhouse that generated electricity for hotel and town.

In the early days the economic base of Katoomba was split between mining and tourism. Eventually the latter won out. Substantial deposits of coal and shale had been located with the assistance of Gundungurra man Billy Lynch. He does not seem to have profited from the discovery, though several Aboriginal families found employment in the mines, living in small, makeshift villages in the valley.

The rugged topography and consequent need for elaborate haulage equipment made the mining a chequered business. The capital investment was substantial. A still passable tunnel was bored through Narrow Neck to connect the Glen Shale Mines of the Megalong with a horsedrawn tramway connected to a hoist that lifted coal and shale up the escarpment. The industry suffered its first very literal collapse in the 1880s when another contrivance, an aerial ropeway that spanned the Jamison Valley, fell to the forest floor having shifted only 500 tons of shale. Cables and wreckage from this accident still litter the track that leads to Ruined Castle and Mount Solitary. Undaunted, John Britty North formed a new operation, the Australian Kerosene Oil and Mineral Company, which took over the mines. By 1903 the shale industry was abandoned. This brought the dissolution of several small workers' villages that had sprung up in the Jamison and Megalong valleys which had provided employment for some of the Aboriginal men. Coal mining was revived briefly around 1925, but it remained a fairly marginal operation.[60]

The site of the Catalina Racing Circuit is also associated with the mining period and, although in no sense a contemporary tourist

ELABORATE HAULAGE
EQUIPMENT WAS NEEDED
TO TRANSPORT COAL
AND SHALE FROM
JAMISON VALLEY TO THE
MAIN WESTERN RAILWAY
LINE. TAKEN AROUND
1880, THIS PHOTOGRAPH
SHOWS THE IMPACT OF
MINING ON THE
RAINFOREST NEAR
KATOOMBA FALLS. THE
TRACK NOW CARRIES
TOURISTS ON THE
SCENIC RAILWAY. THE
FOREST HAS SINCE
REGROWN, CONCEALING
MUCH OF WHAT
REMAINS FROM THE
MINING ERA.

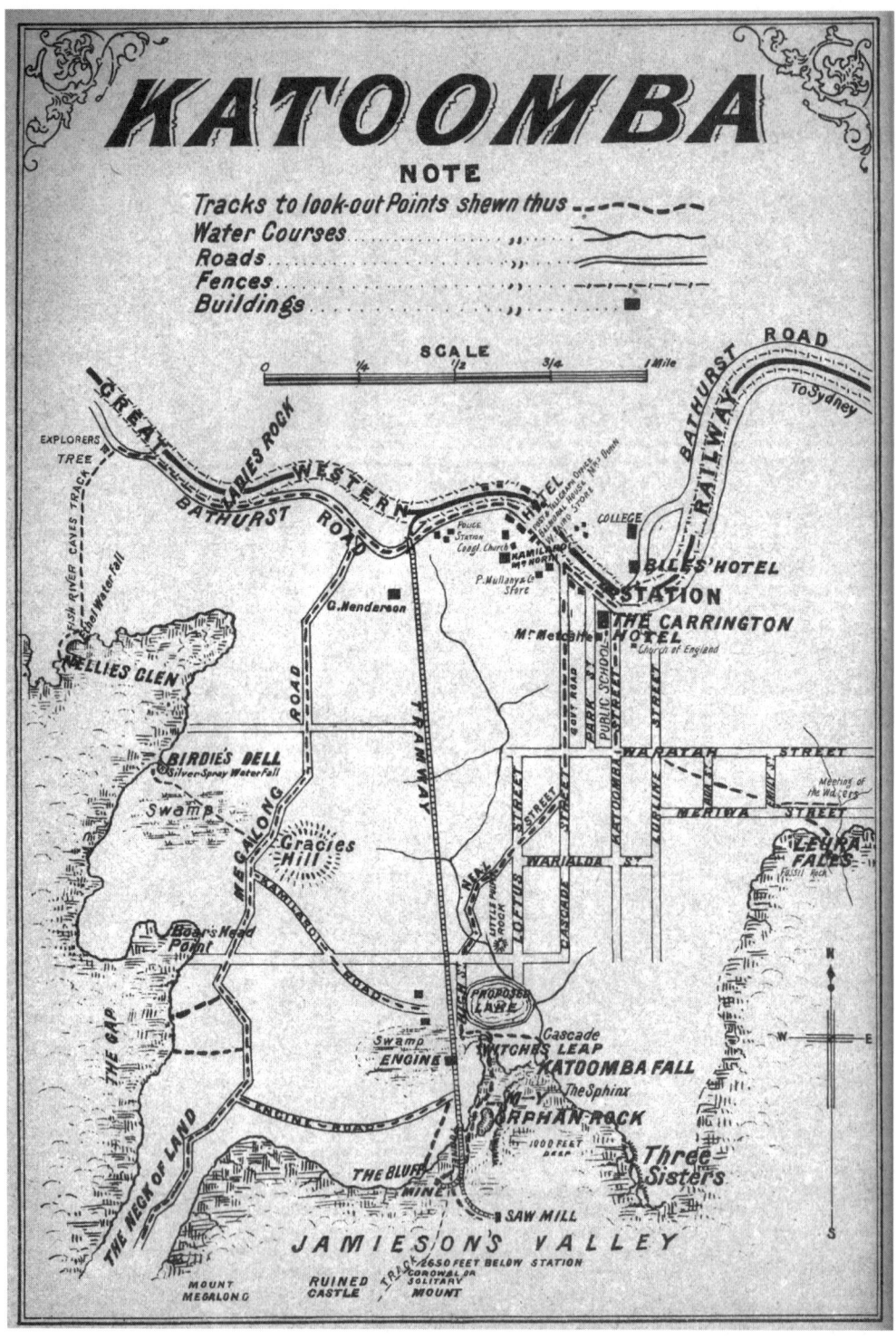

destination, it is historically and environmentally connected with the tourist aspect of the town. The northern reach of Frank Walford Park, just a few minutes' walk from the Carrington Hotel, forms the headwaters of a stream linking plateau and precipice. Katoomba Falls Creek issues from the park and flows southwards, exiting the Walford reserve to flow through an area called McRae's Paddock, a spacious no-man's land backed by houses. It then flows through the recreation and picnic area of Katoomba Park, eventually tumbling into the Jamison Valley as Katoomba Falls. Frank Walford Park, with a swimming pool and recreation centre on the edge and the now largely disused raceway running through the middle, is enjoyed mainly by locals for recreation. Much of the ground is too swampy for conventional housing, which explains the overall lack of development. The park forms part of a wildlife corridor between the Jamison and Grose River valleys. The migration of honeyeaters and bower birds is a regular part of the seasonal cycle. The park also provides a sanctuary in its own right: snakes, quolls, crayfish, possums, wallabies and numerous birds manage to survive despite the competition of feral foxes, dogs and cats.

While most tourists—and indeed many locals—would never know it was there, Frank Walford Park is inextricably tied with that great champion of tourism, Harry Hammon. When he purchased the land and infrastructure for the Scenic Railway, Hammon acquired title to a thin strip of private land that juts into the reserve and constitutes what is perhaps one of the most strangely shaped blocks in the country. It was part of the mining operation: a tramway running beside Katoomba Falls Creek connected the coal hoist with the main western railroad. Hammon was also a keen motoring enthusiast and protagonist in the story of the racetrack. He was central not only to the beginning but to the demise of professional motor sports in Katoomba. For the story of the racetrack is the story of a debt unpaid.

OPPOSITE: THIS MAP OF KATOOMBA DATES FROM 1885. AT THE TOP OF KATOOMBA FALLS IT SHOWS A PROPOSED LAKE THAT WAS NEVER BUILT. ALSO VISIBLE IS THE TRAMWAY THAT CONNECTED THE MINES AND THE GREAT WESTERN RAILWAY. THE AREA KNOWN AS THE GULLY SURROUNDS THE NORTHERN STRETCH OF THE TRAMWAY. IT IS CONJECTURED THAT THE OCCUPANTS OF THE GULLY TOOK OVER ABANDONED BUILDINGS ASSOCIATED WITH THE MINING ERA. WHILE THIS MAY BE TRUE, ARCHAEOLOGICAL EVIDENCE INDICATES THAT THE WELL-WATERED GULLY HAS BEEN AN ABORIGINAL CAMPING GROUND FOR MILLENNIA.

THE GULLY

Frank Walford, after whom the park is named, was a larger-than-life personality not opposed to the odd bit of hyperbole when describing himself. He is remembered as a man of shifting political allegiance and has been accused of shady tactics in party conflicts, cynically drumming up fear of communism when campaigning for mayoral office in 1944.[61]

When he died at Katoomba in 1969, aged 87, the *Blue Mountains Advertiser* published a circumspect tribute, paying homage to his thirty-year service as an alderman, his three terms as mayor, his passion for native fauna and the Boy Scout movement and his tenacity in finding lost bushwalkers which won him 'the honour and medal of "Police Friend"'.[62] Small-town newspapers often have a way of overlooking the more interesting details, especially upon the death of a local personage. There was no mention of Walford's close friendship with Frank Hurley, the photographer hero of Antarctica and New Guinea, nor of his prolific career as a journalist, poet, newspaper editor and writer of fiction. He had also published various popular novels, including *Twisted Clay*, 'an explosive novel of strange passions' according to the cover blurb—a book which, upon its release in 1933, was said (by Walford himself) to have been applauded by *The Times* of London as 'the best book ever written with a lunatic as a central character'.[63] This was Jean Deslines, a fourteen year old from Katoomba, whose downward spiral goes from premarital sex and lesbian tendencies to patricide, prostitution, serial murder, drug running and eventual suicide. It was sufficiently racy to be banned in Australia for almost thirty years.

186

Other aspects of the Walford biography—like the claim that he published 600 short stories and his reputed membership in northern Australia of 'the piratical group known as the "Barrier Rats"'—might have been coloured by the famous Walford hyperbole. But it is that same strange wavering between fact and fantasy, dream and reality, that makes 'Frank Walford Park' an appropriate if rarely used title for the headwaters of Katoomba Falls Creek.[64] There is something about the area that makes it just a little difficult to classify. Among townsfolk it is more frequently referred to as 'Catalina Park', the name bestowed by a businessman, Horrie Gates, who used part of the site as an amusement park in the wake of World War II. These are just two of a cluster of names. To the conservation group that lobbies for its protection, the area is known as 'Katoomba Falls Creek Valley', while for those who actually lived there it is plainly known as 'the Gully' or 'the Valley'.

The conflicting nomenclature reflects the conflicting claims to this patch of ground. The demise of car racing, which some residents want reinstated, has coincided with something of an ecological comeback. Large stands of *Eucalyptus oreades* (Blue Mountains ash) were cleared in the late 1950s to permit an almost complete view of the circuit from any point in the Gully. In recent decades, much of that bush has regenerated and large sections of the track are completely shaded. The native flora is being actively assisted by bush regeneration programs which involve the planting of local species and the reduction of exotics.

So far the bush regeneration program has spared many of the fruit trees in the park. Apples, quinces and plums grow in rather unexpected places, their small but tasty fruit providing a seasonal bounty for those in the know. Some presumably sprouted as wild seedlings. But others, intentionally planted, are among the few identifiable remnants of human habitation. When I walked there with Lynette Stanger, an Aboriginal descendant who had lived in the park from 1946 to 1951 and continued to visit her grandmother on a weekly basis until 1957, we came across the family's apple tree, a solitary sentinel at the house site which was overgrown with acacias and other native flora.

LYNETTE STANGER REMEMBERS THE COMMUNITY

I was introduced to Lynette Stanger by my neighbour Bonnie Colton and she became the main informant for this research, even though she does not claim any sort of role as a spokesperson. We met at a particular time when she felt ready to speak publicly about her experiences. She is not involved in land councils or other Aboriginal organisations but simply wished to speak of her own experiences and what they have taught her. She did this with marvellous eloquence and generosity, even when recalling some very painful events from the family history. There is often a sense of disease when a white researcher takes up an Aboriginal narrative. But I did not feel it here. It was very clear that Lynette was aware of the power of her story and she knew that the recordings we made would be used in a national radio broadcast and a book. She had a strong desire for her story to be placed on the public record.

Whether we were sitting at the Stangers' house in Katoomba or recording in the park itself, I was constantly impressed by the strength of Lynette's spatial memory. She pointed out the main paths used by Gully dwellers and described the location of some of the twenty-five or so households that resided there until the 1950s. With the vegetation re-colonising and the remnants of occupation so scant, every detail of their lives seemed of paramount importance. She quickly built up a picture.

WHEN I MET LYNETTE
STANGER TO MAKE
SOUND RECORDINGS
ABOUT LIFE IN THE
GULLY, SHE SHOWED ME
PHOTOGRAPHS FROM THE
FAMILY ALBUM. THE TOP
PHOTO SHOWS THE
YOUNG LYNETTE
OUTSIDE THE FAMILY'S
HOME IN 1946. LOWER
LEFT SHE IS PICTURED
THE FOLLOWING YEAR
WITH HER MOTHER
LILLIAN BOOBY. THEY
ARE IN FRONT OF THE
APPLE TREE, ALL THAT
NOW REMAINS OF THE
PROPERTY. LOWER RIGHT
IS A PORTRAIT OF ETHEL
ROSE COOPER (NEE
LOCK), LYNETTE'S
GRANDMOTHER.

There would be a fence across here, straight across there, and there
was our apple tree. There used to be a little climbing rose, a very very
soft pink climbing rose that ran along the top of the little fence that
my grandmother had and of course this is where the house was

down in here. [. . .] And you can see how this is all flattened out and you can see where the racetrack has come through just below where the house was.[65]

In Lynette's day the Gully community—sometimes referred to as 'the Blacks Camp'—was not so much a camp but a collection of separate and quite private dwellings. At one level the idea of a community, just 100 kilometres west of Sydney living in humpies until the late 1950s seems extraordinary. Yet in many respects it's the ordinariness that is really striking. During the Great Depression numerous 'Happy Valley' communities had sprung up around Australia. They were places where the unemployed and dispossessed were able to build themselves a simple home. The Gully shared certain commonalities with these communities, though it was far more enduring. By the postwar era that Lynette remembers, nearly all the men were employed. Some worked for the Blue Mountains City Council as road menders, grave diggers or general labourers. The children attended the Katoomba Public School where Lynette is now employed as a cleaner. She told me they had bread and milk deliveries and, although they were not ratepayers, they had sanitation services from the 1940s.

She recalled a myriad of details about life in her grandmother's household, ranging from the dogs and hens they kept, the cut-out butcher's paper used to decorate the kitchen dresser, the coal delivered to Gundar Street on the valley's edge, which her parents would carry to the house on their backs.

I suppose we lived there because they could build little houses that were quite inexpensive. Some of them were just made out of kerosene tins and gum tree saplings and things like that, and lined with hessian and painted white inside and out with clay which was put in a bucket and made into like a—like a whitewash.

Our water came mostly from a well that was fed by a spring and it was beautiful water. And I can always remember being sent to the well with a bucket—with a billy—you know, if Nan had someone visiting. [. . .] And I'd go over there and of course I'd be playing in the water and looking at my reflection in the water and I'd get carried away and then I'd hear coming a call from the house, there'd be this call *Lynette*!

As these transcriptions demonstrate, there's a robust poetry to Lynette Stanger's recollections. The mundane business of doing day-to-day chores for her grandmother opens up a symbolic language that transcends simple nostalgia. It alerted me to the unexpected way in which Darug and Gundungurra heritage has played itself out in the history of Katoomba, contributing, often subtly, to contemporary understandings of community.

This is especially significant because in Katoomba, like most Australian rural towns, the indigenous history (in contrast to the tourist legends) is something of a lacuna in public discourse. The Aboriginal population is small and even when it was identifiable as a discrete unit it could readily be disregarded as 'half-caste' and therefore inauthentic. Certainly, it did not seem obvious to Mel Ward, in seeking Aboriginal legends of the Blue Mountains, to confer with residents of the Gully. Quite possibly the Gully occupants would not or could not have supplied the sorts of stories he wanted to hear. But there is nothing to suggest he ever listened, indeed nothing to indicate, as Lynette Stanger puts it, that 'we were anyone special'. Although the Gully has, in recent years, become the focus of considerable local interest, it was in its day regarded as something of an embarrassment. Rarely—and when it happened, only incidentally—was the Gully mentioned in the local press. Such a situation was not unusual. It is common through much of urban Australia for local Aborigines to be derided as 'half-caste' or 'of mixed blood'. They compare unfavourably with the 'real Blackfellows' who, whether they be up north, out west or in the centre, are always considered to be somewhere else.

According to the national census, in 1996 the adjoining towns of Katoomba and Leura had a population of 13 719 people. Of these, 177 identified themselves on the census form as Aboriginal. It would be interesting, though difficult to determine, how many of those two hundred or so Aboriginal residents of Katoomba have Gundungurra or Darug affiliations and how many are somehow connected with the Gully. Some simply moved into the district. (After all, people come from around the world to experience the Blue Mountains.) Others, such as Lynette, have genealogies that connect them very deeply with the area. That is why she has been able to provide such important insights into the Aboriginal history of the Blue Mountains—the way traditions and attachments have been handed down and also the occasions when they haven't. She talked to me about her grandfather, Matthew 'Nat' Cooper, who was part of a well-known Aboriginal family in the mountains and a renowned bushman. Like Frank Walford, he was often called upon when hikers were lost in the bush in the 1940s.

> He was born in the Burragorang area so he knew the Burragorang Valley and coming up this way, like he would start out in Katoomba and walk out and across the top of Mount Solitary and come up at Wentworth Falls. In those days they walked everywhere and it was nothing, you know, that kind of a walk was nothing [. . .] He knew the area well and it was probably part of their tradition.

She also told me about her grandmother.

> My grandmother originated from Riverstone area [on the Cumberland Plain] and she was of the Darug tribe and my grandfather was from, as I said, Burragorang, and he was of the Gundungurra people.

I asked Lynette whether the words *Darug* and *Gundungurra* were familiar in her childhood or did they arrive later.

> No, not really. It sort of came along later on when a lot of the history was compiled and we were told more and more about this kind of thing. It's a pity that I didn't realise how important my grandmother was at such an early age or I would have liked to have asked her a lot more about her life as a younger person—got to know, you know, exactly what sort of things she had to put up with and conquer, I suppose, in her life.

'So do you feel there was something of an absence of knowledge or discussion about the history of your people?' I asked.

> Yes, there was an absence of discussion about it. I suppose [. . .] nobody ever thought [. . .] that we were anybody special or anybody really any different. We were just part of the community and as such we lived that way and mixed with the people and never sort of made ourselves any different or made a *thing* of it.

Lynette was born in 1946, the only child of Tom and Lillian Booby. The Gully was her first home; her second was a rented house in

192

the town proper, where they lived from 1951. Her grandfather had died when she was a year old but her grandmother, Ethel Cooper, continued to live in the humpy in the Gully. Lynette stayed there on weekends and often visited after school. She knew most of the Gully residents and it remained her second home. Acknowledging all this, the paucity of information about her heritage must stand as a distinctive and revealing feature of the cultural microclimate of the Gully. In contrast to the present milieu, where Aboriginal lobbyists are using every tool at their disposal to recover data about their background, the Gully in the 1940s–50s seemed to be a place of considerable reticence and forgetting.

Among a few stories that Lynette feels might have deeper provenance—there was supposedly a 'hairy man' near Katoomba Golf Course who was to be avoided—she remembers just one resident, Joe Lock (a relative of Granny Lock), who spoke in Aboriginal language when he hit the booze. This poignant memory of one man being the bearer of language could be compared with the cultural awareness of those Gundungurra informants, fifty years earlier, encountered by R. H. Mathews in places such as the Burragorang Valley. They recounted elements of their vocabulary and grammar and related in considerable detail the story of Mirragan and Gurangatch. Only one generation separated this degree of familiarity with traditional law and Lynette's situation of not knowing tribal names. Her grandfather, Matthew Cooper, was born in the 1880s or 1890s and was probably with his family at Aboriginal Reserve 26 in the Burragorang when Mathews made his enquiries. It represents a monumental blockage in the transmission of knowledge and experience—though it is hardly unexplainable. The very location of the Gully community, taking root by the tramway on the swampy ground rejected by settlers, is itself a most potent symbol of the marginalised position of both the Aborigines and the poor white folk who did not fit the suburban norm.

The Aboriginal occupation of the Gully in the post-contact era overlaps an earlier pattern of habitation. This was established by an (admittedly limited) archaeological survey by Val Attenbrow for the Australian Museum which, despite the disturbance the area has suffered, found evidence of pre-European occupation: a set of spear-sharpening grooves in Katoomba Falls Creek and a rock shelter containing stone tools.[66] This is only to be expected given the area's proximity to the main east–west route across the mountains and the Gully's constant supply of water. The community as described here seems to date from the late nineteenth century; one informant believes that the original camp involved the colonisation of outbuildings that dated from the construction of the tramway.[67] Lynette Stanger is certain that her great-grandmother, Alice Cooper Senior, resided in the Gully before 1917. In his search of newspaper records Jim Smith found a report dating from 1903 concerning an 'aboriginal named Lock who had been living in

193

what is known as the camp near Katoomba'.[68] This is the earliest known written reference to the community in the Gully.

The Coopers' connection with Katoomba and the Burragorang is evidence of movement between, and interaction among, the various sites of Aboriginal residence in the Blue Mountains. Smith, in his essay 'Katoomba's Fringe Dwellers' and in self-published working papers, has built up a picture of how Gundungurra life under European occupation revolved around a network of localities that included the Gully. He reveals that in the second part of the nineteenth century modest attempts at Aboriginal self-determination were rebuffed by the colonial administration. In the 1870s Werriberrie (or Billy Russell), a well-known Gundungurra, along with three other Aborigines, adopted a course of action readily available to other inhabitants of the colony. They applied for a land grant in the Upper Burragorang. This was resisted by white settlers and the grant was eventually issued to the Aborigines Protection Board. That the grant should go to a government authority, rather than to an Aboriginal applicant, was completely typical of the paternalism of the era. The Upper Burragorang site was one of six Aboriginal Reserves gazetted between 1878 and 1906. Altogether they amounted to 400 hectares, a minuscule fraction of the original Gundungurra territory, and even then—in moves that pre-empted the removal of the Gully community—neighbouring farmers encroached on the reserves for the purpose of grazing and in one case endeavoured to evict an Aboriginal family.[69]

The Gully community seems to have sprouted of its own volition and was free of the paternalism of the Aborigines Protection Board which subjected many Aboriginal communities to management practices that were highly dictatorial. No doubt this contributed to the appeal and longevity of the Gully. Proximity to Katoomba offered the prospect of economic self-sufficiency, with jobs to be found in the mines or in the town. The community was given focus by a small chapel in the Gully known as the South Katoomba Mission, established by members of the Congregational and Methodist churches in 1906.[70]

As will become evident, the specific circumstances of the community's eviction from the Gully do point to a rather brutal form of racism at an institutional level. But the most overwhelming impression to be gained is the climate of tolerance that was generally typical of Katoomba. Aborigines were active in local sports, especially cricket, and

194

were admitted without question to local hotels. Publicans and police were evidently prepared to turn a blind eye to laws prohibiting sale of alcohol to Aboriginal people. My older neighbours, all of whom are white, have strong memories of visiting the Gully to play, swim, and collect drinking water when the town supply went foul. They all knew the residents and some are still friends with those who remain in the town. Ken Duff, my neighbour, told me how his father would go shooting in the Megalong Valley with Lynette's grandfather, Matthew Cooper. Another neighbour, Bonnie Colton, introduced me to her friend, Jean Murphy—of Gundungurra, Pacific Islander and European descent—who lived in the Gully briefly during World War II and who also subsequently lived in what is now my house. It was Jean who told me about a two-up school that was convened in the Gully every Sunday by Aboriginal men and attended by numerous white townsfolk. It was often raided by police.[71]

Such are the images I've gleaned of the community in the Gully as it existed until 1957, the year everything changed. Some highly dramatic accounts of the eviction still circulate in the town. In an oral history interview recorded for the 1988 Bicentenary, Lolita Martinez, a Katoomba resident formerly known as Lorraine Martin, claimed that the eviction was effected when local businessmen set fire to the humpies and sent the Aboriginal occupants running for their lives.[72] This account of horrific dispersal was then regurgitated in the local press, much to the anger of former occupants and older residents who dismissed it as a fabrication.[73] Internal inconsistencies, and a mass of evidence from

LEFT: ETHEL COOPER AND HER DAUGHTER, LILLIAN, OUTSIDE THEIR HOUSE IN THE GULLY IN THE 1930S. RIGHT: MEMBERS OF THE WEST KATOOMBA CRICKET TEAM SOCIALISING IN KATOOMBA. LYNETTE STANGER'S FATHER, TOM BOOBY, SITS IN THE BACK ROW, SECOND FROM LEFT. HER GRANDFATHER, MATTHEW 'NAT' COOPER SITS AT THE FAR RIGHT. IT WAS ILLEGAL FOR ABORIGINES TO DRINK LIQUOR DURING THIS PERIOD. LYNETTE SEES THE PUBLICAN'S WILLINGNESS TO SERVE ABORIGINAL PATRONS AS AN INDICATION OF RACIAL TOLERANCE IN THE COMMUNITY.

others who remember the events, suggest that the community was not pillaged in this way. Though inaccurate, the Martinez account did have a sort of incendiary effect of its own, encouraging first-hand experiences of the Gully, which had previously been hidden, to be made pubic. Regarding the actual fire—the basis, perhaps, for the Martinez story— and other circumstances concerning the community's expunging, Lynette Stanger recalls:

> There was a Sporting Drivers' Club and they started up an idea that they would build a racetrack and the site they chose was the Gully. And as far as I know [. . .] nobody was consulted that lived in the Valley, no one there was consulted about the building of this track. [. . .] They moved in with their bulldozers and started tearing up the trees and things like that and so my mum would go to some of these fellows, these businessmen who were involved in this club, and she would ask them what was happening and they would ignore her or change the subject [. . .] which I suppose if you look at it in today's terms it would be a really big cover-up of what was going on. [. . .] Anyway, [. . .] the council did approach the white people who were living in the Valley and offered them alternative accommodation like homes, rental homes and things like that. [. . .] The only thing was they never did approach any of the blacks who lived there. And my grandmother became extremely upset about this and so did my great uncle, my grandfather's brother who lived not far from her, and so he decided [. . .] that Uncle Lou, as he was known, would move in with Nan and they just would watch every day, they'd go out and watch the trees crashing down as the bulldozers would come through and one day they stood there and watched Uncle Lou's house just go before the blade of the bulldozer and it was just razed to the ground, and so that was that one. And that's when they really started to become upset and my grandmother said, 'Well, I'm not walking away from my home, the only way I'll go away from my home is when they carry me away. And so we would go and visit her and she'd say things like 'I'm not going to be here for much longer you know. You'd better find a home for this dog and that cat and, oh, that little bowl that somebody gave me. Make sure so and so gets that'. [. . .] Of course a lot of the tracks we used to know through the bush had disappeared

with the building of the racetrack and the bulldozing, you know, so we had to find other ways and that to get to her. [. . .] And anyway, it was the 24th May [1957] [. . .] and we saw her and went home and in the morning Uncle Lou came and said she'd passed away during the night. Before she passed away one of her instructions was she didn't want anybody going through her house or living in her house and that we had to burn it. So the undertakers came to take her away. The bulldozers were working just underneath the house. My mother went out and asked the bulldozer driver whom she knew personally would he mind shutting the thing off as a mark of respect while they took her body away and after that they went to the fire people, the fire station, and received permission to pull the house down and burn everything. And that's how it was. And the only thing that remained were an occasional rose bush or the apple tree. And even though that apple tree has been chopped down a few times it's still there.

CAPITAL DREAMS

It is striking how Europeans of the nineteenth century, when visiting Australian waterfalls, would muse on the excessiveness, the lavishness and even the wastefulness of nature. Typical was William Govett, the colonial surveyor, who regarded the vista from the waterfall that bears his name as one where 'nature itself has been rendered defective, and useless both to man and beast, and where the observer would exclaim and feel, that He who made these mountains alone can declare their use'.[74] It seems part of the capitalist dreaming, faced with the spectacle of water tumbling wastefully into the abyss, that, in Calvinistic spirit, this extravagance must be trimmed and turned to profit. The idea that Katoomba Falls Creek Valley could house something more interesting than a tramway for coal and a few odd humpies has persisted since the earliest days of European settlement. The racing circuit must be seen as the most momentous manifestation of this desire. More common, however, was the idea of damming the creek. An early map of Katoomba in a tourist guide shows the outline of a proposed lake just above Katoomba Falls. Although it was never built, the idea persisted in various guises.

The man-made lake forms a potent image in these visions of development. Perhaps it suggests a semblance of control amidst a spectacle of natural grandiosity which, as Govett suggested, touches on

LAKE BURRAGORANG,
THE WATER SUPPLY FOR
SYDNEY, WAS FORMED
BY WARRAGAMBA DAM,
BUILT AFTER WORLD
WAR II. THE
WARRAGAMBA,
WOLLONDILLY, COXS
AND NATTAI RIVER
WERE HALTED IN THEIR
FLOW. THIS TRANQUIL
VIEW OF A BOATMAN ON
THE NOW DEFUNCT
WARRAGAMBA RIVER
WAS TAKEN BY THE
COLONIAL
PHOTOGRAPHER CHARLES
BAYLISS.

the strangest mysteries of creation. As events transpired, the dream of the lake was not at all a fancy. It was simply misplaced. The lake, on a scale that even J. B. North could scarcely have anticipated, did actually arrive—though positioned down in the river valley rather than on the escarpment. In the wake of World War II, when massive engineering projects around Australia were diverting the courses of rivers and forcing the most dramatic reshaping of ecosystems, a workforce composed largely of European refugees was assembled to construct Warragamba Dam. Tree clearing for this enormous project was carried out by Aborigines, some of Gundungurra descent, whose families had been shifted from Burragorang to the Aboriginal mission at La Perouse on the eastern edge of Sydney.[75] Three million tonnes of concrete made the wall that bridged the Warragamba gorge at its narrowest point. The Warragamba, Wollondilly, Coxs and Nattai rivers were halted in their flow. The Burragorang Valley, with its numerous small farms, its former Aboriginal reserves, the locale for much of Mirragan and Gurangatch's epic journey, was flooded and transformed into Lake Burragorang, fifty-two kilometres long, and the principal water supply for drought-prone

IN THE 1940S
A KATOOMBA
BUSINESSMAN
HORRACE GATES BUILT
AN AMUSEMENT PARK
IN THE GULLY. THE
CENTREPIECE WAS
A SWIMMING POOL
CONTAINING A
DECOMMISSIONED
CATALINA FLYING BOAT.
PATRONS WERE
TRANSPORTED TO THE
PLANE IN A PUNT AND
SHOWN MOVIE FOOTAGE
TAKEN FROM A WORKING
CATALINA FLYING OVER
SYDNEY HARBOUR.

Sydney. In terms that echo the displacement of the Gully—a reminder that the forced removal of communities was reasonably common and politically acceptable during this phase of industrialisation—Owen W. Pearce, a Burragorang farmer, wrote of the lake in the following terms:

> we who were born and bred beneath what is now a dark, deep sheet of water do not see the scenery: when we look upon this lake, our thoughts are of the events which took place in that submerged world in days gone by.[76]

Pearce's poignant sentiments are a reminder that Sydney's symbiotic relationship with the Blue Mountains has a more elemental basis than the lure of escape, adventure, fresh air and spiritual nourishment. It is water from Frank Walford Park and a thousand other tributaries that is drunk, bathed in, excreted, and flushed from the home with more of the same.

Although the big lake happened at Warragamba, the Gully did not entirely miss out. It's as though our tract of land must reflect in microcosm what was happening in the larger picture. The Gully's first flirtation with the tourist industry was marked by the development of a big, pond-like swimming pool, built by Horrace 'Horrie' Gates, who owned the site of Frank Walford Park in the 1940s. It opens up what is surely the most bizarre episode in the history of the Gully. Gates, who was described by one my informants as a 'local entrepreneur and go-getter', was the proprietor of the popular guesthouse Homesdale.[77] The swimming pool was part of an amusement park, the crowning glory of which floated upon the water where it was clearly visible from various aspects including the top of Lynette's apple tree. This was a Catalina flying boat, reputedly bought from an army surplus sale and given to Horrie Gates as a birthday present.

The flying boat was among various amusements, including a Ferris wheel, flying horses and a 'giggle house' that showed Charlie Chaplain films. Visitors were transported in a punt to the plane where they could visit the cockpit and play with the controls. They were then seated in the belly of the aircraft where they were shown movie footage taken from a functional Catalina flying over Sydney Harbour. To further the simulation, the punt would speed round the flying boat, causing the waves to churn and splash against it and hopefully enhance the illusion of flying. Graced with this distinctive installation, the swimming pool became known as Lake Catalina and the area in general Catalina Park.

The amusement park continued for about four years, apparently co-existing with the community in the Gully. But other plans were afoot. In the aftermath of the war, Katoomba was losing its edge as a tourist destination. As the acquisition of a decommissioned aeroplane indicates, domestic aviation was by now established, permitting the emergence of new and different holiday resorts. The town's Chamber of Commerce was particularly active in proposing possible attractions for the town, with much of the focus on racing. In 1948 it was suggested that dog racing be introduced to Katoomba, an idea deplored by the town's clergy who protested 'that wherever this sport has been introduced . . . it has fostered the spirit of gambling, especially amongst children and housewives; and . . . lowers the moral tone of any community which permits it'.[78]

The caustic tone with which the dogs were rebuffed might explain why motor racing, perhaps the most intrusive recreation that could be foisted on an urban area, was deemed acceptable. Lacking the stigma of gambling it could be regarded as a 'clean' sport. Although construction of the track did not begin until 1957, motor racing was being discussed (if not publicly debated) a decade earlier. Members of the Chamber of Commerce were posted at the Great Western Highway when nearby Bathurst was hosting motor sports. On Easter Monday of 1949, a Mr Wiseman counted 6000 vehicles returning to Sydney from the races. It was estimated that £90 000 had been spent there over the Easter vacation, money that the burghers regarded as revenue lost to Katoomba.

The year 1949 brought busy planning, much of it facilitated by the then mayor, Frank Walford. After some conjecture about whether private land could be forcibly resumed for this purpose, it was decided that the council would buy Catalina Park from Horrie Gates, who agreed to sell it for £10 000.[79] The flying boat was removed and the site leased to the Blue Mountains Sporting Drivers' Club Ltd, a company composed of eighty-three local enthusiasts, who—it was claimed at the time—built the circuit from their own resources. A larger organisation based in Sydney, the Australian Racing Drivers' Club, would organise and promote the race events. It was constantly emphasised throughout the process that ratepayers' money would not subsidise the project. Indeed, under the deal eventually signed, it was established that ratepayers would profit from the racetrack, not only through business brought to the town but from a 25-per-cent share of profits.[80]

Doug Macarthur, who was a director of the Blue Mountains Sporting Drivers' Club in its latter days, makes much of the fact that it was largely voluntary labour that constructed the circuit, a real community effort.[81] It is one of the strange ironies of Catalina that a community formation exercise for one group of people could bring about the community break-up of another. For amidst all the meetings, planning, formation of the car club as a limited company and the purchase of land from Horrie Gates, no documents in the mass of records make any reference to the likely impact of car racing on the surrounding residents, let alone allude in the slightest way to the people who lived in the Gully.

THE DEBT UNPAID

In a scenario with parallels to other communities who have squatted or resided without official sanction, the transfer from private to public ownership became the vehicle for removing the occupants of the Gully. The eviction reputedly took the form of written notices to quit.[82]

As those who were evicted made other arrangements, some finding accommodation in the Blue Mountains and at least one Aboriginal family leaving the area altogether, the members and children of the Blue Mountains Sporting Drivers' Club worked on the track, mainly at weekends, over a period of four years. It is sometimes claimed that Jack Brabham, one of Australia's most distinguished racing drivers, designed the circuit. This is not strictly true, but he did make some recommendations on the design. The final course, still in its original state although somewhat run down, takes the form of a triangular star. The three main straights are connected by dramatic corners. The best drivers of the 1960s could get around the track a few seconds shy of a minute. A fence made from Australian hardwood lines the circuit, originally painted with advertisements. Some, as in 'Craven A Corner', gave inspiration for a new nomenclature of straights and bends that became current in the Gully.

The official opening occurred in 1961, bringing a few accidents (although no fatalities) because, as Doug Macarthur recalls, no one had done much practice. Catalina Park did become a significant venue in Australian motor sports, with all the big names performing there. Race events brought many people and considerable business to the town and the impact on the populace was considerable since the cars at that time had no mufflers whatsoever, and the races were accompanied by an equally unmuffled public address system on which the commentators, among them Peter Wherrett, would play rock music, make announcements and tell jokes.[83] Access to the surrounding area was restricted. Occupants of affected houses could drive into their streets if they displayed a large R (for resident) coupon on their cars.

Deeper probing into the building of the racetrack identified a current of dissent against impositions that would certainly prompt an outcry if they occurred today. It transpired that another former occupant of my house is part of the story. When construction began in 1957, a T. A. Humphries, writing from what is now my own address, angrily challenged the council to name any authority on town planning who would justify a racing circuit in a built-up area. His letter, published in a local paper, is notable because, for the first time on the public record, he questioned the fate of people living in the park. '[I]s it not a fact that a married man who has long been unemployed, has been warned to vacate the only home he knows?'[84] Humphries is still remembered as one of the most vociferous opponents of motor racing in Katoomba.

Humphries had been involved in local government before living in the Blue Mountains and was familiar with council procedures. In his initial letter to the *Blue Mountains Courier*, he questioned why the council had gone into secret committee, excluding public and press, when it made a decision about the racetrack. Evidently he smelt a rat. So did three other correspondents—'Sam Square', 'Bombs Away', and 'Jock'—who had written the previous week, all questioning the need for secrecy.[85] The mayor, A. F. C. Murphy, responded to these complaints, prefacing his letter by warning—without apparent irony—that 'anonymous letters are treated with the contempt they deserve'. In this spirit he ambiguously defended the action by saying that 'Council only "goes into Committee" when it is absolutely necessary, and I have no doubt the present Council will continue that procedure'. His letter was followed by a statement from H. C. Muir, president of the Blue Mountains Sporting Drivers' Club, who emphasised that work on the track was being 'financed by the club and business people of the district and not by ratepayers'. In his most extraordinary statement, indicative of the manner in which the Gully residents could be so comprehensively overlooked, Muir declared that 'No homes will be removed. We have gone so far as to have the original survey of the circuit altered to avoid going too close to people living in the area.'[86] While raising a rather serious question about how Muir might have defined 'home', the remark brings to mind the response of Lynette Stanger when I asked her whether the circuit followed the line of any of their footpaths. She said no—'it followed the line of where our houses were'.

To explain subsequent events, which give an impression of what might have been discussed at the secret meeting, it is necessary to touch upon the physical conditions that made the circuit a financial disaster. While races seem to have been successful when they took place, it was very often the case that they didn't. As Lynette's husband John Stanger wryly puts it, race days were an almost certain guarantee of bad weather. The heavens would open, the mist would come down and the race would be cancelled. Hugh Doggett, a council employee who moonlighted as a steward for the race club, remembers helping to unbog as many as 200 spectators' cars in an afternoon. The circuit proved a folly

203

because no one had taken the weather into account, despite the fact that fog and cold are the most notorious features of Blue Mountains winters.

The tribulations of the weather and the consequent financial strain explain why, by 1970, the relationship between the Blue Mountains Sporting Drivers' Club and the Blue Mountains City Council had regressed from clubbishness to animosity. Council minutes contain a document—a brief from the council to its solicitor—revealing that, contrary to all the public assurances, the council had in fact lent the club a sum amounting to $39 000 in decimal currency which covered safety fences, toilet blocks and asphalt—in fact two lots of asphalt because the first was ruined by a shower of rain.[87]

From the very beginning, the club failed to meet its repayments. This led to protracted dispute that went all the way to the Supreme Court.[88] While the records are patchy, it seems that the unpaid debt was finally written off in 1979.[89] Professional motor sports continued in a limited way at Catalina until 1976.

The revelation that public money was lent and never returned makes even more fraught the question of whether a scarcely hidden agenda was motivating Frank Walford and friends when they endorsed the unfortunate notion of building a racing circuit in Katoomba. He resided in Kundibar Street, just a few hundred metres from the Gully, and would have known people who lived there. Quite a few were employees of the council. Touching upon this delicate matter is not appreciated among older denizens. An informant was prepared to say off the record that the racetrack had been welcomed for its added benefit in terms of slum clearance, that the houses in the Gully were dirty and unhygienic. The same was said on the record by Bill Boldiston, a racing enthusiast and supporter of the track, who hesitantly suggested that there was a design to 'clean up this rather embarrassing area'.[90]

APPROACHING JOOLUNDOO

So why go over this old ground and raise from the dead a tawdry episode in local government? Surely it does say something about how power operates in a local community. The council minutes are full of properties being resumed when residents failed to pay their rates. Such is the fate of the poor. But in this case, involving some of the wealthiest people in the town—people whose vision was out of touch with the specificity of the place in which they lived—a blatant refusal to meet their commitments could be quietly forgotten.

Whether the community would be significantly better off if that money had been paid is unimportant. There is a symbolic, as well as a financial, significance to a debt unpaid. The question of an amount owing, of something unreconciled, still hangs around the Gully, and this is felt very personally by people like Lynette Stanger and her family who still bear the grief of these events. That the account might yet be settled is suggested by the subsequent history of the Gully. Around 1980 a shift occurred: the role of the hanging swamp in feeding Katoomba Falls was recognised, and some of those who lived around it began to regard the Gully not as an economic resource but as something intrinsically valuable in its own right.

While there is continuing friction about how Frank Walford Park should be regarded and managed, its Aboriginal heritage is being increasingly recognised. While I was making the final revisions to the manuscript for this book in 2002, news arrived that the Gully had been classified as an Aboriginal Place under the New South Wales *National Parks and Wildlife Act* (1974). The nomination was made by Dawn Colless, a prominent Gundungurra elder, who worked with Dianne Johnson, an anthropologist, in substantiating the claim. The Aboriginal Place declaration has been greeted with jubilation among the Aboriginal people with whom I have spoken. Such official recognition gives state protection to the area, preventing intrusive development. Just as importantly, it is a symbolic victory that gives official recognition to a community that had no official status in its own era.

Although the Gully bears the stigma of a shameful episode involving an unholy alliance of racing and racism, this does not say everything about the town. It seems enormously significant that the Aboriginal inhabitants, as much as the whites, were anxious to record their acceptance of each other. Hence the stories of Ken Duff's father going shooting with old Nat Cooper, of the white and black folk living side by side for half a century, of the humpy dwellers being admitted to pubs. This experience of co-existence is easily overlooked in our own era of land claims and identity politics.

The tales of petrification and the survival of a living community within the Katoomba township that have been juxtaposed in this passage represent a fork in the labyrinth, a possibility of bifurcation, that demonstrates very vividly how myth and history can add to the interpretation of each other. In thinking about the conviction with which Katoomba residents from both sides of the not-so-very-wide racial divide have clung to the vision of a community that was largely reconciled within itself, I am drawn back to the story of Mirragan and Gurangatch as recorded by R. H. Mathews. Why is it that the epic chase of quoll and fish unfolded in the way it did? What was it that the tellers wanted to convey? Myth, as Calasso reminds us, is a fan of a thousand segments. It is impossible to conceive of the Mirragan story as isolated from a flow of narratives that connected with each other, that spread in all directions, that ultimately mapped in their entirety the continent of Australia.

So the story told to Mathews cannot be considered in isolation. It was selected. Nor can it be treated as a 'pure' mythical object. Emerging, no doubt, from ancient tradition, it was the particular story chosen at that moment, around 1900, when the decision was made to share with this white researcher an aspect of Gundungurra culture. We can assume that in the oral tradition there would have been an element of improvisation, of transformation, with each re-telling of the story. This would have been heightened when Mathews recorded the narrative, for the telling was also a work of translation. Again I ask, what message were they wanting him to hear?

The most remarkable thing about the truly remarkable Mirragan and Gurangatch story is its conclusion. Their journey is an epic tale that involves the formation of the Blue Mountains landscape. In that sense it is the ultimate *creative* journey, giving rise to the cosmos as seen by a Gundungurra person. But the story is loaded with a very considerable tension. The journey that forms the world is predicated on the desire of one protagonist to devour the other—to extinguish his existence by incorporating him into himself.

That is where the conclusion of the story is so extraordinary. The final chapter is enacted at a location called Joolundoo waterhole where Gurangatch, fatigued from the wounds and exertions of his journey, is hidden in the lower depths. Mirragan approaches Joolundoo with a group of water birds: Billagoola the shag, Gool-a-gwan-gwan the diver, Gundhareen the black duck and Goonarring the wood duck.

At Mirragan's request, several of the birds attempt to capture Gurangatch. But he is hidden by other, lesser fish, and his head is jammed in one crevice and his tail in another. Finally, Billagoola the shag makes a dive.

> [H]e pulled a large piece of flesh off the back of Gurangatch and started up again. On reaching the surface, Mirragan exclaimed with delight, 'That is a piece of the fish I was chasing'. When the meat was cooked Mirragan and his friends had a great feast and returned to their respective homes.[91]

In this fashion, the fish is caught, hunger is sated, and the co-creators live on in their respective domains. If the tellers of this story were mapping out a cultural future when they spoke to Mathews, it is possible to discern the continuity of that vision among Gundungurra people of the present day. I discovered this when talking to Lynette Stanger and she expressed her views on migration and land rights:

> I believe that the land is everybody's. I don't think land should be taken from people that is rightfully theirs, land that they are dwelling on. [. . .] But I don't believe in this land right business. I think it is our land, it is Australia, there is a piece of ground for everyone to stand on in this place that we call Australia.

LYNETTE STANGER IN THE GULLY IN NOVEMBER 2002. SHE HAD JUST SPOKEN AT A CEREMONY IN WHICH THE GULLY WAS OFFICIALLY DECLARED AN ABORIGINAL PLACE.

'So you believe,' I asked, 'this land is here for those who've been here for a very long time and new arrivals as well?'

> Yes I do, I do indeed. In saying that you'll never take the Mountains away from me, they're my Mountains! But by the same token I don't think anybody is going to go into the valleys around Katoomba and destroy it like they did the Gully. I don't think that will ever happen, and I think it will be there for centuries to come for everybody.

FRANK HURLEY'S PHOTOGRAPH SHOWS AN IMPRESSIVE BOLT OF LIGHTNING OVER THE GROSE VALLEY IN THE
BLUE MOUNTAINS. THIS IS THE LOCALITY WHERE THE EMINENT PREHISTORIAN VERE GORDON CHILDE
FELL TO HIS DEATH IN 1957.

Passage Five

VERE GORDON CHILDE AND THE ABYSS OF TIME

We stand upon the brink of a precipice. We peer into the abyss—we grow sick and dizzy. Our first impulse is to shrink from the danger. Unaccountably we remain . . .

EDGAR ALLEN POE, 'The Imp of the Perverse', 1845

OVERTURE

THERE IS A perception among residents of the upper Blue Mountains that their locality exerts a magnetic force upon certain people who have chosen to end their lives. My own interest in the subject started with an uncertainty about whether the mountains do indeed have a higher incidence of suicide than anywhere else. It immediately struck me as significant that the *perception*, even if it were without substance, was significant to the cultural construction of the area, given the mountains' history of labyrinthine imaginings, the mortification of landmarks, the projection onto the landscape of figures of death. That these suicides were specific to the topography, involving leaps from clifftops—and often from the lookouts demarcated as points of special scenic interest—opened issues that seemed very important. How to regard a landscape in which the freedom to fall is so readily available? What does the act of suicide by falling say about notions of beauty and our relationship with the environment? What is revealed about a society and its history when someone performs this ultimate act of displacement?

I quickly discovered that the statistics kept by government are of little help in investigating whether people travel to specific localities in order to suicide. Only the postcode of the place where they resided is recorded by the statisticians. Whether they do it in their own home or in Timbuktu is apparently of no demographic interest. In order to establish whether there was any basis to the local perception, I arranged to visit the Katoomba Court House where I was allowed access to inquest documents. The coroner admitted me on days when the court was not sitting and suggested that I do my research at the magistrate's bench where I could 'spread myself out'. Sitting less than comfortably in the judge's chair, I started with a pile of inquest documents from 1991. In one of these I found a remark by the district coroner that confirmed all the suspicions: 'As is well known locally, and one has only to consult local Coronial records, a number of persons each year find Echo Point a "convenient" spot in which to end their lives, and such persons are invariably not members of the local community.'[1]

The coroner arrived at seventeen verdicts of suicide that year. Seven were deaths by falling and all but one of these came from outside the Blue Mountains. Of the remaining ten suicides in 1991 (two stabbings, two hangings, two exhaust poisonings and four drug overdoses) another four came from outside the local area.

Reading these documents was a sobering business that opened up perplexing, often inexplicable narratives. Among the deaths by falling was that of a Queensland man aged in his sixties who had flown to Sydney, hired a car and driven to the Blue Mountains, leaping to his death at Horseshoe Falls near Govetts Leap. He had attempted to suicide at the same location eight years before but had been thwarted. His story is echoed by that of a Japanese woman in her twenties who had visited Katoomba on a holiday two years earlier. She flew from Japan to Sydney, stayed briefly in the city, then travelled to the mountains. She jumped from a cliff near Katoomba Falls, leaving a bag with a suicide note nearby. On the very edge, at the point where she had stepped out of them, she left her shoes. It was a telling reminder that acts of suicide are shaped by the culture from which they emerge. A note from her parents to the detective who investigated the case thanked him for his work: 'The funeral and cremation held in Sydney might be even more beautiful than her wish. In an ideal paradise chosen by herself she will be in peace.'

My period in the judgement seat did not last much longer. I had seen enough to indicate that some people travelled considerable distances to kill themselves at places such as Echo Point. There was something about the lure of the mountains.

By this time I was truly familiar with the most extraordinary case of falling yet recorded in the Blue Mountains: the mysterious death of Vere Gordon Childe, then the world's best known prehistorian, who died at Luchetti Lookout near Govetts Leap in 1957. Childe's prominence, and the fact his death occurred after a thirty-six year absence from Australia, impelled my investigation. As I discovered retrospectively, I had been unwittingly drawn into Childe's milieu in the first months of researching this book. During my stays in the mountains I had often wandered through a derelict mansion near the Wentworth Falls lookout and had come to refer to this gloomy place, with its dense border of *Pinus radiata*, as 'the haunted house'. Then I discovered that the property —'Whispering Pines' as it is known, which does indeed boast an extensive repertoire of ghost stories—was the childhood home of Gordon Childe.

I

SETTING

UP THE

LEAP

No dynamic metaphor is directed downward; no imaginary flower blooms from beneath.

GASTON BACHELARD, *Air and Dreams*, 1943

ON THE SOUTHERN wall of the Grose River gorge, a waterfall or 'leap' bears the name of Govett, one of the unlucky surveyors who mapped and measured the Blue Mountains. Although regarded as 'the ablest delineator of ground in the department, and remarkably clever in the fastnesses of unexplored country',[2] Govett resorted to inventing creeks around the Colo River, unwilling or unable to penetrate further into God knows what. As the most rugged and labyrinthine territory of the Blue Mountains region, it is perhaps, inevitable that the Colo should encourage some fanciful cartography. Govett's deceptive 'tracings' (as technically the surveyor's field sketches are known) even hoodwinked that lesser god Surveyor-General Mitchell, a stubborn master who scrutinised the ration books as though they were a tract of land. Few expressions could describe the country with such lucidity as Govett's outburst in an official letter: 'These ounces and fractions of eatables annoy me more than the confusion of Ranges before me.'[3]

Despite his cartographic desperation, and the suggestion of its title, William Govett never leapt from Govetts Leap. Having arrived in Australia in his early twenties and worked as a surveyor from 1827 to 1833, he returned to England where he died from an aneurism in 1848. But the misapprehension that Govett leapt from this mighty precipice, or made '"a daring jump across one chasm", causing Mitchell to name it for his "pluck"',[4] has been resilient. So too has the myth of an insurgent escapee, fleeing his pursuers and leaping into the void. Anthony Trollope must have heard it on his tour, for in 1873 he voiced an expectation:

> that some interesting but murderous bushranger had on that spot baffled his pursuers and braved eternity;—but I was informed that a government surveyor had visited the spot, had named it, and had gone home again. No one seeing it could fail to expect better things from such a spot and such a name.[5]

Govett's descendants, and several others, would bemoan 'the wicked lie' about 'one who should deserve in history recognition',[6] but the bush-ranger fable proved so pervasive that in 1882 a local newspaper would reveal that the outlaw had survived—or perhaps *postponed*—his brush with 'eternity' and lived out his days as a shepherd in the grazing districts of Victoria. In this superb piece of journalism, titled 'The History of Govett's Leap', 'By Z.', Govett escapes a chain gang on the western road

and is chased to the escarpment by an Aboriginal tracker.[7] Confiding all this to the zealous Z., who meets him on his final night, Govett reveals that, in the ensuing fight, he conquers the Aborigine whose descending cry is mistaken for his own.

> 'I seized him by the long strong hair, dragged him to the edge and spurned him over with my foot. To my dying day, which I don't think far off, I shall hear his awful shriek . . . Exhausted as I was, I peered over the edge of the precipice and saw him falling through the empty space. It seemed an age until his body disappeared among the trees a thousand feet or more below.'[8]

The mythology concerning Govetts Leap reveals much about the history of this country. It suggests the enduring pertinence of Burke's proposition that 'we are more struck at looking down a precipice, than at looking up'. With its tale of a falling Aborigine, it readily suggests the

THIS UNDATED PHOTOGRAPH SHOWS THE WATERFALL KNOWN AS GOVETTS LEAP. THE TERM *leap* IS A SYNONYM FOR WATERFALL. BUT THIS WAS FORGOTTEN AS A FERTILE MYTHOLOGY BEGAN TO CIRCULATE ABOUT THE SURVEYOR WILLIAM GOVETT (OR SOMEONE ELSE) LEAPING INTO THE VOID.

cliff-top drama of von Guérard (whose opus also includes a cluster of European tourists at the top of Govetts Leap). Although an obvious fiction, the Govett story draws upon a specific connection between the Aborigine and the Fall that is played out in whitefellow mythology throughout many parts of Australia. David Roberts has written about one such narrative—the reported Bells Falls Massacre near Sofala in New South Wales—remarking on the common association of

> some violence or Aboriginal death with a local landmark, such as the tale of 'Blackgin's Leap' in Tenterfield in northern New South Wales, or the 'brief and disjointed' local traditions of the New England district. Roger Milliss found similar oral traditions in the Moree/Bingara region, stories illuminating a past felicitously commemorated in the names of local landmarks such as Gravesend Mountain and Slaughterhouse Creek.[9]

Roberts' 1995 article on the Bells Falls Massacre is an interesting speculation on the place of colonial violence in folkloric traditions. The story, as recounted by a barside raconteur, explains the fate of the local Wiradjuri in the following way:

> 'They're all killed mate', he said solemnly. Then, gesturing out towards the south-west . . . he told me that a great number of Aborigines had been shot at Bells Falls Gorge. By his account, it had been a 'huge massacre': 'They rounded all the blackfellas up at the top of the gorge, and shot at them until they all jumped off. . . . Neither he, nor indeed any[one] in the Sofala/Wattle Flat district, knew exactly who committed the massacre, precisely when it occurred or for what reason.[10]

Roberts undertook extensive research, even scanning the gorge with a metal detector in search of bullets, but was unable to uncover any firm evidence of the massacre. Although there is abundant documentation of violent conflict between Aborigines and settlers in the district during the 1820s, he found himself wondering whether the details were deliberately concealed to protect the perpetrators or whether the massacre is the apocryphal residue of a regrettable past. The abundance of narratives concerning 'leap'-type massacres is incommensurate with their improbability. Why would people being persecuted and chased head like lemmings for the nearest cliff? It is more appropriate to regard these leap type stories as a distinctive genre in colonial discourse that reflects back on those who have brought it into being.

A notable feature of the Bells Falls narrative—and to the empiricist surely its most suspect quality—is that it purports to explain the end of a 'tribe'. In lieu of a narrative where violence is serial, ongoing, where clashes and encounters are repeated, where flour and waterholes are poisoned, women raped or seduced, children of mixed race spawned—in lieu of the whole cultural confusion of colonisation, a moment of finality is ascribed to a solitary event.

In the climate of the nineteenth century, when many of these place names were bestowed, the doctrine that Aboriginal Australians were a dying race was at its height. Great attention was directed at Aborigines regarded as the 'last fullblood' or the 'last of their tribe'. The demarcation of leaps as places of dramatic death signalled the putative completeness of this collective passing, memorialising and assimilating the violence of territorial possession. The designation of 'leaps' was specifically concerned with the marking and containment of otherness within the landscape. In emphasising the transition from presence to absence, inscribing images of death within the landscape and establishing the Aborigine as death's representative figure, 'leaps' have certain commonalities with the mortification of landmarks like Orphan Rock and the Three Sisters.

That this moment of passing is so frequently encoded as a fall is immediately interesting. Falling exerts a particular fascination, resonating with the great Fall of Lucifer as a defining event in the Judeo–Christian tradition. The reality that the falling Aborigine has maintained a strong presence in cultural memory is vividly illustrated by the surprise crescendo of Charles Chauvel's motion picture *Jedda* (1955), in which the Aboriginal heroine, who has left her white adopted parents to abscond with a notorious outlaw, the 'wild' blackfellow Marbuk, is dragged over a fatal precipice to avoid otherwise inevitable capture by police.

One of the most memorable moments in Australian cinema, the climactic fall of Jedda and Marbuk is often read as a warning on the dangers of assimilation. By strange coincidence, it was shot in the Blue Mountains. While most of the movie had been made on location in northern Australia, in the last days of production, already over-budget, footage was destroyed in another Icarus fall—a plane crash that forced the startling scenic transformation from the red country of the interior to the blue–green hills of the coastal ranges. The fall itself was enacted on the remote plateau of Kanangra Walls.[11]

The imagined fall of the Aboriginal figure—what we might call a 'Jedda syndrome'—provides a way of projecting the fall onto someone else. So why have Europeans been so enraptured by the fall in negotiating the colonial vista? Why should a visitor like Trollope hope for 'better things' than the prosaic information that Govett made a map and went away? This is the question—literally, the life and death question—that hangs around this country: a territory inscribed and superinscribed by a modality of falling. As the following descriptions, among them the words of Govett himself, will make abundantly clear, perceptions of the precipice are influenced by a strange mixture of terror and desire. In this scenario, the words of Sartre (anticipated so graphically by Edgar Allen Poe) are as unavoidable as the abyss itself: 'Vertigo is anguish to the extent that I am afraid not of falling over the precipice, but of throwing myself over.'[12]

This desire has helped shape the cultural construction of the Blue Mountains landscape. In considering a territory where the temptation to launch oneself into the void is so palpable, it becomes possible to explore the alienation between the topography and its coloniser, and to consider how the meaning of suicide might be better understood by attentiveness to both the politics and the poetics of space.

~

Inquest: Scene 1

[From the coronial inquiry into the death of Vere Gordon Childe. 22 November 1957[13]]

ALEXANDER GORDON HAVING BEEN SWORN: ON HIS OATH STATES AS FOLLOWS:—
I am a Broadcasting Supervisor and reside at 'Denbie', Douglas Street West, St Ives. I am a first cousin to the deceased. As far as I know his age was sixty-five and he was single. Until the end of 1956 he was Director of the Institute of Archaeology at London University. He retired from

that position and arrived in Australia about 14th April, 1957... I had lunch with him on the 11th October. That was the day he actually came to Katoomba and we discussed then what he was doing. He was investigating the gullies and the layout of the Blue Mountains. He had looked at it from this side and he was going around looking at them from other positions as well... He was preparing some sort of paper on their conformation. He told me then he was going to Katoomba that day and that he was going to stay at the Carrington. He was in good health and an extremely active man... To the best of my knowledge he was in comfortable circumstances financially... Despite his retirement he retained an interest in the remainder of his life. He was feeling the heat rather badly and he proposed to return to England earlier than his passage was booked. I asked him about what he was proposing to do in England and from his reply he had obviously plans for further archaeological investigations in Europe.... I have possession of reports and maps of his work exploring the Blue Mountains and they indicate the detail he went to in his work that he had not finished.

~

the sky, surely, is open, and that is how we shall go.

Ovid, *Metamorphoses*

~

Although Govett never fell, the Celtic *leap* or *lep* as a synonym for waterfall, fits well with the cultural legacy of a surveyor who charted with such fascination the phenomenon of verticality. Govett, after all, was responsible for an unaccomplished watercolour, *Accident on the Road at Victoria Pass* (c.1835).[14] This scene, in which Govett depicts his theodolite and himself standing in the foreground while in the mid-ground an upturned bullock, wagon and possessions go careering down a precipice, was inspired by an incident on the western extremity of the road across the Blue Mountains. The bullocks, Govett wrote, 'as soon as they had turned the corner took fright at some Black fellows who were loitering by, and off they went... I was a spectator and beheld with some amazement the loss of Government property and of my own rifle.'[15]

If this painting suggests a concerted, albeit clumsy, attempt to translate the rapid, almost invisible motion of falling into a gesture of perpetual attenuation—beast and vehicle are ever poised in the progress of descent—Govett's writings display a consistent disposition. Describing the southern head of Sydney Harbour, Govett observed that:

> Many persons cannot endure to look down a perpendicular precipice, nay, some feel a sensation of giddiness before they reach the brink; and it requires a firm nerve to stand by the edge of this tremendous rock, and coolly look below to watch the foaming surge: it is truly awful and terrific.[16]

Known as The Gap (another highly suggestive appellation) this site, like Govetts Leap, is favoured for suicide by falling.

Govett's colonial descriptions are pervaded by the modality of falling. This is how he set the scene for an English audience when he published a series of magazine articles about Australia in 1836:

> Govett's Leap is situated at one of the sources of the Grose River; it is distant rather more than two miles from the main western road which leads from Sydney across these mountains into the rich Bathurst country, and is nearly sixty-five miles westward of Sydney. Two small swamps commencing near Blackheath, (a dreary spot which the road crosses,) afford two streams a continual supply of water; and these, after their junction, rush rapidly over the cliffs into the chasm and fall into the deep abyss. Although the quantity of water is by no means considerable, (the breadth of the course which it has worn, not exceeding twenty feet,) yet the entire fall, which is estimated at full twelve hundred feet, gives this cascade a grandeur worthy of notice.
>
> The *perpendicular* height of the cliff, or wall of rock over which the stream *first* pours itself, is at least two hundred feet, and then, falling, in a succession of broken cataracts, into misty hollows, it forms, at the depth of a thousand feet lower, the bed of the River Grose. The chasm, or aperture of the mountain which apparently yawns for the small stream, is like an amphitheatre of about a hundred yards in breadth, and the water gliding into it seems again transformed into its parent vapour, for not long after its fall, it assumes a misty

appearance, and a moment's gaze into the dark void is sufficient to appal the stoutest heart. When, however, fear is overcome by curiosity, and the brink of the precipice is approached, wonder is increased at every step, by the dreadfully abrupt and perpendicular sides, the frightful depth of the gulf, the whispering echo of the place, and the deep hollow-sounding dash of the water.[17]

It is significant that Govett's description follows an established conduit, travelling the road from Sydney, reaching the stream, then charting its course from heath to cliff and finding its primary interest in the moment of falling. Thus, the action of descent establishes a prevailing logic to Govett's evocation of the landscape. Hungry and devouring, the chasm becomes a mouth which 'yawns for the small stream' and which, despite its horror, invites the visitor to peer into the void.

Remember that waterfalls were the locations of greatest scenic interest to Blue Mountains visitors of the nineteenth century. Seldom simply beautiful or grand, there was usually a violent, perverse or even devilish connotation to these spectacles. Trollope would write of the Grose as a sinister place, 'a green, dark, crowded valley',[18] while for Govett it was a 'dark void'. Both authors charted a cosmology of elevation versus depth, light versus dark. The trajectory of the waterfall was especially compelling for it connected these opposing realms. Many visitors would imitate its confluence by throwing a stone and watching its progress. Such missiles had vicarious purpose, functioning prosthetically as they simulated a bodily descent. 'Great astonishment is here excited,' wrote the surveyor who never leapt in person, 'at the length of *time* which elapses, when a huge block of rock is rolled headlong over, before you hear it strike, and the rebounding echoes thundering from rock to rock, redouble the surprise.'[19]

~

Inquest: Scene 2

[From the coronial inquiry into the death of Vere Gordon Childe]

THIS DEPONENT ON OATH STATES:—
My name is James Walley Morey. I am a Senior Constable of Police stationed at Blackheath. At about 2pm on 19th October, 1957, Henry

Newstead, a taxi driver of Katoomba, informed me that he had brought a man known to him as Professor Childe from the Carrington Hotel, Katoomba to Govetts Leap, Blackheath. The Professor left his cab at Govetts Leap and walked off across the cliff top towards Evans Lookout. The usual practice for taxi drivers driving Professor Childe was for them to wait for him and then return with him to his hotel. As Professor Childe had not returned at 12 midday Newstead said he went to look for him and a short way along the track leading to Evans Lookout he found a coat lying on a tree beside the track. Further on at a point called Luchetti Lookout he found other articles which he presumed to belong to the Professor. . . I took possession of a blue-green sports coat which was lying on a tree which had fallen across the track. On the pocket of the coat was a small diary with the name Professor V. G. Childe inscribed in it with the sum of £15-10-0, a pipe and a tobacco pouch with a letter of credit from the Commonwealth Trading Bank of Australia in the name of Professor Vere Gordon Childe. . . About 200 yards further along the track at a point called Luchetti Lookout I found on the outside of the safety fence on the western side of the lookout a brown felt hat with the initials V. G. C. cut into the sweat band. About a foot from the hat I found a pair of bifocal glasses lying on the rock with the lugs open. About six feet north of the glasses and about one foot from the cliff edge I found a prismatic compass standing on a piece of cardboard and some papers apparently to make it level. The compass was open and was sighted on a feature known as Pulpit Rock with a bearing of about two degrees east of north. On a piece of paper beside the compass were written the words *Mount Banks, Mount Hay, Table Rock, Pulpit Rock*—they were all features in that vicinity and would all be clearly visible from that lookout. I made a search of the surrounding bush and cliff edge and could find no trace of the professor and no marks to indicate that he had fallen over the edge of the cliff. There was nothing there to indicate the presence of any other person. This lookout is on a promontory that projects from the cliff line. The safety fence is three-sided. . . The compass was about six inches from the cliff edge on the western side of the fence. The compass was not on a tripod. To take a reading from the compass as it was resting you would have to be prone on the ground and to take a reading with glasses is very difficult. The rock that the compass was bearing was on the other side of the valley.

220

The head and shoulders would be six inches from the cliff edge and because of the widening of the promontory his feet would be about four feet from the cliff edge. The surface was stony and there was a slope to the rear where his feet were but the front was level. It would be difficult to take a proper compass reading inside the safety fence. From the edge of that lookout there is a sheer drop to the foot of the valley. It is 1,200 feet and there is a ledge about 200 feet from the bottom.

In the afternoon we made a search of the bottom of the cliff and discontinued at dark. On the morning of 20th October in company with other police and civilians I continued the search of the valley bottom and at 9 am in company with Malcolm Longton and Frank Boyce of Blackheath I located the body of a man who was later identified to me as Professor Vere Gordon Childe lying on a ledge 1,000 feet below Luchetti Lookout and 200 feet from the floor of the valley at the bottom of Bridal Veil Falls. The body was badly smashed and mutilated and with the aid of police and civilians we brought it to the cliff top at Govetts Leap and then by ambulance to Dr Siedlecky's surgery at Blackheath and life was pronounced extinct, and then to Katoomba Hospital Morgue where Dr Siedlecky made an external examination of the body on 21st October, 1957. From the observations made by me I formed the opinion that Professor Childe, who was an eminent archaeologist, was taking compass bearings of features of the locality of Luchetti Lookout. He placed his compass in position, took off his hat and glasses, and was either getting down to take the reading or getting up after taking one when he either misjudged the nearness of the cliff edge owing to his short sightedness or slipped and accidentally fell over the edge to the valley below. From a police point of view there are no suspicious circumstances. Where the body was lying was almost directly under where the compass was at the top of the cliff. I took a reading with the compass from the floor of the valley and it was almost directly on his reading.

~

that dreadful moment when my entire self trembles on the edge of being and not being

J. W. Goethe, *The Sorrows of the Young Werther*, 1774

~

222

To visit Govett's Leap today is to observe a curious shift in emphasis. Although the cataract retains its old name on the topographical map, on sign posts—as in the local vernacular—it appears as Bridal Vale Falls. No longer thought of as a waterfall, Govetts Leap has become a *locality*: the section of the escarpment *adjoining* the waterfall with its car park, picnic area and nearby visitors centre, which also serves as access point for an intricate network of walking trails. From the car park, a short flight of steps leads out to the cliff edge. As the visitor descends, a squat obelisk in memory of Govett and the already visible panorama of the gorge are framed by a stone and concrete arch.

The notion of the *lookout*, which physically regulates the spectacle of Blue Mountains landscape, is worthy of contemplation. The *Oxford English Dictionary* defines *look out* as either a vista or a person (watchman or sentry). In Australia, however, it more commonly refers, as the *Macquarie Dictionary* puts it, to 'a place on a high vantage point, especially a mountain, from which one can admire the view'. Frequently, these high places have been transformed or enhanced by some sort of environmental modification. The writer Cathie Payne, in a rare rumination on this subject, has accurately described the lookout in architectural terms as a 'balcony' unto the landscape. Lookouts are part of an elaborate, if often subtle, network of environmental modification. Tracks and roads provide access, signposts guide the visitor, trees are lopped to increase visibility. And since the most spectacular sites are often hazardously exposed, safety rails are installed to protect the beholder. Thus the lookout—a literal and symbolic focal point within the landscape—will manifest the cautionary portent of its appellation, combining the experience of supreme visibility with a cry of warning.

As Payne describes it, and as the arch at Govetts Leap makes very clear, the lookout is 'a well installed frame for viewing the rest of the country'.[20] And like the pictorial frame, with which it is linked (as both a site for picture-making and through the culture of visuality that sustains it), the lookout attains a degree of invisibility within the landscape. A subtle and generally unexpressed code will govern the construction and maintenance of the lookout, preventing its overt conspicuousness and allowing sufficient surrounding foliage to obscure it from other points of view. Since the tendency within this visual order is to see the vista and not the cultural artifice that shapes it, the lookout plays a special role in mediating the vision of an apparently unmediated nature.

Lookouts come about through processes of inscription. Lines of access are drawn upon the landscape; a proliferation of imagery encourages other visitors and contributes to the cultural resonance of the locality. William Govett mapped the waterfall in 1831, recording it simply as 'cascades'; the following year the *N. S. W. Calendar & General Post Office Directory* would recommend a visit to the 'wild scenery' of Weatherboard Falls, and at Blackheath 'another fine cataract, named Govett's Leap'.[21] The vistas from these points, to the south and north respectively, would become the quintessential Blue Mountains views, both about a mile from the western highway and both with waterfalls to emphasise that anxious connection between the upper and lower realms. It is a pervasive breach, that relief in the landscape, never entirely broached by the tourist trails that, since the late 1800s have snaked their way into the valley, following, on occasions, the older Aboriginal routes. Trollope expressed it well in 1873 when he wrote that 'In looking down from cliffs upon the sea, one is conscious that the foot of the rocks may be reached. A boat, at any rate, will place you there, if the weather be fair. But here the mind becomes aware of no mode of entering the abyss.'[22]

Although unstated, there *is* a mode that will bring him down with great rapidity. A sense of it pervades his text.

~

Inquest: Scene 3

[From the coronial inquiry into the death of Vere Gordon Childe]

HENRY NEWSTEAD ON OATH STATES:—

I am a taxi driver and I reside at 8 Darley Street, Katoomba. I remember the Saturday morning 19th October. I was engaged in my occupation as taxi driver and he came over to the rank. I had seen the deceased before that. He had travelled in the cab before but not with me. I knew the deceased by sight. He came up to me in my cab at the taxi rank. That was about 7.40. I usually have my watch. I arrived at Govetts Leap about 8 o'clock. . . . I didn't notice anything abnormal about him. He seemed to be smoking heavily on his pipe. He got out of the cab at Govetts Leap and he looked at his watch for about ten seconds. I waited for him to say something and then he said, 'I will take these.' He took a compass and some papers from the seat and left a map on the seat which I gave to Constable Morey.

   I waited in the cab until about 12 o'clock. Some people came along and told me something. I had just been looking around and I was near the cab and these people came and told me they had found a coat. That would be about a mile-and-a-half to two miles from the cab. I went to have a look and I found his coat before I came to the lookout. I found his hat and glasses and compass. They were on the ledge outside the safety fence and alongside it. I looked around to see if I could find him and then I shouted out. I could not see any further sign of him and then I went and reported it to Constable Morey. While with me he did not show any signs of being ill. He did not seem to want to talk. That may have been just a mannerism. [He] gave me no impression he was unsettled.'

Q. He didn't ask you to wait?

A. No, but we always waited.

Q. Did he always use the same cab?

A. Yes.

Q. Had you talked about him?

A. Yes. Mr Benham had driven him three times before, once to Bell and once or twice to Kings Tableland.

Q. Did he tell you what the deceased used to do?

A. Sketch the mountains and things, I think.

~

vertigo is a sign of the most fundamental crisis of the self, a radical
(and, for Kierkegaard, religious) disorientation that is qualitatively
different from the merely relative loss of reference that occurs when
calculation fails.

John M. Hoberman, 'Kierkegaard on Vertigo', 1987

~

The story I'm telling might have been different. Another history lies in
the shadow of what has been. The gaping channel that is the Grose River
Valley could have permitted a different thoroughfare, a different mode of
viewing. Thomas Mitchell, who was fascinated by the 'stupendous,
perpendicular cliffs', the 'silvery line of the Grose' and who published a
marvellous lithograph of the valley, once proposed that its broad channel
could provide a new route for the western road with 'a tunnel, of about
a mile, through a ridge at the head of it, to reach the Vale of Clywdd,
and so avoid the mountains' with their difficult ascent.[23] In the late
1850s, Mitchell's idea was rehabilitated when the valley was surveyed as a
possible route for the railway line to Bathurst.[24] But ultimately the
ruggedness of the terrain, with its 'round boulders, which were as large
as houses, and over, or between which we found it impossible to
proceed',[25] prevented the fulfilment of those grand engineering visions.

Image-makers, too, would be strangely obstructed when they took
to the valley. Eccleston du Faur was a draughtsman in the surveyor-
general's office and a tireless promoter of Blue Mountains scenery. In
1875 he organised one of the colony's earliest artists' camps in the Grose
River Valley. Amateurs and professionals attended, the latter including
W. C. Piguenit, a distinguished landscape painter, and the photographer
Joseph Bischoff, who was fully equipped with glass plate negatives and
chemicals so that he could photograph and develop his plates in situ. Du
Faur had arranged a number of axe-wielding assistants to clear the
interfering vegetation.

Tim Bonyhady has discussed the problems presented to Bischoff
when he visited the valley. On the one hand, the cliffs of the Grose
seemed insignificant when compared with the photos of Yosemite that
had originally inspired du Faur. In addition, it was difficult to conceal the
zealous axework of du Faur's labourers from the photographs. A

225

foreground of fallen trunks and branches did not resonate with notions of the picturesque. As Bonyhady points out the truly successful images were those like *The Valley of the Grose* which shows riverbed and forest untampered with.[26]

Bischoff had other problems in the valley. He found himself frustrated by the lack of 'a single dull, still day, with diffused lights, by which alone satisfactory results can be obtained in such scenery'.[27] Gael Newton, a curator and historian of photography, proposes that his lack of success in the Grose had the effect of discouraging further exploration of this aspect on the mountains. In contrast to the great images of Yosemite and other escarpments in the American west, which are pictorially depicted from the base looking up, Bischoff would reveal the futility of working from the valley floor. Newton writes of the legacy of this experiment: 'Artists and photographers since have rarely bothered with the difficulties of the narrow valley when all the drama required can be had more comfortably from above.'[28] Newton's claim is substantially correct, though there were some artists, including W. C. Piguenit and the colonial photographer Charles Bayliss, who made impressive images of Blue Mountains valleys.

The valley that Trollope deemed impossible to reach would encourage recreational exploration on the part of bushwalkers and play a seminal role in the history of environmental protection in Australia. In 1931 a group of hikers visited the valley and met a farmer who had acquired a lease (with option to buy) on a magnificent stand of *Eucalyptus deanei*. In the ensuing campaign to protect it, the area became widely known as Blue Gum Forest. The farmer declared he was planning to fell the trees and plant a walnut orchard in their place. Led by Myles Dunphy, who achieved legendary status as a pioneering environmentalist and advocate for a Blue Mountains National Park (eventually gazetted in 1959), the bushwalkers succeeded, despite the Depression, in raising funds to buy out the farmer and have the area protected as a recreation reserve.[29]

The long history of recreational hiking in the Blue Mountains is evidence of a social trajectory in which visitors to the area acquired an increasing intimacy with the landscape. While remaining mindful of this, it is still curious how the sense of a vertiginous terrain remains dominant in popular imagery, highlighting the aura of sadness, danger and imminent death that Delia Falconer addressed very movingly in her novel

JOSEPH BISCHOFF TOOK
Valley of the Grose
DURING THE ARTISTS
CAMP OF 1875. THIS
PHOTO WAS SUCCESSFUL,
BUT ON THE WHOLE
BISCHOFF FOUND IT
DIFFICULT TO OBTAIN
PICTURESQUE VIEWS
FROM THE HEAVILY
FORESTED FLOOR OF THE
VALLEY. THE MAJORITY
OF ARTISTS HAVE
DEPICTED THE GROSE
FROM THE TOP LOOKING
DOWN.

The Service of Clouds. Her evocation touches upon a very real history in which people in a range of circumstances go to the Blue Mountains with the expectation that they will die. Among other contemporary representations of the mountains, it is very often the conservationist rhetoric that, far from emphasising the communion between people and nature, is most energetic in driving home the sense of alienation. I am referring here to an issue touched upon in Passages One and Two: the longstanding connection between notions of wilderness and the

labyrinth, exemplified by the Maxvision film *The Edge*, in which the Blue Mountains environment becomes a symbol of impending global collapse.

Amidst such spectacles of cliff-top drama—the fascination of awful heights and dreadful depths connected by falling water—one can almost forget the fundamental appeal of an elevated view. For this reason, Mitchell's lithograph *Valley of the Grose* is doubly exceptional.[30] A view from the escarpment somewhere near Mount Hay, the image shows a patch of light in a darkened valley caused by a break in a clouded sky. In the foreground, where a jagged anvil of rock is cantilevered over the cliff, an eagle stands with wings alert, poised to fly. Thus Mitchell, as an antidote to the abundant imagery of falling—the preoccupation with the abyss—drew attention to the great and compelling fantasy of soaring through the air that comes when standing at an eagle's eyrie; when watching with envy and delight the airborne movement of a bird.

Flight, remember, is the corollary of falling. Or should I say that falling mocks our dreams of flight? It is the limit of bodily capability that finds its most potent expression when a human subject leaps into the void. Hence the connection between flight and fall that the psychologist Binswanger discerned in the kites and eagles that appeared in his patients' dreams—gliding boldly through the sky or tumbling to earth as a bundle of feathers. Hence, also, the connection between flight and fall in mythology of the labyrinth. Daedalus, its architect, escapes the isle of Crete on wax-bound wings accompanied by Icarus, his son, who flies too high in 'his eagerness for the open sky'. The wax melts. The boy is engulfed by the sea.

It is in the light of this profound connectedness between fall and flight—and the particular imaginative challenges it poses—that, in the spirit of Bachelard, we can 'study the imagination of the fall as a kind of sickness of the imagination of rising, as an *inexpiable nostalgia* for heights'.[31]

~

Inquest: Scene 4

[From the coronial inquiry into the death of Vere Gordon Childe]

Verdict of Coroner John Ebenezer Tonkin

And I, as such Coroner, being charged to inquire (on the part of Our said Lady the Queen), when, where, how, and by what means the deceased came to his death, having made such inquiry, declare and find that the deceased on the nineteenth day of October 1957 at Luchetti Look-out, Blackheath in the Penrith Police District in the said State died from the effects of injuries accidentally received, namely a compound fracture of the skull and multiple fractures, when he fell from a cliff top.

~

'He says it is the beginning of the coming universal wish not to live.'

Thomas Hardy, *Jude the Obscure*, 1896

~

A tourist landscape that is organised around the excitement and drama of the precipice invites accidents as well as suicides. With an absence of evidence suggesting foul play, suicide or accident were the alternative verdicts available to the district coroner in 1957 upon the death of Vere Gordon Childe.

The desire to quantify and tabulate the phenomenon of death is enshrined in the legislature of industrialised nations. If a death is violent, suspicious or unexplained, if it occurred in state custody, as a result of an anaesthetic, or in other 'suspicious' circumstances—in short, if a death is deemed at all 'unnatural'—an enquiry or inquest will be carried out by the coronial court. Historically, death by suicide has opened up a curious anomaly in the coronial system. A factor that makes suicide statistics no-toriously shaky is that the reputation of the deceased and the sentiments

of their family are so often prioritised over the State's determination to rationally investigate the cause of death.

It is often observed that, in cases of likely suicide, coroners hand down a finding of accident if there is doubt—often very slight—about the cause of death. Attributable to the social stigma of suicide, such determinations are a hangover from the old crime of *felo de se* (felony against the self) which required the 'civil death' of the suicide. This law, which survived in New South Wales statute until 1912, regulated the disposal of the subject's body and required the forfeiture of their estate to the Crown. Although it persisted in legislature, this rule of forfeiture had, by the nineteenth century, fallen into disrepute and in practice it was frequently circumvented. *Felonia de se* were defined as suicides that resulted from a *willed action* and were *part of an evil design*. Coronial juries often felt that depriving heirs of their inheritance was misplaced punishment. It became widely known that forfeiture of property could not occur if a jury found that the suicide was deemed to be of 'unsound mind' or 'state of mind unknown'.[32]

THOMAS MITCHELL'S *Valley of the Grose* DEPICTED THE SPECTACULAR GORGE WITH AN EAGLE ON THE EDGE, ITS WINGS UPLIFTED. THE DANGER OF THE PRECIPICE IS JUXTAPOSED WITH THE FREEDOM OF FLIGHT.

The actions of John Ebenezer Tonkin, the District Coroner of Katoomba who investigated Childe's death, suggest a marked reluctance to arrive at verdicts of suicide. In Tonkin's jurisdiction, there were two other deaths by falling in 1957, both of which occurred near Echo Point. The cases involved women, both from Sydney: one 'in a state of extreme melancholia' according to police reports; the other was staying with her husband in the mountains having suffered a nervous breakdown. In the latter case, a policeman advised the coroner:

> I am of the opinion that the deceased threw herself over the rocks to the valley, a distance of approximately 200 feet below. This is supported by the fact that the deceased left Prince Henry Walk about 20 feet from the Spooner lookout, walked down a sloping bank to the edge of the precipice where the earth was disturbed.

The coroner nonetheless concluded that she 'died from a fractured skull and multiple fractures received when she fell from a cliff top but how she came to fall the evidence does not enable me to say'.[33]

Tonkin reached a similar conclusion in the case of the woman with melancholia. She had caught a train to Sydney, gone to Echo Point and left her handbag a metre from the wire enclosure beneath which her body was found. The bag contained a hospital contribution book with her husband's name, an evening edition of the *Sun* newspaper and a sum of money. The placement of such 'calling cards', identifying both the subject and location of the body, is common in many cases of suicide by falling—as the coroner must have known. Quite possibly, he was endeavouring to protect the financial interests of her husband. Like the woman who had suffered nervous breakdown, her life was insured.

The placement of a note or personal items at a site of suicide opens a broad issue concerning the inscription of an environment and the cultural resonance of a site of death. In the case of Gordon Childe, the 'message' conveyed by the things he left on the clifftop, is certainly mysterious. If not to guide his searchers, why would the professor have draped his coat, with wallet in pocket, across a fallen tree some two hundred yards from Luchetti Lookout? Given Coroner Tonkin's demonstrated tendency to avoid verdicts of suicide, it is more than possible in the case of Childe, a well known figure whose death made headlines, that he acted on similar aversion. Then again (and this cannot be ruled out), the placement of the map, compass and spectacles may, on the balance of evidence, have genuinely convinced him of his finding.

Suppose for a moment the coronial verdict is wrong. If so, Childe's death becomes truly perplexing. The map and instruments are not what they seem—aids in interpreting the landscape—but props in a deliberate hoax that will fool the officers of the law; a set of signs around his own premeditated death. They are both 'false' signs, perpetrating a deception that will result in an erroneous verdict, and 'genuine' signs in that they reveal the complexity of his purpose. Perhaps, also, they are metaphorical signs, designed to evoke meaning in the manner of a text or work of art. Assuming all this, the last sign-making gestures of the professor would only become *more* perplexing if it were known that he prepared some communication—a letter, say—to be opened at some future time which revealed his deception by declaring his suicidal intent.

In fact, none of the above is supposition. So far as can be determined, it is true. V. Gordon Childe, the eminent archaeologist, wrote such a note and apparently created an elaborate deception around his own death. If his initial purpose was to hide his suicide, it seems that his overriding intention was to throw it into focus, encouraging some serious engagement with the locality and the events surrounding his self-destruction.

233

In responding to this challenge, it might be possible, in the mode of A. Alvarez (whose 1971 study of suicide *The Savage God* was written in the wake of Sylvia Plath's death), to circumvent some dominant trends in 'suicidology' as literature on this subject is jargonistically known. While such study is frequently justified by moralising rhetoric of 'suicide prevention', most of it is simply enumerative. Taking the lead from Durkheim, whose major book *Suicide* appeared in 1897, the sociological model does little more than count the dead. Thus constrained, it can ask no qualitative questions about the lives that might be lost or dragged back from the brink, just as it is drastically ill-equipped in dealing with the issues that suicide, at the most basic level, will inevitably raise. These, surely, are the BIG questions: 'Who am I?'; 'What is the meaning?'; 'Why should I go on?' That the possibility of choosing life or death—there for all of us—opens up the very substance of being is the basis of Wittgenstein's assertion (paraphrased by Alvarez) that suicide is 'the pivot on which every ethical system turns'[34] and Camus' declaration that there is 'but one truly serious philosophical problem and that is suicide.. . . . All the rest—whether or not the world has three dimensions, whether the mind has nine or twelve categories—comes afterwards. These are games.'[35] Yet since Camus, who was writing in 1942, suicide has been almost abandoned as a philosophical question. Alvarez's remark concerning suicide study since Durkheim remains acute: '"To be or not to be" had given way to "the reason why".'[36]

The pointed way in which V. Gordon Childe threw light on the manner of his passing emphasises the reality that the history of suicide in modern times has involved a systematic negation. The specificity of the act is buried in the mausoleum of statistics. Under the rubric of compassion, but equally motivated by fear of contagion, a specific instance of suicide becomes almost unutterable in public media. In the jurisdiction of New South Wales, this is vividly symbolised in the legal history. Acknowledgment of the right to suicide—that life in effect is private property—was made belatedly, with decriminalisation being enacted in 1983.[37] This was three years after the *Coroners Act* of 1980 had decreed that where 'the death of a person was self-inflicted, no report of the proceedings shall be published'.[38] Recognition of the right to kill oneself came at the expense of the right to have it known. The law states that in cases of 'public interest' the coroner is entitled to over-ride the prohibition. But on the whole, the mundane frequency of suicidal deaths is systematically ignored or only tangentially referred to in such brief reports as: 'A man was found with a shotgun wound to the head. There were no suspicious circumstances.'

The prohibition of reporting is often justified as compassion for the family of the deceased—a courtesy that is not extended, however, to the relatives of murder victims, disaster casualties, the sufferers of almost any other accident or transgression. Perhaps, indeed, it *is* a consideration to friends and family to be relieved of painful details splashed in headlines. But with that relief comes the deletion of this significant theme from the narrative of public life and the consequent muffling of the suicide's cry: a censoring of the circumstances, personal and social, that influenced the choice to end a life.

234

The press reported that Malcolm Longton, fifteen years old, was the first to glimpse it. He saw 'a boot protruding from the bush'. So he called the other searchers, seventeen in total, and they placed it on a stretcher and manoeuvred it to the base of Govetts Leap. Then, in the dry heat of early summer, they began the climb along the walking trail, relieving each other every hundred yards.[39] The body, which Constable Morey would describe at the inquest as 'badly smashed and mutilated', was also incomplete. Some years later, a botanist fossicking for a rare plant around the waterfall found the cap and boot of the professor, the latter still containing fragments of his foot. His broken watch was also lying among these remnants.[40] The famous archaeologist had himself become an archaeological find.

Childe's fall is poignantly symbolic, anticipating his departure as an intellectual figure. It is difficult to reconcile the present obscurity with Childe's prominence some forty years ago. He was, in the words of his biographer, Sally Green, 'the most eminent and influential scholar of European prehistory in the twentieth century'.[41] An obituary by his young colleague D. J. Mulvaney headily described Childe's major work *The Dawn of European Civilization* as 'comparable with *The Origin of the Species* in its significance for prehistoric studies'.[42] Distinguished within his field, he was also one of those exceptional scholars who attracted a substantial audience outside. It has been said, without exaggeration, that on the international stage Childe was the best known of Australian writers. *What Happened in History* (1942), the most popular of his publications, had sold 300 000 copies at the time of his death.[43] This was one of more than twenty books and hundreds of essays by Childe that spanned the fields of archaeology, history, epistemology, labour politics.

That Childe is now almost unknown beyond the disciplines of prehistory and labour studies is an interesting phenomenon. But then Australia has a tradition of coolness towards those who have 'made it' overseas. For Childe this has been compounded by his decidedly leftist politics. It is salutary to realise that, when he returned to Australia in 1957 after an absence of thirty-six years, the Australian Security and Intelligence Organisation (ASIO) was on his trail, monitoring his lectures on prehistory and compiling memoranda on his dinner party pronouncements.[44] Such was the paranoia of Cold War Australia. That

If suicide is allowed then everything is allowed. If anything is not allowed then suicide is not allowed. This throws a light on the nature of ethics, for suicide is, so to speak, the elementary sin. And when one investigates it it is like investigating mercury vapour in order to comprehend the nature of vapours. Or is even suicide in itself neither good nor evil?

LUDWIG WITTGENSTEIN,
Notebooks 1914–1916,
1961

V. Gordon Childe
and students
excavating at the
prehistoric village of
Skara Brae on
Orkney in the 1920s.

236

Childe's possible suicide could have been associated with 'factors of counter-espionage significance' was actually raised by the Director General of ASIO in October 1957.[45] But on the evidence available, it is difficult to assimilate Childe's death with the cloak-and-dagger sentiments of the security chief.

Certainly, his death *was* political—in every sense of the term. And while the factors that shaped his politics are the substance of public history (the rise of communism, the two world wars, their aftermath), the way in which Gordon Childe died opens questions about the sense of place, the perception of home, the dynamics of narrative—a politics of *being*—which is rarely countenanced in what usually passes for political debate. In seeking such terminology, and thus scrutinising the limits of that extreme no-go zone—the embracing of death—the story of Childe's fall unfolds.

The elements have already been established. The map, compass, notebook and spectacles sit at a lookout on the top of the escarpment. The body, shattered, lies below. Those few seconds of failed flight connect the sites to create a strange moment in scenography. It was—and still is—disturbing. Hence the rapidity with which it was all dismantled. The body, what they could find of it, collected; the map and possessions stashed away. Yet even now they survive in memory as an enduring image. With this in mind we might approach the no-go zone: to treat Childe's death, in the words of Camus, as though it were a 'work of art'.[46]

THE DEPARTURE

Childe's fall spirals around moments of departure and return. He had left Australia in 1921, aged twenty-nine. He did not return until retiring from the directorship of the Institute of Archaeology, University of London, at the age of sixty-five. His refusal to visit even briefly throughout this lengthy interval can be attributed at least in part to disillusion with his native land. Certainly, the theme of rejection ran strongly in the early years. While Childe's success as an academic and author, the professorships at Edinburgh and London, and his honorary doctorates from Harvard and Pennsylvania, may have aroused a certain envy at home, it is telling that he left Australia by the volition of others. For several years, Childe had sought academic appointments in Australia, with the most extraordinary lack of success. His qualifications were certainly impressive: triple first class honours from Sydney, a Bachelor of Letters from Oxford where he had studied under the renowned excavator of Crete, Sir Arthur Evans. His knockbacks on returning from Oxford were so frequent and discriminatory that questions were even raised in Parliament. Why should a young scholar with impeccable credentials be vetoed for a lowly tutorship by the University of Sydney senate?[47]

Previously, Childe had been squeezed from the position of Resident Tutor at the university's Saint Andrews College. Finally, he left Sydney in disgust, travelled north to Queensland and taught at Maryborough Grammar School where he was tormented by students and castigated by parents, colleagues and the local newspaper for his political views. He took a menial job (as government clerk) and applied again for an academic position at the University of Queensland, to be rejected in favour of a far less qualified candidate.

Throughout this period, Childe's leftist sympathies, and in particular his opposition to the Great War, were bones of contention with the authorities and inspiration for an earlier phase of government surveillance. ASIO was not formed until 1949, but during World War I army intelligence officers co-ordinated the monitoring of suspect persons. As Mulvaney has written, Childe's mail, like that of other malcontents, 'was intercepted and summarised on official forms by the censors to which they appended their pungent and outrageously biased political and moral observations'.[48] Childe's movements and job aspirations were noted by these officials and circulated around the country. In the face of such obstacles, he decided on a new career in which his principles might serve him to advantage.

Thus began what Childe later described as his 'sentimental excursion into Australian politics'.[49] He returned to Sydney and in August 1919 became the private secretary to John Storey, leader of the Labor Opposition in New South Wales. In the elections the following year, Storey was elected premier with a delicate majority of just one seat. Childe wrote Storey's speeches and began detailed study of the labour movement in Australia, attaining 'unrivalled grasp of its structure and history'.[50] In 1921, having experienced the inner circle of state politics, Childe was transferred to London to serve as research and publicity officer for the New South Wales Government. He was delighted at his proximity to the libraries and galleries of Britain but the position brought rapid disappointment. Premier Storey had died while Childe was en route to England and his successor, James Dooley, was defeated in the elections of 1921. The new conservative government acted quickly to relieve Childe of his position, and for a while it seemed he would be stuck unemployed in London without so much as a return passage from the State.

Eventually, he decided not to go back at all. As Sally Green writes, Childe was 'feeling particularly disillusioned with Australian politics . . . He had very little money in hand . . . and was soon badly in need of a job'.[51] He managed to survive in London on slender resources while he wrote his first book, *How Labour Governs* (1923). It is striking evidence that it was his own side of politics, not the conservatives, with which he was most disillusioned. Still considered a seminal study on unionism and labour politics in Australia, this book makes a scathing critique of how the Australian Labor Party had forsaken its working-class allegiances on entry to the parliamentary system. In his devastating conclusion, Childe would remark on how the 'Labour [*sic*] Party, starting with a band of inspired Socialists, degenerated into a vast machine for capturing political power. . . . Such is the history of all Labour [*sic*] organisations in Australia, and that not because they are Australian, but because they are Labour [*sic*].'[52]

Childe considered writing a sequel to *How Labour Governs* but never did so. Green suggests he was becoming increasingly torn between involvement in contemporary politics and his interest in past societies. The struggle played itself out during the first half of the 1920s, when he was associated with the Labour Research Department, a Marxist body, and visited the museums and galleries of post-war Europe.

239

Supporting himself as a book translator and as a librarian at the Royal Anthropological Institute, London, he read almost every book in the collection, completing a panoramic survey of prehistorical literature which allowed him to produce his first major work in archaeology, an attempt 'at distilling from archaeological remains a preliterate substitute for the conventional politico–military history with cultures, instead of statesmen, as actors'.[53] *The Dawn of European Civilization* (1925) was the first attempt to synthesise a great mass of inchoate archaeological data, gathered over many years across hundreds of sites. It proposed, as Childe himself put it, 'the irradiation of European barbarism by Oriental civilization'.[54] To his colleague Stuart Piggott, it represented 'our Ariadne-clue to the labyrinth of Neolithic and earlier Bronze Age Europe'[55] and, as Sally Green observes, it 'established his reputation overnight'.[56] It won Childe the Abercromby chair of prehistoric archaeology at Edinburgh in 1927, a position he held until 1946 when he became director of the Institute of Archaeology in London. Childe's 'big picture' approach to prehistory, involving the assimilation of masses of data, would become the hallmark of his archaeology. His enduring accomplishment was on the page, rather than in the field. The ancient village of Skara Brae on the Scottish isle of Orkney was his most significant excavation.[57] Launching his career with a work of synthesis— and he published many more—Childe became a unique and revered figure on the archaeological scene. That first book in prehistory became known affectionately as *The Dawn*, and was still in print (in its sixth edition) at the time of his death, having acquired almost mythological status. Archaeologists seeking an obscure reference would often fondly remark, 'You'll find it in a footnote in *The Dawn*'.[58] While the tension between changing the future and understanding the past remained a presence throughout Childe's life, the past had gained the upper hand.

THE RETURN

Childe returned to his homeland after thirty-six years in Europe. It had been a time of extraordinary productivity that brought, in his public life, all the hallmarks of success. About the private Childe, practically nothing is known. He had a wide circle of colleagues but all who left account of him have testified to the opacity of his personal life. He never married and never had a lover (so far as anyone seems to know). Rumours of homosexuality sometimes circulate. Whatever their foundation, there was much about Childe that remained inside the closet. He is remembered for his eccentricities which seemed to shield the inner self. He wore a black, wide-brimmed hat and short trousers in the worst of weather, and enjoyed the shock effect of being seen to read the *Daily Worker*, prominent in his office or requested when he stayed at good hotels.[59]

With a dearth of information about the private man, Childe's appearance has been the cause of comment and speculation. Max Mallowan cruelly described him as 'the ugliest [man] I have ever met, indeed painful to look at'.[60] Sally Green describes him thus:

> He had, especially in his younger days, a very odd face, not helped by his thick spectacles and gingery hair, together with a thin frame and awkward movements. He was always extremely sensitive, and his unfortunate physique can only have contributed to the reserve and detachment from his fellow human beings which characterized him throughout his life.[61]

A former student, Howard Kilbride-Jones, remembers that he 'preferred to lecture in a darkened room, with female students assembled in the front row'. He mumbled and sometimes dribbled through his lectures and when he was questioned his nose went red. Such shyness was counterpoised by displays of extroversion; what Childe would call his 'Childe-ishness', a word he liked. Almost as common as reports of ugliness are memories of his fast cars and appalling driving. Kilbride-Jones was one of the few students sufficiently game to ride with the professor, travelling to archaeological sites with Childe in his open tourer, a Hudson Terraplane.

> Childe drove the Hudson all over Scotland at eighty miles an hour, his poor eyesight causing it to be known eventually as Childe's terror-plane. He liked to share the car with me because I could drive it faster than he could, and Childe adored speed. I can see him now, sitting in the passenger seat, the brim of the black hat driven hard against his face by the force of the wind, a look of complete happiness on his face.[62]

For the moment, allow Childe's European career to flash past like scenery observed from the Terraplane. He has arrived in Australia, sixty-five years old, returning to a place that cannot be other than a space of memory. He had been brought up in North Sydney where his father was rector of St Thomas's Church of England. A severe and conservative man who regarded his parish duties with a certain disdain, the Reverend Stephen Childe was then married to Harriet Gordon, the mother of Vere Gordon Childe. She was the daughter of a wealthy lawyer, and with her money Stephen Childe built in 1899 the Chalet Fontenelle, named after the Enlightenment scholar who inspired him. This is the substantial residence on the clifftop at Wentworth Falls that is now known as Whispering Pines. So fond was the Reverend Childe of his Blue Mountains retreat that when, between 1901 and 1906, he held the post of Rural Dean of North Sydney, it was 'often commented that he was a great "Rural" Dean—so rural that he almost lived in the rural surroundings of Wentworth Falls'.[63]

Although there is evidence of a fond relationship between Childe and one of his half sisters (the father had been married previously and would do so a third time on the death of Harriet), differences over politics and religion created an enormous gulf within the family. His conservative father was in general agreement with the state government's decision to sack his son in London and his step-sister, an Anglican nun in

242

The Childe family's mountain retreat was called Chalet Fontenelle. Now it is a guesthouse called Whispering Pines.

Queensland, responded with panic when she heard that the red Gordon was heading north in 1918.[64] When Childe returned to Australia, it is likely that this divide was opened anew. Despite the gratification of belated recognition—lectures and broadcasts around the country; an honorary doctorate from Sydney University which had twice denied him a job—he had entered the Australian version of American McCarthyism: the ultra-conservatism of Prime Minister Robert Menzies. He may have sensed that ASIO was on his trail; certainly, he was disappointed by the failing fortunes of his old university friend and leader of the Opposition, H. V. Evatt, with whom he stayed.[65] Perhaps the most consistent ray of hope—or source of pleasure—that appears in his letters of that period is his fondness for the mountains. 'They are as good as remembered and to me compare favourably with West Highlands or Tyrol,' he told a friend. To another he declared that,

> I have employed the past couple of months with enormous zest satisfying my youthful craving to understand the complicated arrangement of the pale blue ranges that bounded the wide valley on the precipitous edge of which we had a summer house. Now I have reached most of the vantage points in taxis and climbed to some.[66]

243

A place of memory and a source of ecstasy in those final months, the mountains had been working on his mind well before he left Europe. In January 1957 his colleague Edward Pyddoke reported to a mutual friend a conversation he had with Childe about what he would do when he returned to England. 'He replied that he doubted if he would return from Australia and that he would in all probability throw himself over some convenient cliff.'[67]

In retrospect, there seems abundant evidence that Childe was contemplating if not deliberately planning his death. He had retired early from the directorship of the Institute of Archaeology. He sold his library at auction, destroyed his personal papers, gave up his flat in London. He wrote his last book, *The Prehistory of European Society*, on the voyage to Australia, compiling a list of friends to whom copies should be sent. Most telling, though, are his final essays. He drafted an autobiographical sketch, a kind of obituary, titled 'Retrospect', in the weeks before his death. For Childe, who throughout his life had defended his theories with the utmost assiduity, it was a startling self-evaluation.

Now I confess that my whole account may prove to be erroneous; my formulae may be inadequate; my interpretations are perhaps ill-founded; my chronological framework—and without such one cannot speak of conjunctures—is frankly shaky. Yet I submit the result was worth publishing.[68]

Another essay, admittedly less devastating, was written in the same period and posted via surface mail to London. He was dead by the time it arrived. Titled 'Valediction' by its editor, it outlined 'the main tasks confronting archaeology in Britain'.[69] As recently as 1992, a further document came to light that has the flavour of valediction. At a conference celebrating the centenary of Childe's birth, the Russian archaeologist Leo Klejn presented a letter written in December 1956, previously unknown in the West, in which Childe made the most severe denouncement of archaeological methods in the Soviet Union.[70] As a well-known Marxist, a supporter of Soviet scholarship and a frequent visitor to Russia, the letter, coming in the wake of the Soviet invasion of Hungary (at which Childe was privately dismayed), suggests a traumatic collapse of his ideals.[71]

THE NOTE

Jack Lindsay, son of the artist Norman, and prolific expatriate author, was among the friends convinced all along that Childe's death was suicide.[72] On learning of the fall, Lindsay was immediately reminded of their weekend visits to Mount Tambourine in Queensland in the wake of World War I. 'I can still see Childe standing near the cliff edge, staring with vague intentness into immensity, swaying a little with bent shoulders and sliding his glasses down to the end of his nose.'[73] Perhaps this memory of Lindsay's is nothing more than a retrospective insertion. Yet if not, it does suggest that since his early days, the might of the precipice and the trajectory of the fall had been at work in Childe's imagination. This is consistent with his passion for speed and possession of the earthbound Terraplane.

Such details become important if we are to remember what sociology so frequently ignores: that suicide depends on a specific relationship between the human body and those material elements that will wreak its destruction. That this relationship is shaped by an individual's disposition and is utterly integral to their wish to die was emphasised by Alvarez when, in his remarkable epilogue to *The Savage God*, he described the drug overdose with which he himself attempted to end his life.

> Seneca, the final authority on the subject, pointed out disdainfully that the exits are everywhere: each precipice and river, each branch of each tree, every vein in your body will set you free. But in the event this isn't so. No one is promiscuous in his way of dying. A man who has decided to hang himself will never jump in front of a train.[74]

Certainly, there are cases that contradict this assertion, but even statisticians will support its substantial truth. Britain saw a one-third reduction in its suicide rate after 1963 when highly lethal coke gas was replaced by natural gas for domestic use.[75]

For Childe, it might well be inferred that leaping was the only method. I would add, more hesitantly, that, given his association with the ranges, the Blue Mountains could be the only place. The great question around his death is not its cause but the mystery he chose to generate in dying the way he did. The success of his ruse is amply demonstrated by the bizarre sequence of events that precipitated the ultimate unveiling of his suicide note. Prompted by the autobiography of Sir Max Mallowan, a colleague of Childe's and renowned excavator of Nimrud, the revelation occurred over several issues of the journal *Antiquity*. Max Mallowan was married to Agatha Christie who had been a bridge companion of Gordon Childe's. They might have marvelled at the exposition. Occurring in the pages of a usually sedate archaeological journal, it has all the implausibility of one of Christie's own drawing-room denouements.

There had been no signs of anger, depression or aggression— supposedly the symptoms of a suicidal person—in the final months of Gordon Childe; this was the conviction of Laila Haglund, a young prehistorian, who had stayed with him at the house of Professor James and Mrs Eve Stewart at Mount Pleasant near Bathurst just before he died. She took umbrage at Mallowan who, like Lindsay, was convinced Childe took his life.

> It is time this myth about Gordon Childe's suicide was knocked. It seems to be prevalent in Europe; I sometimes wonder whether some

245

of his colleagues and contemporaries there think that he *ought* to have felt suicidal.

I had the pleasure of knowing him at the time of his death and remember him as ebullient and full of enthusiasm... He was full of plans. There was so much he wished to see done in Australian prehistory... But it was all part of a large co-ordinated scheme. Listening to him was at times rather like hovering over the continent and looking down in a godlike manner.... At the time of his death he was particularly interested in the geology of the Blue Mountains, and I am convinced that it was this interest that brought him to his death. Though mentally alert he was physically somewhat tottery. I can easily see him fold his coat, put it down on the rocks, place the compass, take off his spectacles to do some sighting, peer around, perhaps step back a bit to line up certain features—quite forgetting that he had a cliff edge behind him. I cannot imagine him stepping— bleakly or desperately—over that edge to end his life![76]

In the same issue of *Antiquity*, Childe's hostess at Mount Pleasant, Eve Stewart, also wrote of his love for the geology of the mountains:

I got the impression of a man full of enthusiasm for a new project. There was certainly no hint of a bleak future; I would have said that he was rejoicing in his retirement because he was free to devote *all* his time and energy to the things which interested him. The enthusiastic tone of the letters he wrote us, between April and October 1957, endorse this impression.

As to suicide—definitely NO![77]

Contrary opinions quickly followed. In the March 1980 issue of *Antiquity*, W. F. Grimes, who had succeeded Childe as Director of the Institute of Archaeology at the University of London, reported a conversation in 1956. It was similar to that recorded by Edward Pyddoke.

Childe and I dined together in Soho. We drove back to NW3 in his car. In the hundred yards between Primrose Hill station and Chalk Farm (where I was to leave him) the following conversation took place:

G: What are you going to do when you retire?

C: I know a 2000-ft cliff in Australia. I intend to jump off it.

G: Good god! Why are you going to do that?

C: I have a horror of a prostate operation.

G: But surely thousands of men have had that and come out of it without difficulty?

He made no further comment and seconds later I got out of the car.

The conversation is *verbatim*. I saw no point in arguing or remonstrating. Childe knew his own mind, though he rarely—very rarely—revealed it in personal matters.[78]

Following receipt of this recollection and ensuing discussion between the correspondent and *Antiquity* editor Glyn Daniel, Professor Grimes revealed the existence of a letter he received from Childe after his death in 1957. Attached was this covering note:

THE CARRINGTON

KATOOMBA

BLUE MOUNTAINS, N.S.W.

20/10/57

Dear Grimes,

The enclosed contains matter that may in time be of historical interest to the Institute. But now it may cause pain and even provoke libel actions. After ten years it will be less inflammable. So I earnestly request that it be deposited in the archives and be not opened till January 1968 supposing that year ever arrives.

Yours sincerely,

V. Gordon Childe[79]

Showing unhesitating respect for his colleague's last request—and mind-boggling lack of curiosity!—Grimes kept the letter under wraps, even after the deadline of 1968 had expired. Thus, Childe's suicide note, which takes the form of an essay on suicide, written from the Blue Mountains just before his fall, did not become public until 1980. I reproduce the text in full.

THE CARRINGTON

KATOOMBA

BLUE MOUNTAINS, N.S.W.

The progress of medical science has burdened society with a horde of parasites—rentiers, pensioners and other retired persons whom society has to support and even to nurse. They exploit the youth which is expected to produce for them and even to tend them. While many are physically fit to work and some do, others are incapable of looking after themselves and have literally to be kept alive by the exertions of younger attendants who might be more profitably employed otherwise. And in so far as they do work, they block the way to promotion against younger and more efficient successors. For in all persons over 65—there are of course numerous exceptions—are physically less capable than their juniors and psychologically far less alert and adaptable. Their reactions are slowed down; they can only gradually and reluctantly, if at all, adopt new habits and still more rarely assimilate fresh ideas. I am doubtful whether they can ever produce new ideas. Compulsory retirement from academic and judicial posts and from the civil services has of course done something to open the rewards of seniority to younger men, and has rescued students and subordinates from inefficient teachers and incompetent administrative chiefs. In British universities the survival of the old system during my lifetime has provided cautionary examples of distinguished professors mumbling lectures ten years out of date and wasting departmental funds on obsolete equipment. These instances probably outweigh better publicized cases of scientists and scholars who in their colleagues' opinion are 'forced to retire at the height of their powers'. But even when retired, their prestige may be such that they can hinder the spread of progressive ideas and blast the careers of innovators who tactlessly challenge theories and procedures that ten or fifteen years previously had been original and fruitful (I am thinking for instance of Arthur Evans).

In fact if the over-age put 'their knowledge, experience and skill at the service of society' as honorary officers or counsellors of learned societies, public bodies, charitable institutions or political parties, they are liable to become a gerontocracy—the worst possible form of leadership. In a changing world their wisdom and maturity of judgement do not compensate for their engrained prejudices and stereotyped routines of behaviour. No doubt the over 65s are competent to carry out routine investigations and undertake compilations of information, and may be helped therein by their accumulated knowledge. Yet after 65 memory begins to fail, and even well-systematized information begins to leak away. My personal experience is confirmed by observations on senior colleagues. And new ideas, original combinations of old knowledge, come rarely if at all. Generally old authors go on repeating the same old theses, not always in better chosen language.

I have always considered that a sane society would disembarrass itself of such parasites by offering euthanasia as a crowning honour or even imposing it in bad cases, but certainly not condemning them to misery and starvation by inflation.

For myself I don't believe I can make further useful contributions to prehistory. I am beginning to forget what I laboriously learned—forget not only details (for these I never relied on memory), but even that there is something relevant to look up in my note-book. New ideas very rarely come my way. I see no prospect of settling the problems that interest me most—such as that of the 'Aryan cradle'—on the available data. In a few instances I actually fear that the balance of evidence is against theories that I have espoused or even in favour of those against which I am strongly biased. Yet at the same time I suspect this fear may be due to an equally irrational desire to overcome my own prejudices. (In history one has to make decisions on inadequate evidence, and, whenever I am faced with this necessity, I am conscious of such opposing tendencies.) I have no wish to hang on the fringe of learned societies or university institutions as a venerable counsellor whose authority may slow down progress. I have become too dependent on a lot of creature comforts—even luxuries—to carry through some kinds of work for which I may still be fitted; I just lack the will-power to face the discomforts and anxieties of travel in the USSR or China. And, in fact, though I have never felt in better health, I do get seriously ill absurdly easily; every little cold in the head turns to bronchitis unless I take elaborate precautions and I am just a burden on the community. I have never saved any money, and, if I had, inflation would have consumed my savings. On my pension I certainly could not maintain the standard without which life would seem to be intolerable and which may be really necessary to prevent me becoming a worse burden on society as an invalid. I have always intended to cease living before that happens.

249

The British prejudice against suicide is utterly irrational. To end his life deliberately is in fact something that distinguishes *Homo sapiens* from other animals even better than ceremonial burial of the dead. But I don't intend to hurt my friends by flouting that prejudice. An accident may easily and naturally befall me on a mountain cliff. I have revisited my native land and found I like Australian society much less than European without believing I can do anything to better it; for I have lost faith in all my old ideals. But I have enormously enjoyed revisiting all the haunts of my boyhood, above all the Blue Mountains. I have answered to my own satisfaction questions that intrigued me then. Now I have seen the Australian spring; I have smelt the boronia, watched snakes and lizards, listened to the 'locusts'. There is nothing more I want to do here; nothing I feel I ought and could do. I hate the prospect of the summer, but I hate still more the fogs and snows of a British winter. Life ends best when one is happy and strong.[80]

250

IN THE MID-1980s, the local studies librarian John Low recorded an interview with a Mrs C. of Katoomba, one of the last people to see Gordon Childe alive. She worked as a receptionist at the Carrington, the grand hotel of Katoomba. Childe had stayed there often since returning to Australia and Mrs C. had come to know him well. He had spoken about his geological explorations and told her about a book he was writing on the mountains; how he wanted to examine some rock strata at Govetts Leap.

Mrs C. related that on 18 October 1957, the last evening of his life, Childe was drinking in the hotel's private bar where he found himself 'the butt of some cruel jokes directed at his rather ugly appearance'. He left the bar and sought the company of the receptionist. In this final encounter an unusual gesture was made.

> He offered her his typewriter as a gift and would hear of no refusal. She didn't want to take it and remonstrated with him to keep it but, not wishing to cause him distress, finally accepted it and placed it in the hotel safe with the intention of returning it later.[81]

Of course, that opportunity never arrived.

Presumably, Childe had finished with his typewriter when he completed his final testament, mailed in confidence to W. F. Grimes. Thus Gordon Childe, as he contemplated the abyss into which he would hurl himself, maintained a correlation between life, death and authorship. An intensely private man who had become a public figure through his publicatons, Childe chose to dispense with his tool for writing as he approached the end.

Already, I have written of suicide as an act of inscription, unique among ways of generating meaning for it comes at the cost of erasing the self. Suicide is negation in its purest form; a negation that is met with further negation: the elaborate net of coronial, statistical, psychological and sociological conventions that will go to almost any limit in muffling or assimilating the suicide's cry and so denying its status as an expressive act.

Childe's death was uniquely adapted to this theatre of twofold negation, seeking in the first instance to fiddle the tune of what he himself described as the irrational 'British prejudice against suicide' by leaving evidence conducive to a finding of accidental death. His final testament would demonstrate the fiction of the coronial finding and in

Laughter only assumes its fullest impact on being at the moment when, in the fall that it unleashes, a representation of death is cynically recognized. It is not only the composition of elements that constitutes the incandescence of being, but its decomposition in its mortal form.

GEORGES BATAILLES,
'THE LABYRINTH',
1935–6

the process outwit society's negation of suicide by emphasising the fraught reality that in leaping into the void Childe attained an apotheosis in his power of articulation. Childe's suicide note was the final missive of a prehistorian, so it is not far-fetched to regard it as an archaeological moment of the future. Indeed, the manner in which he secreted the letter ahead in time, providing diagnostic certainty to an enigma he himself had perpetrated, suggests a perverse antidote to the complaint in his letter that in history 'one has to make decisions on inadequate evidence'. This was the predicament of a scholar who, in the words of his colleague Mortimer Wheeler, 'made the study of man as nearly a science as perhaps that wayward subject admits'.[82] That Childe's ruse is indicative of an epistemological crisis—that his way of knowing had reached an impasse—is intimated in his lament that 'the balance of evidence is against theories that I have espoused'. Connected, surely, with the loss of faith in 'all my old ideals'—a revealing jeremiad from a Marxist of the 1950s—this seems more convincing in explaining his action than the claim of poverty, the excuses of concern for friends, the fear of defamation, the need for a routine operation.

Were the feelings of those who knew him protected by his action with its belated revelation that he chose to die? And who would sue a dead man for libel and how could he care if they did? No, that leap into space, that cry 'Enough!' which echoes through the valley still, demands a closer, more attentive listening: a fundamental respect for the gift and for the loss of life. Here the remarks of Camus and Wittgenstein come readily to mind, proposing that suicide is the first question of philosophy, or, by implication, that the fundamental challenge for living is a reconciliation between ways of being and the ways we think.

Childe was a theorist in the grand sense of the term, a follower of Marx and Durkheim and almost the last archaeologist to tackle such panoramic subjects as the birth of Europe and the rise of 'man'.[83] He was a late figure of the Enlightenment, milking the metaphor with titles such as *The Dawn of European Civilization* and *New Light on the Most Ancient East*. With his confidence in social evolution, his determination to bring scientific principles to archaeology, Childe embraced Bacon's dictum that, in 'discovering the right road' through the 'forest' or 'maze' of raw experience, it is 'prudent either to wait for day or procure a light and then proceed'.[84]

If Childe, as Stuart Piggott claimed, provided the 'Ariadne-clue' to early Europe, he was also in the mould of Daedalus, a builder of labyrinths with his lofty paradigms. To make sense of his appeal to flight, his Icarus fall, and even of his deprecation of Arthur Evans in his final note (the excavator of Crete, Evans was Childe's teacher at Oxford), it is as well to recall the admonition of Borges when he tells the story of the labyrinth through the mouth of the Minotaur. In the relentless tedium of his dance through infinite corridors, the bodies of his victims are his only means of marking place, distinguishing 'one gallery from another'. The arrival of Theseus, his 'redeemer', he awaits with anticipation. 'I hope he will take me to a place with fewer galleries and fewer doors'.[85] In this scenario, death, and only death, can mark a place in the labyrinth.

∽

all classical and medieval mazes share a remarkable characteristic: *they are unicursal, with no forked paths or internal choices to be seen.*

Penelope Reed Doob, *The Idea of the Labyrinth*, 1990

∽

The story of Childe's passing is as abundant in pathways as the labyrinth itself. At a certain point, the interpreter must simply choose a way. My account here is swayed by the theme of place: how the relationship between real and imagined places poses particular problems in the topography of colonisation. Childe's suicide is particularly pertinent to such an investigation, involving as it did a return to the country that both spawned him and spurned him. That return was a return from Europe— the continent that must have been another world to the Australian schoolboy and university student who read classics and philology, that became more real at Oxford under the tutelage of Arthur Evans. Then came the Australian return—an interval, as events transpired—the time of political action and academic rejection leading to the London posting where Europe and its antiquities offered sanctuary to the leftist misfit, dismissed by the state he had recently served. This was the trigger for what would become Childe's life project: elucidating the birth of European culture; establishing a genealogy of technological progress; documenting savagery, barbarism, the rise of civilization—the stages through which 'mankind' had passed.

For thirty-six years, Europe was his stamping ground. He travelled its width and breadth; he was literate in the major languages. As a prehistorian he plumbed the depths. His Eurocentrism has been regarded as his greatest weakness and the probable cause of his demise as a theorist. The Childe scholar Bruce G. Trigger gives the example of his belated consideration of Mayan culture in 1950 which convinced him that America had produced its own 'fully developed civilization that lacked irrigation, metallurgy, ploughs, sails, wheels, or domestic animals—all of which he had interpreted as prerequisites of civilization'.[86]

How would the homeland, Australia, have seemed to this Europhile after such a lengthy lapse? Even as it became more distant, itself more other-worldly, there remained the 'Australian-ness' he continually carried. In the heart of empire, the position of the colonial is always strange. Although it is difficult to imagine these days, Britain was regarded as 'home' for many Australians of Childe's generation. That sense of attachment, complicated by his 'colonial' background, was part of Childe's outsider status which, despite his prominence, he perpetually endured. With his radical politics, his unfortunate appearance, his cultivated eccentricities, his sentences that 'often ended in a falsetto squeak',[87] Childe retained a foreignness in the European scene.

Perhaps the emigrant is made doubly foreign in returning 'home'. The motherland—or is it fatherland?—despite outward similitude will rarely correspond to the space of memory. With its combination of familiarity and strangeness, it is an experience of 'the uncanny' as Freud so memorably defined it in 1919.[88] Childe's suicide note complains that he likes 'Australian society much less than European'. The idealist who in his youth had fought and suffered for the labour cause was appalled at returning to postwar consumerism and the urban sprawl.

'Australia today is far from a socialist society . . . but the working classes . . . have got what they want,'[89] he complained to the Australasian Book Society in Melbourne, treating his audience to 'a merciless comparison between the tepid suburban life of Australia and the vital culture of Iceland in the tenth century'.[90] Among all the disappointments, however, there were moments of undoubted reverie, including his visits to Bathurst where he was the guest of James Stewart, Professor of Archaeology at Sydney University, and his wife Eve. James Stewart was descended from early Bathurst settlers and his residence was a considerable mansion modelled on a Scottish baronial hall. The generous bounty of the Stewarts' excavations in Cyprus (Eve, also, was an archaeologist) were stored there for the long process of analysis and documentation. It was there that Childe met Laila Haglund, a young archaeology student from Sweden who was staying with the Stewarts for an extended period. He was delighted to find that this young woman was a pipe smoker, and often they would enjoy their tobacco and the contents of the Stewarts' well-stocked liquor cabinet well into the night. Such encounters, and the joy of a sudden trip to the distant mining town of Broken Hill which he regarded as 'more vibrant and culturally conscious than any place which he had visited',[91] seemed to anticipate the epiphany described in his final note: 'I have seen the Australian spring; I have smelt the boronia, watched snakes and lizards, listened to the "locusts".' Stimulating the senses in a most personal way, the experience of a place he loved, vibrant in its seasonal uniqueness, offered solace and an enduring image as he prepared to step away from Planet Earth.

~

death is power's limit, the moment that escapes it; death becomes the most secret aspect of existence, the most 'private'.

Michel Foucault, *The History of Sexuality*, 1976

~

In the opening pages of this passage, I sketched a history of Govetts Leap. Through a series of encounters, works of art and narratives—the powerful descriptions of Govett and Trollope—I suggested certain traits in the cultural pattern. As a possible conduit through the mountains, the Grose River, which heads at the cliffs of Darling Causeway, is a most notorious dead-end. It is one that has most frequently been depicted from the top looking down, allowing the modality of falling to be inscribed and reinscribed in landscape impressions. They include the mythology surrounding Govett himself and the bizarre newspaper 'interview' in which the bushranger, aged and just alive, claims to have survived his struggle with an Aboriginal tracker whom he pushes over the cliff and whose descending cry is misinterpreted by his pursuers as Govett's own.

This fiction is representative of a wider trend in topographical nomenclature, with its network of 'leaps' across the country upholding a kind of 'Jedda syndrome' by commemorating moments (actual and imagined) in which Aborigines are driven over or elect to throw themselves from cliffs. In the logic of this taxonomy, the confusion that permits the escape of the fictional Govett—a providential case of mistaken identity—is very much at home. The naming of 'leaps' after fallen persons is usually racially specific. The colour—the blackness—of the 'fellow', 'gin' or 'tribe' that fell, and rarely their specific names, is the quality emphasised in most of these attributions.

Acknowledging that this history has contributed to the cultural resonance of Govetts Leap (a backdrop to Childe's fall, though not a causal factor), the nuances of the site must be considered in order to establish its significance, its appeal, its terror and perhaps its ultimate pleasure, for an archaeologist who, from his distant home in London, appears to have selected the cliff line of the Blue Mountains as a place to die.

Several witnesses have reported that Childe's explorations in the Blue Mountains were motivated by a book he was writing on geology. As an explanation for these rambles, the story is somewhat odd. Childe, like any archaeologist, had a professional interest in the distribution of rocks and soils. His fascination with metal and metallurgy and his glorification of smiths as early travellers and conduits of social transformation (based on no more evidence than a line from Homer[96]) were emphasised in both his academic and more popular publications. Yet how he might have contributed to an understanding of Blue Mountains geology is less than clear. Travelling with notebook and sketch pad by foot and taxi, he had neither the resources nor the detailed knowledge to rival the geological specialists at work in the 1950s. This begs the question, then, of whether he was considering a work within his own discipline. Was he considering the archaeology of Aboriginal culture? Or could it be that the reported book was part of the ruse that would disguise his suicide? Is it like the map and compass at Luchetti Lookout, a sign both false yet full of meaning? Was it intended to raise the significance of geology in his symbolic world?

The section concerning Govetts Leap in a publication on Blue Mountains geology suggests the particular fascination of the Grose River Valley to an archaeologist.

The spectacular view from Govetts Leap is probably one of the most famous for its display of the deep mountain gorges. The bottom of the gorge is made up of Permian marine mudstones, and the lower slopes consist of the soft Permian coal measures. Overlying the coal measures are the very thick Triassic sandstones, forming the vertical cliffs.[93]

The title of this booklet, 'Layers of Time', encapsulates an elemental fascination. From the colonial era, visitors to the mountains have been dazzled by the splendour of temporal immensity. For Charles Darwin, a young man at the time of his visit in 1836, it represented a limit to the age of the Earth. He rejected the now-accepted theory that erosion formed the valleys, unable to 'fully appreciate the geological time span involved'.[94] Since then, the view has aged. Frank Hurley, addressing a popular audience in 1953, would write in colourful prose of erosion and time as 'those patient mills of Nature . . . grinding down the sandstone into grains'.[95] While evoking in such dramatic form the age or longevity of the Earth, the valleys with their layered strata from Permian, Triassic, Jurassic and Crustaceous periods symbolise not only the magnitude of earthly time but its orderly sequence of successive ages. D. J. Mulvaney characterised an archaeologist's point of view when he referred, in Childe's obituary, to the widespread faith in a 'single sequence of evolutionary progress from ape to Athens, akin to a geological sequence as read in rock strata'.[96] Although Mulvaney distanced his colleague from such simplistic linearity, Childe himself had evoked that sense of temporal layering when he argued in *Man Makes Himself* that geology and archaeology are the twin foundations of prehistory: 'Geology has traced the building up of the earth we inhabit; under the aspect of palaeontology it follows the emergence of various forms of life, through vast periods of geological time.'[97]

From such statements, it can be inferred that the dramatically stratified valley of the Grose had a very particular resonance in the philosophy of Gordon Childe. The space into which he threw himself was very much the abyss of time. Writing in the 1930s, that layering of geological sequence had suggested to Childe a methodology in which 'the historian's "progress" may be the equivalent of the zoologist's evolution'.[98] Such statements, read in the context of his final action, suggest the terms of his epistemological crisis. In 1957 when he came to smash himself, he would do so against the lowest strata.

~

the life of a man is of no greater importance to the universe than that
of an oyster

David Hume, *The Life of David Hume*, 1777

~

When Laila Haglund reminisced in *Antiquity* that listening to Childe in his
final days was 'like hovering over the continent and looking down in a godlike manner', she remarked on how 'much he wished to see done in
Australian prehistory'. In these final days this interest was expressed in
several forums. Six days before his death, he gave a 'Guest of Honour'
address for the Australian Broadcasting Commission in which he complained that Australia's prehistory was 'less well-studied in 1957' than
Europe's was in 1857. He also denounced the prejudice that 'The true
prelude to Australian history was written in the British Isles and Con-
tinental Europe, while the aborigines stagnated in illiterate savagery.'[99] To
H. V. Evatt's wife Mary he voiced concern that Aboriginal 'rock pictures'
ought to be conserved.[100] Yet somewhat inconsistently, D. J. Mulvaney,
speaking at the Childe Centennial Conference in 1992, has described his
meeting with Childe in Melbourne in the following terms: 'I was doing
my first excavation in Australia and had spread out all the stone tools. He
spent two minutes looking at them, and then wished me luck—he had
no interest in them whatsoever.'[101] Concordant with Childe's recorded
opinion on Australian archaeology—it's 'all horribly boring unless you're
a flint fan'[102]—this encounter is especially revealing. Mulvaney would
come to assume Childe's mantle as the best known of Australian archaeologists. But where Childe had gone to Britain and made his name in
European prehistory, Mulvaney had returned in the 1950s after postgraduate study at Cambridge, convinced his calling was in Australia. 'I
hankered after the Iron Age but knew I must return to Stone.'[103] Their
meeting, then, represents an auspicious crossroad. In the ensuing decades,
the excavations of Mulvaney and colleagues would establish the antiquity
of Aboriginal occupation, contributing to the political future of a people
derided by Childe in numerous publications as an evolutionary dead-end.

At the Childe Centennial Conference in London, the prehistorian
Colin Renfrew remarked in his summation on the mysterious sadness of

258

Childe's suicide, going on to observe that 'the almost unspoken question' of the proceedings was why Childe had so thoroughly ignored Australian Aborigines:

> whereas one might have thought that an interest in the indigenes of his homeland would have led him to hunter–gatherer studies, as it leads so many Australians today, and indeed leads so many archaeologists from all over the world to Australia, this was not the case for him.[104]

Childe made no endeavour to acknowledge, let alone enter, the world view of indigenous Australians. He barely gave them status as social actors. Bruce G. Trigger has described his position as one in which Aborigines 'evolved along "blind-alleys of superstition". Hence the "painful" rites and "puzzling", "incoherent" beliefs about totems found among such groups.' The slaves of mysticism rather than agents of reason, they never attained the 'peculiar vigour and genius'[105] that Childe discerned in Europeans.

Renfrew is substantially though not entirely correct when he argues that Childe avoided comparisons between Australian Aborigines and the hunter–gatherer societies of ancient Europe. Unarguably, the Aboriginal references in Childe's writing are extremely slight. But references, distinctive for their fleetingness, *do* exist in many of his publications. The practice is established in the opening lines of Childe's archaeological foray, *The Dawn of European Civilization* (1925):

> The material basis and spiritual context of modern life are the cumulative result of the achievements and discoveries of the past. Europeans share with the Chinese and even with the Aborigines of Australia a part of this cultural heritage.[106]

Sadly, Childe's oeuvre would never fulfil the promise of this vision-splendid where Europeans share with Chinese and Aborigines a common heritage. While his theorising did significantly complicate the technological history of early Europe, arguing that cultural transformation had arrived from elsewhere—diffusing along the Danube from the Near East[107]—'primitive' societies in general, Aboriginal in particular, were treated with increasing disparagement. His approach has been described by prehistorian Michael Rowlands as especially concerned with 'the development of reason as a core cultural value in the West'. He located its birth very deep in prehistoric time: 'A superstitious and magic-ridden Neolithic world was superseded, he claimed, by a rationalist Bronze Age dedicated to the development of science.'[108] The treatment of 'primitives' became ever less flattering in the build-up to his mysterious advocacy of Aboriginal prehistory in 1957. In *Social Evolution* (1951), 'the extinct Tasmanians' were described as 'the most backward of recent savages'.[109] In *Society and Knowledge* (1956), he would conjure the vision of 'a palaeolithic savage' whose 'physical equipment was comparable to that of the Arunta of Central Australia today, and his conceptual outfit may well have been similar'.[110] Shifting his tense to locate his subject firmly in the past, Childe claimed that the Arunta:

> could perceive, of course, that some sensation clusters were like his own body and others were not. But the names he learned did not emphasize this distinction. Among the Arunta the same name, translated 'black cockatoo', is equally applicable to birds, to men, and even to trees and rocks![111]

Of course, such vulgar phenomenology does no more than reduce and bastardise a language and culture that is very far from being crude or simplistic. But hunter–gatherer societies really were the blind spot in Childe's world view, symbolising a subordination to 'mysticism' that he found utterly abhorrent. This attitude was congruent with his materialist conception of history and was doubtless influenced by the considerable breach with his clergyman father.

Childe's notion of human development, as he explained in *Social Evolution*, was broadly concurrent with that expressed by Henry Lewis Morgan in 1877 which formed the inspiration for Engels' more famous work, *The Origin of the Family, Private Property and the State* (1884). Morgan had divided humanity into the three hierarchal stages of Savagery, Barbarism and Civilization, noting that traces of all three were extant in the 'human family' of his own age. Engels would reproduce this argument with particularly vivid imagery in discussing the Iroquois Indians:

> just as Cuvier could with certainty conclude, from the pouch bones of an animal skeleton found near Paris, that this belonged to a marsupial and that now extinct marsupials once lived there, so we,

with the same certainty, can conclude, from a historically transmitted system of consanguinity, that an extinct form of the family corresponding to it had once existed.[112]

In broad terms, Childe subscribed to the hierarchy of Savagery, Barbarism, Civilization—although he cautioned against the simplistic application of biological theory to human history, arguing that social evolution was not the unilinear process propagated by Soviet archaeologists for whom the influence of Engels was so very strong.[113]

Nor was Childe a social Darwinist. Indeed, he felt personally impelled to counter the propagandist misuse of racial stereotyping found in Nazist archaeology.[114] In his important address to the Prehistoric Society in 1935, certainly informed by the situation in Germany, Childe argued strongly against notions of racial purity, proposing that 'the science of genetics has exploded the old, simple conception of race'. Childe argued that physical uniformities in skeletons were the signs of 'prolonged isolation and inbreeding' and that racial mixture was a more typical sign of cultural vigour.[115]

Amidst such carefully framed arguments, his denigration of traditional, non-European societies still stands as an extraordinary anomaly in his social conscience. As human skeletons, living or extinct, they cast weird shadows in his textual Europe. Sometimes he might select African societies as atavistic exemplars of the 'primitive'. The Dinka and Shilluk people of the Sudan were described as a '"living museum" whose arrested social organizations illustrated early stages in the development of the ancient Egyptian civilization'.[116] But, in a gesture not entirely incidental, Australian Aborigines were more frequently preferred for such comparisons, serving in the work of this impersonal writer—'the most detached person I knew' (Jack Lindsay)—as oblique lines of anchorage between the textual Europe of his theorising and his place of birth.

~

What a thing is Man, this lauded demi-god! Does he not lack the very powers he has most need of? And if he should soar in joy, or sink in sorrow, is he not halted and returned to his cold, dull consciousness at the very moment he was longing to be lost in the vastness of infinity?

J. W. Goethe, *The Sorrows of the Young Werther*, 1774

~

261

Though retrograde skeletons warned of dead-ends, the European narrative of Childe's prehistory was one of progress. Born into a climate of confidence that the 'universe was moving forward towards new horizons',[117] it was typical of a scholar influenced by Marx to regard the unfolding of history as a developmental journey that would reach its highest level with the arrival of a socialist state. To Childe, archaeology could readily yield a 'science of progress' because tools and technology represented the basic element of study.[118] By scrutinising changes in artefacts, the prehistorian would detail a path of transition from one temporal order to the next.

While such a schema was implicit in the developmental structure of an early work like *The Dawn*, Childe's tableau of progress acquired urgency in the 1930s as he witnessed the rise of dictatorship with increasing trepidation. Although he had never been a card-carrying communist[119]—preferring to remain independent of the Party—Childe was privately dismayed by Stalin and his pact with Hitler. Trigger notes that the explicit purpose of Childe's two best-sellers, *Man Makes Himself* (1936) and *What Happened in History* (1942), was to encourage 'renewed faith in cultural progress'.[120] In 'Retrospect' Childe himself described *What Happened in History* as an attempt 'to convince myself that a Dark Age was not a bottomless cleft in which all traditions of culture were finally engulfed. (I was convinced at the time that European Civilization—Capitalist and Stalinist alike—was irrevocably heading for a Dark Age.)'[121]

For good reason, Childe was concerned for his personal safety as the 'Dark Age' loomed, convinced that his Marxist credentials would put him on the list for extermination if Hitler reached Britain. William J. Peace has documented how Childe made tentative preparations for emigrating to the United States, depositing a financial nest egg with a Boston bank in 1939. An American job, however, was not forthcoming and in August that year Childe expressed thoughts of suicide to Jack Lindsay, doubting he 'could be of any use in the forthcoming catastrophe:. . . a retreat into rather than across the Atlantic would seem most reasonable'.[122]

The grim reality of totalitarianism was the nemesis of Childe's confidence in social evolution. The reality of that bold socialist experiment, the Soviet Union, was taking grip of him; the horrors of

Nazism he understood and abhorred. The possibility that his grand vision of human development might come to an abrupt terminus is certainly implicit in his instruction to W. F. Grimes that the letter not be opened 'till January 1968 supposing that year ever arrives'. Trigger describes his intellectual position at the end of the war in the following way:

> Childe, now confronted by the spectre of the Atomic bomb, believed that there was no certainty that Western civilization would evolve in a rational manner, rather than vanishing like that of the Maya, or fossilizing like that of the Chinese.[123]

His despair at the state of the world worsened during the 1950s. Under the grip of the Cold War, the United States, to which he had previously considered emigrating, became hostile to his work. His slim volume *History* was regarded as politically unacceptable and rejected by several American publishers until Schuman Books finally bit the bullet in 1953, six years after its British release.[124] Amidst such trials was the Soviet invasion of Hungary in 1956 at which Childe was personally distressed, though he refused to sign a public letter deploring it because it 'would have given too much satisfaction to his life-long enemies'.[125] There is little doubt that these factors must have weighed heavily on his decision to suicide as it did for so many communists during this era when the dystopian reality of their utopian vision became blatantly evident. This is the specific dilemma explored in Frank Hardy's *But the Dead are Many* (1975), the most powerful novel in Australian literature to grapple with the suicide theme.[126] Indicative of a loss of faith on enormous scale, the communist predicament was sharply encapsulated in the title of Arthur Koestler's essay 'The God that Failed'.

In so many ways the postwar era brought a new world—a world for Childe that offered little hope. In the wake of the Hungarian invasion, he complained to his cousin, Alexander Gordon, that the 'world situation in 1956 is distinctly unpleasant—but probably not really worse than in 1956 B. C. say under Shulgi of Ur'.[127] In archaeology, Childe was witnessing the end of the era of the great syntheses that had made his name. Specialisation was taking over.[128] In the midst of this, the discipline was quivering at its own technological revolution, a by-product of atomic research, which would thoroughly explode Childe's speculative chronologies of European habitation. Green points out that

Childe did not live to see how extensively radiocarbon dating would shatter his schema. To judge by his last letter, and his subsequent fall, a temporal re-ordering of such immensity was something he never wished to see.

~

The sterility of the bourgeois world will end in suicide or a new form of creative participation.

Octavio Paz, *The Labyrinth of Solitude*, 1961

~

Anecdotes have been handed down of the Childe-ish professor, the outsider and maverick, enjoying a certain association between himself and the 'primitive'. Howard Kilbride-Jones remembered from Edinburgh days,

> the poster of the nude Australian aborigine, on whose head someone had sketched in outline the wide-brimmed hat: this poster was stuck on the wall of the library of the Society of Antiquaries of Scotland and left there for a week—a joke gone agley since Childe basked in the publicity it generated.[129]

There was also the occasion at the Institute of Archaeology in London when Childe declared, upon examining a newly commissioned bust of himself, that it looked like neanderthal man.[130] In 1956 on the occasion of his final lecture at the Institute, Childe acted out the association with a theatrical gesture. As seen in a sketch by Marjorie Maitland Howard, he appeared before his audience wearing Central Asian dress and brandishing an Aboriginal spear.[131]

Such incidents provide some picture of the man himself. Despite his shyness he enjoyed the limelight and could wear a joke. There is a danger, certainly, in over-interpreting such acts. Yet jokes can be incisively revealing—an insight to the teller, to the recipient, to the things at which we fear or laugh. There are jokes that can bring us closer; others, like those at Childe's expense on his final evening, that are simply cruel. If the power of a joke is to stretch an accepted order, elasticise a boundary, whether it be of credulity, good taste, language, politics or faith, then the odd gestures in which Childe assumed the mantle of the 'primitive'

264

do stand out as a point of tension. In a period of scholarship stretching back more than thirty years, phantasms of difference, of otherness, had been projected as so many cul-de-sacs within a historical landscape that a new science would ultimately 'prove' to be a work of the imagination. How might Childe's clownish identification with 'the other' relate to this?

At this point it is worth returning to Ernst Cassirer's volume on *Mythical Thought* which I quoted in Passage One. Cassirer insists that 'knowledge does not master myth by banishing it from its confines'. Myth, in contradistinction, is a founding principle. '[T]he actual point of departure for all science, the immediacy from which it starts, lies not so much in the sensory sphere as in the sphere of mythical intuition'.[132] Is it possible that Childe, as he watched his landscape begin to crumble in those final years, sensed something of Cassirer's message: that all along his science of humanity had been an act of faith?

We know nothing of his thoughts as he left the Carrington, hired Henry Newstead's cab and progressed along the highway to Govetts Leap. He said little. He smoked a lot. He walked the edge of the Grose River Valley, that mighty channel that almost drives a passage through the mountains, terminating at a cul-de-sac of cliffs. In a stratified landscape where temporal orders are all in order, he unfolded the map, unpacked the compass, surveyed a view in which a deathly gap separates the archaeologist from the deepest past.

In his own terms, perhaps to his own satisfaction, Childe had already rationalised his passing. His legacy, he hoped, had been established. He had no need for further time. In the chapter, 'My Beliefs', of *Society and Knowledge* (1956) he had written that

> Society is immortal but its members are born and die. Hence any idea accepted by Society and objectified is likewise immortal. In creating ideas that are thus accepted, any mortal member of Society attains immortality—yes, though his name be forgotten as completely as his bodily form dissolve. Personally I desire no more.[133]

Several ironies are evident in the terms employed by Childe to couch his death. While his legacy *is* substantial, with some of his methods attaining a certain 'immortality', many more are obsolete: significant but overgrown byways in a disciplinary history. Conversely, the curiosity

265

of his suicide—its ultimate statement on a way of thinking, a mode of being, a relation to the past, the future, the flow of time—make Childe's death a most enduring work. The man who at the dawn of his career had castigated the megalithic as a society in which 'the cult of the dead overshadowed all other activities' would inscribe his sundown with the following assertion: 'To end his life deliberately is in fact something that distinguishes *Homo sapiens* from other animals even better than ceremonial burial of the dead.' This became Childe's contribution to those essentiating categories that purport to define humanity. For many linguists it is the power of speech. For Lévi-Strauss we cook our meat. Childe's intellectual project might have placed him among those who believe that the transformation of nature through technology is the defining characteristic of human beings. But at the end of the day this was discarded. The ability to unmake himself became the quality that maketh man.

Freud claimed that the suicide is driven by 'murderous impulses against others re-directed upon himself'.[134] Although reductive, although so predictably Freudian, the connection between suicide and homicide retains value if only to emphasise the basic violence of taking any—even one's own—life. A retort that belies the nihilism of Childe's distinguishing human characteristic is that regard for the sanctity of life could just as easily be posed as the foundation of mortal endeavour. It is not the human but the animal that kills without question, kills without compassion. It is the human that questions the necessity of death, that knows the sheer banality of killing, that has, on occasion, made of that banality a monstrous perversion but in the process shown it for what it is.

If killing invokes the animal, to kill oneself invokes the god. Suicide is thus situated around the tension between the earthly and the divine. Camus turned his attention to the issue of suicide as part of a project that considered the absurd. While proof of the absurdity of life is everywhere apparent to one who looks for it, Camus discerned a special dilemma in the plight of 'modern man'. Absurdity, he argues, attains a pinnacle of acuteness when man surrenders to his own finitude; when the possibility of immortality is finally closed. In such a schema, where the world is rationalised to the extent that the only event beyond mortal control—the only 'act of God'—is the timing of one's death, it is only a minor leap, according to the absurd logic, to become the god and take one's life. Camus' *The Myth of Sisyphus* is an attempt to re-negotiate this line of reasoning. In the process, he contemplates the limit of rationality, quoting Karl Jaspers on the impossibility of constituting the world as a coherent unity.

> This limitation leads me to myself, where I can no longer withdraw behind an objective point of view that I am merely representing, where neither I myself nor the existence of others can any longer become an object for me.[135]

In considering the death of Childe, his wilful transformation from subject to object, I find myself at the site of his departure: a set of possessions sitting at the lookout; the body, shattered, lying below. The famous hat, emblazoned with the initials V. G. C., was left as calling card. The bifocal spectacles sat nearby. A map and compass, tools for his geological foray, would become instruments of a parodic science that mocked the investigative game of cause and effect. Finally there was the piece of paper, as Constable Morey recounted, with 'the words *Mount Banks, Mount Hay, Table Rock, Pulpit Rock*—they were all features in that vicinity and would all be clearly visible from that lookout'. The prismatic compass was open and Morey peered through the lens. Fortunately he knew his landmarks if not the possible significance of the landmark's name in the greater scheme. Whether it be a genealogical memento, an appeal from the son of a man of the cloth, or even a line of reference to some greater category, the possibility of which he would maintain in memory, none of us will know. But the compass was sighted on the feature known as Pulpit Rock.

Koestler's essay 'The God That Failed' narrates his experience of the Communist Party in the 1930s and his ultimate abandonment of the cause. It is a moving piece, especially relevant because Koestler also committed suicide, though his seems a clear case of euthanasia. His title and his opening assertion—'A faith is not acquired by reasoning'[136]—provide telling insight into the dilemma of those dialecticians like Childe for whom all that was solid melted into air. Like Childe, Koestler envisaged the loss of faith as an aerial descent, but unlike him—and here lies Childe's tragedy—he was able to survive it for a considerable period, to move on to something else, by negotiating that collapse in symbolic not physical form.

267

The tight-rope had snapped, but there was a safety net spread under it. When I landed there, I found myself in a mixed company—veteran acrobats who had lost their dialectical balance, Trotskyites, critical sympathizers, independent 'cryptos', new statesmen, new republicans, totalitarian liberals and so on—who were sprawling in the net in various contorted positions. We were all hellishly uncomfortable, suspended in no man's land, but at least we did not have to regard ourselves as completely fallen angels.[137]

For Koestler this was a state of 'suspended animation', an absurd position, certainly, floundering grotesquely in a congress of clowns. And yet that state of suspension did provide a certain way of coming to ground and in the process becoming something else.

Childe's reluctance to seek the safety net, his decision to step bleakly into the void, can be seen as an ultimate failure to acknowledge otherness; an otherness both beyond and within. It was otherness with which he toyed in holding a spear before his audience, but which, in the end, could only be a game. If otherness is only deadness—the brittle skeletons exhumed during his excavation of Skara Brae in Orkney— then the reality of otherness is one of mortal danger. To embrace it, to acknowledge its embeddedness within oneself, might lead to the embarrassment of uncertainty or clownishness but is, nonetheless, entirely necessary as a death-defying leap. That Childe's downfall concerns something greater and more pertinent to the contemporary world than the personal anguish of an ageing professor is emphasised by its connection with the disenchantment and eventual loss of the great liberating promise of the modern era. With this philosophy in tatters, what paths are open to its fundamental if elusive promise of a new world?

This question floats around the valley as Childe's body is carried up along the walking trail, the stretcher bearers relieving each other every hundred yards. It is a question for philosophy, but more than that a question of action; a challenge that must be lived in a theatre not of gesture but negotiation. For Camus hope is the essential ingredient for life without a Master—an ingredient he senses in the plight of the most extreme absurdity: the lot of Sisyphus, 'futile labourer of the underworld', whose eternal duty it is to roll 'a rock to the top of a mountain, whence the stone would fall back of its own weight'.[138] Certainly, hope is required to fly out in the face of gravity's inexorable logic.

I have often wondered whether a sense of hope could have somehow infused the sentiments of futility that Childe expressed in the build-up to his departure. A very strange experience—compelling evidence of how a research topic can reach out and envelop the researcher—makes me wonder whether there was indeed such hope. Having completed a draft of this passage, I posted it to Isabel McBryde, another eminent Australian archaeologist, who had expressed interest in my research. Upon reading it, she took up a pen to reply but was stopped by a phone call. It was Laila Haglund.

Thus I came to meet both Laila and Childe's hostess at Bathurst, Eve Stewart, who, well into her eighties, was living just a short walk from the Childe family home at Wentworth Falls. When I met her I was surprised to hear that, even in light of the letter to Grimes, she still does not believe Childe committed suicide. Certainly, he must have been thinking of it, she acknowledges, but the conclusion that he did so was the mischief of certain 'bigwigs' in London.

Laila Haglund is more circumspect, admitting that suicide was possible though hugely out of character with the man she had come to know. When I visited her at her home in the inner-Sydney suburb of Balmain, she uncorked a bottle of red wine and endeavoured to capture something of those conversations in Bathurst some forty-two years earlier. She emphasised that she was a young student when she met Childe. She had not yet read his work. He was a distant if illustrious name. As she remembers them, those brilliant evenings with their pipes were more monologues than conversations. It was as though Childe was thinking aloud, and although most of the detail has slipped through her fingers, she is convinced that much of what they spoke about was the book he intended to write about Australia. These investigations were not purely geological, as has been suggested, but were very much to do with Australian prehistory. When I expressed surprise at this, and pointed out how out of keeping it was with his published statements, she admitted that she too had been equally amazed when, in the years following his death, she read his work and encountered a position so divergent from what he expressed.

As we endeavoured to thrash this out, Haglund gave me one of my most important insights into how Childe, returning to Australia with decades of archaeology behind him, would have seen the country. For an archaeologist, she emphasised, it does not take much looking to find evidence of human habitation in the Australian bush. I was reminded again of that evocative comment by Eugene Stockton who has done the bulk of archaeological research in the Blue Mountains: 'As a teenager I began to find stones which did not belong to the geology of the area . . . Holding a stone tool in my hand I wondered at the last hand to grasp it: it was like a handshake across the centuries.'[139] I mentioned this to Laila and she told me that Eugene Stockton was a good friend. Recently he had entrusted to her his archaeological library which she considered an enormous honour.

The conversation returned to Childe, and she told me of his influence on her life. She decided, as a result of their friendship, that she would commit herself to the subject of Australian prehistory. He advised her on where to study and the skills she would need to learn. He judiciously warned her that on starting out she could expect no practical assistance whatsoever. Haglund became one of the first independent consultant archaeologists in Australia, part of a movement that would take the study of Aboriginal society in a very different direction from the rigid prescriptions of Childe's writings. Acknowledgment of the essential legitimacy of Aboriginal culture has brought about a significant and still ongoing transformation in the discipline of archaeology. My own recent experience of working in a team of cultural heritage practitioners has convinced me of the scale of this shift. The emphasis on digging and uprooting graves or other sites has been reconsidered. Aboriginal participation in archaeological survey has become standard, and the remains of post-contact sites—of places like the Gully in Katoomba—have been recognised for their historical and cultural significance. Far from determining the atavistic status of Aboriginal society, archaeological evidence can be vital in the process of returning land to traditional owners.

There, indeed, is cause for hope.

271

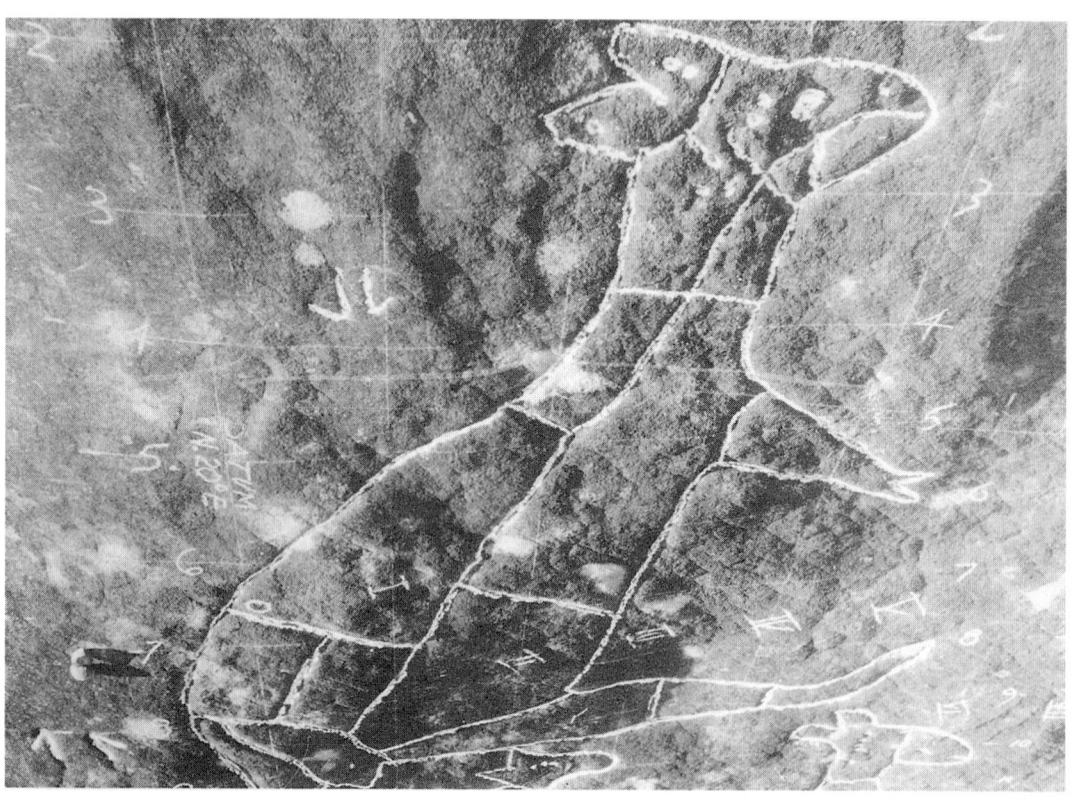

A POIGNANT EXPRESSION OF CONFLICTING CULTURAL VALUES. I FOUND THIS UNIDENTIFIED PHOTOGRAPH OF AN ABORIGINAL

ROCK ENGRAVING AT A FLEA MARKET. THERE IS NO EXPLANATORY INFORMATION, BUT THE KANGAROO HAS BEEN HIGHLIGHTED

WITH CHALK AND A GRID HAS BEEN SUPERIMPOSED OVER IT, EVIDENTLY FOR THE PURPOSE OF DOCUMENTATION.

CODA

Who gave us the sponge to wipe away the entire horizon?

FRIEDRICH NIETZSCHE, *Dawn*, 1881

I TWO
CAVES

ONCE YOU ADJUST to the not-so-difficult idea that to journey through history is to journey through time, something so simple as a walk through the bush becomes a temporal rather than a purely spatial digression.

So it was that on an afternoon in late December, a few days after Christmas, I met with a friend and we visited a district on the south-western fringe of Sydney that is sometimes referred to as the Cow-pastures. That the area should bear this name is due to one of the many agricultural hiccups that characterised the early years of European settlement in Australia: that time of failed crops in hostile soil and limited rations from a begrudging government in London. Among the livestock carried to Australia by Governor Phillip's fleet was a selection of domestic beasts that would become a food source for the colony. They included a bull, a bull-calf and five cows, one of which went mad and had to be shot. The six survivors, a wilful little herd of Afrikander cattle purchased when the fleet stopped at Capetown, had lived less than six months at the fledgling settlement of Sydney Cove when, in June 1788, 'either from not being properly secured, or from the negligence of those appointed to take care of them, [they] strayed into the woods'.[1] The cattle were considered lost until 1795 when two convicts, motivated by Aboriginal reports, travelled fifty kilometres from Sydney to discover a wild herd grazing on the plains country near the Nepean River.

These animals were the progeny and perhaps the remnants of the original escapees: tamed creatures gone feral—a familiar theme in the Australian imaginary where a varied selection of birds, plants, animals and people have broken the boundaries of domestication to run amok in that uncultivated domain we designate 'the bush'. The six Afrikanders evidently thrived on the heavily pastured lowlands and, over the ensuing decades, grew into a herd that numbered several thousand head. They feature as a distinct if minor theme in the annals of early settlement.

For the colonisers, an aura of ambiguous symbolism was attached to the feral herd. Too wild to be captured or handled, let alone trans-ported to town and slaughtered in the conventional manner, they rep-resented a potential but unmanageable food supply in a colony that for many years teetered on the brink of starvation. But a food supply that could not be harnessed was as good as useless—in fact, worse than useless in a penal settlement which was predicated on the regulation of movement. In 1795 Governor Hunter issued the first in a series of public orders promising the prosecution of anyone who chose 'to destroy or annoy' the cattle. Joseph Foveaux, a military officer, articulated the concern of the authorities when he wrote to Lord Castlereagh in London, warning that banditti might establish themselves in the adjacent hill country beyond 'the reach of controul [sic]' where the 'wild herds will supply a never failing source of subsistence'. Macquarie was forced to deploy guards to prevent access to the Cowpastures and in 1817 proclaimed the slaughter of wild cattle a capital offence.

Here was food unable to be consumed by the law-abiding populace. Yet it might be eaten by unauthorised mouths. In this respect the cattle represented a riddle, a problem. Yet to the capitalist mind the spectacle of domestic animals flourishing without human intervention was also a promise that hostile land might be converted to future wealth. For Hunter's successor, Governor King, the cattle offered the prospect of a personal fortune. Two of the original strays had been the property of Governor Phillip (the rest belonging to the government), who had bequeathed his one third share of the descendants to his successor. However, King never touched this gold. The highly bred horses and skilled stockmen required to muster and tame the beasts never existed during his governorship of New South Wales. But eventually resources were committed to containing the cattle. Macquarie pursued a policy of enclosure, driving the Afrikanders into fenced areas, and by the early 1820s most had been incorporated into government herds or banished to the mountains. As Jack Thompson and John Perkins have observed (in a short article from which much of this information has been drawn) the lessons gleaned from the management of the Cowpastures herd facilitated the development of an 'appropriate technology' that was 'applied in the expansion of settlement into the interior, a process in which cattle were to play a major role'.[2]

Quite a myriad of hopes, fears, dreams and realities were invested in those feral occupants of the Cowpastures—a reminder that animist imaginings were not the exclusive domain of Aborigines. The colonisation of Australia was contingent on a specific set of human–animal relationships. Horses carried the intruders, dogs accompanied them, pigs, cattle and sheep followed in their wake or, as we have seen, sometimes led the way. Although it is unusual for the authors cited above to describe stock horses as a form of 'technology', the metaphor has some value if it conveys the notion that relationships between humans and animals were central to social and economic life, just as so many lives today are shaped and influenced by machines. Perhaps insufficient attention has been paid to the role of animals in shaping the object-world of our pre-industrial ancestors, too little consideration of the processes involved in domesticating other living beings. As the story of Mirragan and Gurangatch demonstrates, Aboriginal Australians had totemic associations with animals. Early in life children were assigned a creature or other element of the cosmos that would remain their personal totem. For the Dharawal who shared territory on the Cowpastures with the Darug, it was taboo to consume their totem. To do so would be akin to cannibalism.[3] It is also pertinent that Aboriginal Australians had no domestic beasts apart from the dogs that had accompanied them on their migrations from the north. The wild animals of the bush were an integral part of spiritual life but never became the functionaries of human beings.

A preoccupation with the manifold meanings of those aberrant cattle might explain the motivation for my own passage through the bush on that December day. It was bushfire season and the forest was ready to explode at the slightest spark. We were passing through a tract of bushland in the vicinity of the Cowpastures looking for Bull Cave, a place where the Aborigines before their dislocation had drawn charcoal pictures of the Afrikander cattle. Having read about these in a journal article, it struck me as somehow important that I should view these drawings; that the prospect of observing an Aboriginal interpretation of the feral animals might assist in my project of trying to better understand the intercultural relations of colonial Australia.

Finding the cave turned out to be quite difficult. Vandalism of Aboriginal sites is so endemic that they are rarely signposted. Few residents of the Sydney metropolis would be aware that over 6000 such sites have been registered in the area and 30 000 throughout the state. A few have been demarcated public attractions and can thus be readily visited, while the rest have been left to people with local knowledge. Inevitably, such a policy is of limited efficacy. The National Parks officer who I had consulted about the rock shelter we were seeking had warned me that, although a steel grille had been installed to protect the images, they had recently been defaced by some spray paint-wielding graffitists.

I had with me a printed description that located the site but found it was useless without a topographical map which I'd neglected to bring. After stumbling about for some time in the undergrowth, uncertain whether we were on the correct side of a dehydrated creek—

the only familiar landmark we could identify from the description—we heard some voices and climbed up to a walking track where a young couple, aged perhaps twenty, were taking an afternoon stroll. He was a tall youth with dark hair and olive skin and she was short, with a round face, and her head was covered. They were obviously Moslem. I asked them whether they knew the whereabouts of a cave with Aboriginal drawings, to which he replied yes, that they were going there themselves and that he would happily show us the way. We gratefully accompanied them and within a few minutes had been led up the hill to a small opening in the sandstone that someone had partially covered with branches in an attempt at concealment. We used a second, uncovered entrance—the cave formed a narrow tunnel—and crawled into the darkened cavity.

I quickly realised that it was not Bull Cave at all, but another of the many Aboriginal sites in what was once a frequently inhabited area. The little gully, abundant with rock shelters, had obviously been highly favoured by the Aboriginal communities at a time when the creek's catchment was undisturbed and it would have flowed more generously. The walls of the cave were decorated with red hand stencils. These markings, common throughout much of Australia, were created by blowing an ochre-based pigment against a hand placed on the rock. A little educated guesswork suggested that we had come to a place of great significance. Gavin Andrews, a National Parks officer with responsibility for Aboriginal cultural heritage and himself of Dharawal lineage, had told me that while white hand prints on rock were often associated with death, red prints, which he described as 'signatures', symbolised blood or life and would often mark the birthplace of the print-maker. Among the signatures we found an impression of childhood: a tiny hand print, ten centimetres in length, dwarfed by the surrounding adult ones. Guided by Gavin Andrews' comment about the red hands, I surmised that this could have been a birthing cave, a hypothesis supported by what I understand of the strict gender divisions that operate in Aboriginal communities. According to the anthropologists Ronald and Catherine Berndt, birth would 'take place outside the main camp in a special shelter or wind-break'.[4] I realise that my birthplace theory is speculative but it does seem to fit with the overall topography of the area. The shelter was too small for a family or clan to inhabit but it would have functioned admirably as an intimate space where the pregnant woman, accompanied by her mother, sisters or female friends, could have the necessary privacy to bring her child into the world. The entrance to the cave was streaked with smoke, perhaps the residue of fires kindled for night-time vigils.

My senses were bombarded with light as I left the cave's cool interior and the dry forest assumed the washed-out, slightly unreal appearance of an over-exposed photograph. More vivid than this pale exterior were my impressions of the smeared smoke and ochre outlines—minimal remains of lives once lived—which seemed to urge an imagining of originary moments, the occasions when earth and spittle, borne by breath, had captured the transient conjunctions of hand and rock. Yet such imaginings, once awoken, seem compromised by the sharp juxtaposition of marks of presence and conditions of absence. (These, you might remember, were the sensations that provoked this project.)

I watched the Moslem man replace the leaf litter we had disturbed, and he spoke with great conviction about his excitement at having recently found this place and that his only hope was that no one would damage it. We urged them to help us find Bull Cave but they said they had to go home, and once more my friend and I began combing the sandstone ledges.

This time we tried the eastern bank of the creek, and coming upon a line of low, overhanging cliffs that looked decidedly promising, we followed them until we saw in the distance a rusted steel grid that covered the gaping mouth of Bull Cave. Despite Gavin Andrews' warning that the site had been damaged, I was completely unprepared for the spectacle that awaited. The graffitists, having broken the barricade, used red paint to scrawl messages and pictures across the interior of the cave, partially covering the cattle, ochre hand prints and other markings left by the Aboriginal owners. The overwriting included: 'this is Bullshit', 'fuck off', 'ACDC' (a reference to the heavy-metal rock group), the profile of a smiling face, a cock-and-balls symbol, a peace sign and, most bizarrely, the 'signatures' of the intruders who had placed their own hands upon the rock and sprayed over them with red aerosol, mimicking the Aboriginal method.

We travelled through a lot of time that afternoon. Times past: ochre blown against a hand, wandering cattle, spray paint used for irreverent deeds. Future times: forks in the labyrinth of Chronos. Two caves: damaged and undamaged, respected and disrespected. A maze of alternative futures.

THE ROCK SHELTERS we encountered on that dry December day remind me of the contrasting views I described in the early pages. There was the view to the Blue Mountains from Mount Wilberforce Lookout and the view to the city which I associate with the future, seen from Dame Mary Gilmore Park. The two vistas represent a forked passageway, a prospect of bifurcation. This might explain why, in seeking to evoke the hieroglyph that is the landscape of the Blue Mountains, I was so captivated by those recurring references to the labyrinth.

Reviewing the twists and turns that make up this collection of passageways—a personal attempt to engage imaginatively with the country that produced me—I return to the initial problem that underlies these enquiries: how to draw a history out of dreams? This question, with all its methodological challenges, seems particularly urgent because the dilemmas associated with the habitation of colonised territory—the disjunctions and ruptures that will frustrate though ultimately modulate any attempt to find communion with the spirit of this place—cannot be resolved through recourse to an entirely materialist approach to history. To regard as a totality what is only a partial means of apprehending truth is to negate the flow of life in its constant variegation—to experience the dilemma of Gordon Childe. In approaching the landscape as a dreamscape, my attention turned to the morphology of myth. I became convinced that this collective mode of singing the country would permit access to experiences, both actual and anticipated, that might at one level open up the tensions and aspirations that underlie the meeting of the coloniser and the colonised while permitting a mode of exposition that is itself a process of encounter.

The image of the artificial horizon provided an opening to a project that might be seen as a series of lenses which provide varying foci on the politics and poetics of reflection. Here was an object of considerable richness that could be regarded in its practical sense as a mechanism that brings the heavens down to earth, levelling the irregular world, while providing a metaphor for the dreams evoked by the view to the horizon—the reality that our perceptions are the product of artifice. There were specific reasons for allowing a scientific instrument to serve as such a central metaphor in a study of myth. They include, but go far beyond, Blaxland's rather puzzling request that Macquarie lend him an artificial horizon. The point at which this study departs radically from celebrators of myth such as Joseph Campbell is my conviction that for all the 'timeless' or 'universal' concerns that are the stuff of myth, its ability to convey meaning is contingent on the cultural specificity, the temporal uniqueness, of the moment at which it appears. To work effectively as a mythographer required close attention to histories of perception and theories of knowledge. Inevitably, given the intellectual currents of the period discussed, my interest includes the legacy of science.

Hence the concern with surveying and instrumentation, with numerical systems that anticipate or defer infinitude, with the natural history museum of Melbourne Ward, and the endeavour of Childe to make 'the study of man as nearly a science as perhaps that wayward subject admits'. While disrupting the demarcation that is often drawn between myth and science, demonstrating how they bleed into and infuse each other, I hope that my exposition—a set of lenses, certainly, but lenses focused on a series of reflections—has opened certain possibilities for cultural study.

Was it an image exactly or was it a *tendency* I discerned in the history of modernity that influenced the physical arrangement of these passageways, these digressions? It seemed that the enduring significance of the myth of the labyrinth in an age of science was connected with the mystery of mortality—that troubling reality which Western medicine might defer but which science as a project has done little to explain. Death is still the domain of myth. In Passage One I cited a paragraph from Thomas Hardy's *The Return of the Native*, an observation concerning landscape in an age of industrialisation which remarked on the incubation of a 'recently learnt emotion' that would force a re-definition of beauty in nature. Egdon Heath is the locale for Hardy's tragedy: 'a place perfectly accordant with man's nature—neither ghastly, hateful, nor ugly: neither commonplace, unmeaning, nor tame; but, like man, slighted and enduring; and withal singularly colossal and mysterious in its swarthy monotony'. Egdon Moor is crowned by a 'bossy projection of earth above its natural level'—a Celtic barrow or burial mound—which 'formed the pole and axis of this heathery world'.[5] In the opening pages an itinerant reddleman spies a female figure rising from the crest of this 'semi-globular mound like a spike from a helmet' who turns out to be Eustacia, the *femme fatale* of the novel. Rainbarrow, as it is known among the locals, forms the central stage in Hardy's drama, a bleak icon that serves as a perennial reminder that these contemporary events are shaped and swayed by the remnants of the pagan dead. As a series of flawed and ultimately tragic passions embroil the protagonists in the story, and Eustacia is increasingly regarded as a witch among the occupants of the moor, Hardy develops a theme in which premature death is the legacy of an unreconciled past.

Early in the book I charted a set of conjunctions in the colonial imaginary: the frequency with which the Aboriginal Australian has been positioned as the figure of death within the landscape and the tendency for the phenomenon of death to mark a place in the labyrinth. This association between death and otherness seemed the most frightening and ultimately the most untenable aspect of European imaginings in the colonial context. Although I have not cited it until now, a passage from the Russian critic M. M. Bakhtin profoundly flavoured my exposition. Inspired by the compassion with which Dostoyevsky could give life to even the most grotesque characters, Bakhtin proposed that

> I achieve self-consciousness, I become myself only by revealing myself to another, through another and with another's help. The most important acts, constitutive of self-consciousness, are determined by their relation to another consciousness (a 'thou'). Cutting oneself off, isolating oneself, closing oneself off, those are the basic reasons for loss of self. . . . The very being of man (both internal and external) is a *profound communication. To be* means to *communicate.*[6]

Led by this comment, which seemed to echo Octavio Paz's succinct warning that the 'sterility of the bourgeois world will end in suicide or a new form of creative participation', I structured this work as a journey through a labyrinth that would encounter the spectre of death in varying guises (the snake and the Aboriginal man, the convict corpses in sight of the mountains, the stony sentinels of petrified women, the skulls in Ward's museum), coming at last to the figure of Childe on the clifftop, the consummate image of 'private man', whose course of action emphasised the unsustainability of the gulf between self and other.

But I could not end there as first intended. Hence this coda. There is too much life running through the labyrinth to allow the gesture of suicide to be the final act. As Emmanuel Levinas has written, 'there is a vocation of an existing-for-the-other stronger than the threat of death'.[7]

281

In thinking about the capacity to embrace otherness and its eventual abandonment as a distinction, the connections between the world and oneself must be heightened. To experience the cosmos in totemic form one must acknowledge the environment, the landscape and especially the animal within. The memory of those cattle who escaped domestication, their images inscribed among the hand prints in an Aboriginal shelter, runs contrary to the logic of the Theseus story, a tale of admonition in which the Minotaur, a creature both human and animal, is banished and eventually destroyed. I have already drawn a contrast between this narrative and the foundational chase of Mirragan and Gurangatch, recounted by Gundungurra informants around 1900, where the feats of the Burringilling—creatures both human and animal—carve out the southern Blue Mountains landscape. It is salutary to realise that the logic of this story has a certain resonance in the folklore of those Blue Mountains residents who lived their lives not on the plateaus but in the valleys of the Megalong, the Burragorang, the Kanimbla—working as farmers along the rivers created in the course of Mirragan and Gurangatch's mythic chase.

This is another story of pursuit, related by Bernard O'Reilly who lived his early years in the Kanimbla Valley. (His family later pioneered the Lamington Plateau in southern Queensland where Bernard shot to national fame in 1937 for having, in almost miraculous circumstances, located the survivors of a plane crash who were stranded in the rainforest.) The story appears in a book called *Cullenbenbong* (1944) and it concerns a wild stallion known as Cronje, named after the Boer guerrilla general who long evaded capture. He is described as 'the last of a long line of high-blooded rebel stallions which for seventy years were lords of the great, uninhabited mountain region away to the south'.[8] Three generations of settlers had tried to expunge the horses, but

> Like the bad brigands which they were, they swooped down from their mountain eyries at night while the peaceful settlement slept— swiftly they struck, killing quiet horses to left and right and then before the settlers could take their Sniders down from the racks they'd be gone, carrying off valuable mares back to their strongholds.

Although Cronje and his pack of wild horses (or brumbies) were the bane of the Kanimbla settlers, he was such a magnificent creature that though men sometimes had him cold over the sights of their rifles, their bushman's love of a splendid horse would not let them pull their triggers, even though this be a killer and a menace. They swore instead that they would capture him alive or die in the attempt—one did.

O'Reilly, born in 1903, did not participate in the extraordinary series of chases in which the young men of the district attempted to capture Cronje so they could break him in and possess what was certainly one of the finest stallions in Australia. He dates these exploits as occurring in the 1880s. They were well and truly the stuff of legend by the time 'a small red headed boy' listened at the hearth 'while old men lived their purple hours over again'.

The first attempt to capture Cronje started near Jenolan Caves where the brumbies had been sighted. The stockmen conceived a plan where riders would chase the pack to a landmark known as Alum Gap which led into the settled district of Cullenbenbong Creek. Relays of men on fresh horses were posted at various points along the route and at Alum Gap itself a double line was positioned funnel fashion to drive Cronje and his cohorts through the pass. The chase proceeded according to plan until they reached the funnel at Alum Gap where

Cronje suddenly knew there was something wrong, and all his wild instinct told him that once down that gap there would be no return. He plunged to a dead stop from the top of his wild gallop, propping his front legs stiffly as his hooves ploughed up the loose rocks, then he turned and rushed the runners, straight into a murderous barrage of stockwhips.

Although one rider, young Pat Cullen of Cullenbenbong Creek, anticipated Cronje's about-face and almost headed it off, his horse plunged into a wombat burrow and Cronje cleared the fallen beast and 'crashed off around the mountain side, rocks from his flying hooves rolling into the gorge two thousand feet below'. Far from being discouraged the men were even more determined 'that an animal of such speed and stamina should not waste his life in the ranges'.

Subsequent attempts followed, all fairly similar. They successfully drove him into a stockyard, built for that purpose.

He was like a great wave which rushes into a rock walled inlet and leaps at the black cliffs to fall back and leap again. He was a mighty dynamic power a thousand times too great for the small space in which he was locked. It was like the fury of a thunderstorm confined to four walls. It became a question of whether the fence would break or the horse would dash himself to pieces, and then there was a crash and a splintering of rails, the defiant blast of his whistle, the flash of mirrored backs in the dappled sunlight, and Cronje led his wild mob to freedom.

Next they tried to drive him into the Lockup, 'a cliffwalled valley with a bottle neck entrance' west of the Great Divide. They almost succeeded but Cronje must have known his liberty would be 'gone forever, and this led him to do the most desperate deed in the whole history of brumby running'. He turned and rushed at a solid wall of horses and men.

They yelled as one man, but Cronje came on, straight into the hail of stockwhips with never a faltering stride, and then with one mad, magnificent leap—a leap so high that his hooves brushed the ears of the men on either side—he cleared two horses side by side, and went thundering off into the ranges, as wild and free as the wind in the turpentines.

They made one last attempt to catch him. This time they would drive him into a cliff-locked gorge near Jenolan called the Pit of Hell. There they would 'yard him at their leisure when his panic and fury subsided'. The run was a long one and the chasers were well prepared. After two miles Cronje abandoned his mob and ran solo.

Unhampered by his string, all his brilliance came into play. He had the flashing speed of a swallow and the subtle knowledge of an old fox, and at bay he was as dangerous as a Bengal tiger. All the hereditary instinct and cunning, all the speed and endurance born of generations of running were incarnate in one supreme wild horse, Cronje.

Their attempt to drive him into the Pit of Hell was as futile as all the others, but in evading the entrance Cronje fled to the top of a plateau, running 'knee deep through acres of purple boronia and snowy flannel flowers, along the cliff edges where endless billows of mighty ranges stretched into the blue distance'. The men would follow him until he dropped.

The dilemma of Cronje was the dilemma of Jedda and Marbuk, a choice between captivity and the void. He 'ran blindly to the cliffs, then turned to find himself trapped'.

> He trotted back to the cliff, stamped and whistled, tossed his mane proudly and then plunged; his body flashed in a beautiful arc and disappeared into the blue air beyond the cliff rim. With a cry of agony and horror the men rushed to the edge and looked over. Cronje had landed lightly as a rock wallaby on a narrow ledge over twelve feet below, but now they held their breaths as he leaped for a narrower ledge lower down. He landed with four feet stiffly propped, and rocks from his hard feet spun out into the gorge. Slowly he worked to where the ledge ended and gave on to an almost perpendicular slope of loose rock particles like alpine scree.

Against all odds, Cronje leapt and danced his way down the scree slope. A rockslide was set in motion by his weight. Bounding down the moving surface, he struck firm ground. His pursuers looked on while 'the whole mountain side which he had traversed was a running river of rock'. Eventually Tom Boyle broke the silence with the following words: '"Goodbye old cove, we will never run you again." And they never did.' O'Reilly relates that Cronje escaped the great bushfire of 1903 and made his way to the head of the Kowmung River. 'There he was seen years later, still as free as the mountain winds.'

Cronje's phenomenal escape and the eventual acknowledgment by the settlers that he would remain forever uncaught and untamed recalls the fate of the wayward Afrikander cattle. Macquarie reported that 237 very fine wild cattle had been reclaimed to government herds in 1820, and a further 872 in 1822. But it is known that the wild herd was considerably larger than this. The policy of enclosure and the often unauthorised practice of hunting the feral breed 'had the effect of driving many of them to seek areas distant from human molestation in the rugged valleys of the Blue Mountains and their spurs'. The judge and historian R. Else Mitchell set out on a quest to locate the herd in the 1930s, searching the area around Kanangra Walls and Mount Guougong.

> Although Mitchell saw only six beasts, he thought their numbers were much more substantial. Those seen were of gigantic proportions, mainly of a rich red brown colour with very glossy hides. They quickly fled and took to the hillsides. The party cornered one in the brushwood and examined it from a distance of from 20 to

285

30 yards. Its horns were long and curled as Highland cattle are depicted in old drawings; the hips were prominent and protruded considerably. Mitchell concluded that they were almost certainly descendants of the wild cattle of the Cowpastures.[9]

A question thus arises. Are the descendants of the First Fleet cattle still running wild in the Blue Mountains? That feral cattle live near the Kowmung River in Kanangra-Boyd National Park is well established. The National Parks and Wildlife Service of New South Wales shot 84 between September 1997 and February 1998.[10] The policy of attempting to eliminate all non-indigenous fauna is associated with the desire to manage the Kowmung as a 'wilderness' area. This is a matter of grave concern to Steve Johnston, a nearby resident and member of the Kowmung Wild Cattle Committee, who argues that research must be carried out to establish whether or not the cattle are Afrikanders and thus of significant heritage value.

The destruction of the cattle raises the question of when—if ever —the environmental ethos will acknowledge a foreign creature as a legitimate inhabitant of the Australian landscape. When I met Steve Johnston, a horse and cattle man who goes by the name of 'Avalanche', he showed me his file of information on the wild cattle of the Cowpastures. I took out some photos of Bull Cave, bringing the site to his attention. By way of exchange he showed me a photo of another cave, also adorned with Aboriginal markings. It is called the Livery Stable, located in the Gardens of Stone National Park north of Lithgow, and in the nineteenth century it was the refuge for bushrangers, Captain Starlight and his gang, who once stole a fine horse called the Duke of Athol. To celebrate their prize they inscribed in charcoal an image of the stallion. Another horse was drawn beside it. The two drawings partially obscured a series of Aboriginal figures painted in red ochre.

Avalanche told me a story concerning the management of the cave. A group of white conservators, supervised by an Aboriginal elder, turned up one day to remove graffiti. They had erased one charcoal horse and were beginning on the second when the elder queried what they were doing.

'You've had that for a hundred years,' he said. 'Remove it now and what will you have in forty thousand years' time?'

So one black stallion remains, vividly symbolising how the signs of oneself might be absorbed or simply acknowledged by another.

286

THE ABORIGINAL DRAWINGS in Bull Cave have been literally fucked over. A bulging, upright penis, spray-painted in red, expresses with cartoon clarity the persistence of a particularly troubling strain of violence. In this depiction of the penis, the sexual act—potentially an act of communion—becomes blatantly expressive of contempt. The phallus is used as a conduit for aggression and rape forms a medium of exchange. Yet even here a lesson might be drawn. The two sets of inscriptions clearly demonstrate that even where their relationship is acrimonious, the delineation between Western and Aboriginal cultures is not so terribly clear-cut. Both sets of artists have expressed themselves through signs of the other.

For this reason I'm compelled, in interpreting the site, to resist the temptation of looking *beyond* the graffiti. To envisage a pristine set of Dharawal drawings is nothing less than a delusion. The site, in all its present ugliness, is representative of a social condition. The vandalism is typical of an imaginative trajectory that still regards the Aboriginal body as virgin territory, as land that has yet to be invaded.

My own experience of Aboriginal sites around Sydney suggests that their history, if described in its complexity, would necessitate an archaeology of vandalism. Generations of colonisers have smashed glass, etched their initials, painted slogans or done imitative drawings upon or alongside Aboriginal inscriptions. The colonial history has transformed these sites, often in weird or tragic ways. I have visited a place in the Blue Mountains where the outline of a kangaroo is engraved on a smooth platform of sandstone. Carved footprints lead away from the animal—towards what? It's impossible to know. They terminate at an unnatural drop, the beginning of a quarry where rock was extracted by convict labourers to build a guard tower. When David Campbell wrote his poems about Aboriginal sites in the 1960s he too was forced to deal with this phenomenon. Observing a rock engraving that had been bisected by the excavation for a septic tank, he sardonically observed that 'a Picasso may yet be used to bung a hole'.[11]

So Bull Cave, like any site, must be regarded as a work-in-progress. Only then can its diverse meanings be appreciated. This rock shelter has a long history of visitation which continues through the post-contact era. Earlier graffiti, some of which has been removed, is said to date from European occupation of the cave during the Great

Depression.[12] David Campbell, when he visited, was struck by the continuing sense of dialogue engendered by the site:

In Peter Meadows Creek sun orchids shine.
Lovers came to Bull Cave
And wrote their simple histories: *Lynette was here*;
And in faint charcoal: *My friend was murdered by blacks*.[13]

It might be argued that Bull Cave was a complicated (though still retrievable) site of wreckage when, in 1993, it was entered and sprayed in red automotive paint, one of the most indelible on the market. No solvent has yet been found that will remove it without destroying the other images.

I describe it as a site of wreckage, however, because the wire mesh that bars the cave is, to my mind, a more profound violation than the red paint. It was constructed in 1982 with the financial aid of a federal body, the Australian Heritage Commission.[14] The most basic quality of the site, that it forms a natural shelter, is thus denied. The cave is reduced to spectacle and has to be experienced through the impediment of a metal grid. The Afrikander cattle, creatures that escaped, are now locked and double locked within a violated pictorial surface. Two cattle are discernible but only one is sufficiently unobscured to permit close observation. Its form is elongated, the snout forms a sharp point. Originally, it appears, they were painted in ochre. Later they were retouched in charcoal. Was this done by an Aboriginal artist or someone else? The penis or prepuce is visible and the head is hornless. The latter detail permits an accurate dating of the drawing. It was almost certainly inspired by the herd that escaped in 1788 and not their descendants. In transporting them from the Cape it is likely that the horns of the first Afrikanders (unlike their wild offspring) had been removed.

It is tempting to consider how the observers of these first cattle might have described them as they watched them grazing or marked their outlines in the cave. What word would they have used to describe them, and what word for the alien beings that brought them here? Perhaps no one knows. The Aboriginal languages of Sydney have been largely lost. This is part of the semantic gulf that haunts the occupation of this continent. Sometimes just a few bastardised place names are all that remain of a language. The implications of this loss affect us all. We are

deprived of the most finely tuned terminology concerning the specificity of place, the specificity of ourselves. For strangest of all is that there
is no word for the newcomers, the arriving people, in the public lexicon
of Australia. When using conventional terms such as 'British', 'European',
'white' or the increasingly common 'non-Aboriginal', I'm constantly
aware of their reductiveness, their failure to embrace the diversity of a
migrant society. They shirk the fundamental problem that in order to
arrive somewhere, and I mean *really* arrive, one must see oneself through
the eyes of another.

It's a sign of some hope that attempts are being made to fill this
lacuna. *Yarmul: For the Lies We Sing* is a long, dialogic poem by Chris
Mansell which deals with this issue directly. In establishing a polyphonic
movement between outsiders—the 'aliens too bereft to speak'—and
some Wiradjuri people of New South Wales with whom she has spent
time, she resolved the problem of locating herself (a 'non-Aboriginal')
by using the Aboriginal term *Gubba*.[15] This word has a fascinating
lineage, thought to be a corruption of 'government', although in the
Blue Mountains, as Bernard O'Reilly recalled, it was also a word for evil
spirits or devils.[16] Perhaps it is indigenous or perhaps it is one of our
words. Maybe it is both.

A notion of Gubbahood or something like it is necessary for the
retrieval of Bull Cave from its present state. Some day in the future it
might stand uncaged, no longer prone to acts of racist aggression. With
its curious mirroring of signs—pictures of cattle, the word 'bullshit'; a
penis on the bull, a cock and balls symbol; hands stencilled in both ochre
and spray paint—the harmonious potential of mimicry, of doing
something in the manner of someone else for no other reason than
because *that is their way*, is violated. Mimicry equals ridicule under this
rubric.

But to merely complain about the bigotry of the Bull Cave graffitists would negate the complexity of *their* semiotic gestures. What
'bullshit' are they referring to? Who is being told to 'fuck off'? Is it the
Dharawal or Darug (who still visit the site) or is it the caged entrance, a
mark of prohibition that is most resented? There's a boulder some metres
from the cave where an ochre signature of life stands unbarred and un-
molested. Perhaps the physical barrier of the wire grill is emblematic of
an internal barrier—the demarcation between outer and inner self. The

great and no doubt intended irony of the graffitists' gesture is that the mesh is now repaired and their markings interred in the same cage as those they cover.

Hovering around Bull Cave are questions of insoluble difficulty. Aboriginal markings are not static or complete objects. Their continued existence traditionally depended on touching up, re-engraving, over-inscribing and ongoing maintenance. Hand prints, like their makers, would eventually perish; new hands and new lives must replace them. Without traditional maintenance, the Aboriginal art sites in the Sydney region are fading away. Is that an appropriate outcome given that the system that produced them is no longer operative? Should they be re-touched in simulation of that system, or should they be placed under glass?

Of course there are no right answers to these questions, and it would be mistaken to think that the problems they stem from can be resolved within the representations themselves. Just as the dreaming state will reflect the actions of the awoken consciousness, the cultural trace, in its humble materiality, is a pale reflection of the social exchanges that form the basis of interactive life.

Such thoughts preoccupy me as I walk along the ridge above the cave and look about me at a place that is and is not mine. How to account for the Gubba legacy, the immediate one—this country between escarpment and ocean? I am walking through the Cowpastures by the river Nepean which becomes the Hawkesbury where another cave I know, secret and undamaged, bears a charcoal outline of a sailing ship and beside it the white hand stencils of death. The Hawkesbury meets the ocean at Broken Bay and from there you go south to find the metropolis, the city of Sydney, spilling out from the harbour, spilling to the north and south and towards—I can see them now—the westerly line of plateaus, 'a bluish curtain, rising but little above the horizon, and preserving a considerable uniformity'.[17]

Notes

Introduction

1. T. Mitchell, in 'Report from the Commissioners', p. 1.
2. Mitchell, *Field, note and sketch book 1828–1830*. Unless stated, this is the source for remaining quotes from Mitchell.
3. Mitchell, *Three Expeditions*, vol. II.
4. Péron, *A Voyage of Discovery*, p. 286.
5. Barrell, *The dark side of the landscape*, p. 22.
6. Baker, *The Civilised Surveyor*.
7. Meredith, *The Last Kooradgie*, p. 15.
8. Werriberrie, *My Recollections*, p. 9.
9. Mitchell, *Three Expeditions*, vol. I, p. 242.
10. Ibid., pp. 239–40.
11. Stockton, *Blue Mountains Dreaming*, p. 5.
12. Eugène von Guérard, *Weather Board Creek Falls, Jamiesons Valley, New South Wales* (1862). Collection of the National Gallery of Victoria, Melbourne.
13. Clare, *Bodgie Dada & the Cult of Cool*, p. 119.

Passage One

1. Webster, *Metallographia*, p. 311.
2. Oxley, *Journals of Two Expeditions*, pp. 31, 153.
3. Blaxland to Banks, 10 November 1816, in Richards (ed.), *Blaxland—Lawson—Wentworth*, p. 150.
4. Perry, *Australia's First Frontier*, p. 29.
5. Cited in Houison, 'John and Gregory Blaxland', p. 10.
6. Macquarie to Bathurst, 28 April 1814, *HRA* series I, vol. VIII, p. 150.
7. *The Edge* publicity kit, March 1996.
8. Introduction to Thomas (ed.), *Uncertain Ground*, p. 12.
9. New South Wales National Parks and Wildlife Service, *The Greater Blue Mountains Area World Heritage Nomination*.
10. Rothenberg, 'Indians & Wilderness', p. 11.
11. Jackson, *A Sense of Place*, p. 76.

12. Cited by D. Foster, 'A Walk in the Southern Blue Mountains', p. 196.
13. Langton, 'What do we mean by wilderness?'.
14. Rose, *Nourishing Terrains*, p. 19.
15. Tape recording by J. Barker in Thomas, *This is Jimmie Barker*.
16. Benjamin, 'Theses on the Philosophy of History', p. 255.
17. W. Mitchell, 'Imperial landscape' in *Landscape and Power*, p. 10.
18. Moffatt, *Fever Pitch*, p. 6.
19. Gurr & Harrowsmith, *Blue Mountains Story*, p. 2.
20. Gilmore, *Old Days: Old Ways*, p. 84.
21. Clark, *A History of Australia I*, p. 169.
22. Cited in Currey (ed.), *Reflections on the Colony of New South Wales*, p. 49.
23. 'Samuel Marsden', *ADB*.
24. D. Foster, *The Glade within the Grove*, pp. 33, 31, 35.
25. Evans, 'Evans's Journal' in Mackaness (ed.), *Fourteen Journeys*, p. 21.
26. Macquarie to Cox in Anon., *Memoirs of William Cox*, p. 50.
27. Whitaker, 'The Convicts who Conquered the Blue Mountains', p. 2.
28. 'Journal kept by Mr. W. Cox' in Anon., *Memoirs of William Cox*, p. 62.
29. Cited in W. Foster, *Sir Thomas Livingston Mitchell*, p. 440.
30. Hawkins, 'Journey from Sydney to Bathurst' in Mackaness, *Fourteen Journeys*, p. 106.
31. See Speirs, *Landscape Art and the Blue Mountains*.
32. Hawkins, 'Journey from Sydney to Bathurst', p. 110.
33. Blaxland, *A Journal of a Tour of Discovery* in Richards, *Blaxland—Lawson—Wentworth*, p. 72.
34. Macquarie, 'Tour over the Western or Blue Mountains, 1815' in Mackaness, *Fourteen Journeys*, p. 67.
35. Field, 'Journal of an Excursion' in ibid, p. 124.

36 Hawkins, 'Journey from Sydney to Bathurst' in ibid., p. 113.
37 Hardy, *The Return of the Native*, p. 5.
38 Hudson, *Over the Blue Mountains*, p. 4.
39 Commonwealth Bureau of Census and Statistics, *Demography Bulletin*, no. 65, 1947, p. 153.
40 Perry, *Australia's First Frontier*, p. 27.
41 Blaxland to Banks, 10 November 1816 in Richards, *Blaxland—Lawson—Wentworth*, p. 151.
42 Ibid., p. 150.
43 Macquarie, 'Tour over the Western or Blue Mountains, 1815', p. 73.
44 Macquarie to Bathurst, 24 June 1815, *HRA*, series I, vol. VIII, p. 556.
45 Goodall, *Invasion to Embassy*, p. 38.
46 Macquarie to Liverpool, 17 December 1812, *HRA*, series I, vol. VII, p. 559.
47 Cited in Houison, 'John and Gregory Blaxland', p. 19.
48 Ibid., p. 7.
49 'John Blaxland', *ADB*.
50 Castlereagh to King, 13 July 1805, *HRA*, series I, vol. V, p. 490.
51 Memorandum of Agreement, ibid., pp. 491–2.
52 Houison, 'John and Gregory Blaxland', p. 7.
53 Macquarie to Liverpool, 17 December 1812, *HRA*, series I, vol. VII, p. 559.
54 Cited in Houison, 'John and Gregory Blaxland', p. 10.
55 Macquarie to Liverpool, 17 December 1812, *HRA*, series I, vol. VII, p. 560.
56 Blaxland, *A Journal of a Tour* in Richards, *Blaxland—Lawson—Wentworth*, p. 65.
57 'William Lawson', *ADB*.
58 'D'Arcy Wentworth', *ADB*.
59 *ADB* and Melbourne, *William Charles Wentworth*.
60 Wentworth, *Australasia*, p. 15.
61 'William Wentworth', *ADB*.
62 Kendall, 'Blue Mountain Pioneers' in *Poems*, p. 303.
63 Blaxland, *A Journal of a Tour* in Richards, *Blaxland—Lawson—Wentworth*, p. 68.
64 Richards, *Blaxland—Lawson—Wentworth*, p. 82.
65 See Stockton (ed.), *Blue Mountains Dreaming*.
66 Cassirer, *The Philosophy of Symbolic Forms*, vol. 2, pp. xvi, xvii.
67 Nietzsche, *The Birth of Tragedy*, p. 53.
68 Weiss, *Unnatural Horizons*, p. 87.
69 John Low, personal communication.
70 Blaxland, *A Journal of a Tour* in Richards, *Blaxland—Lawson—Wentworth*, p. 64.
71 Wentworth to Bathurst, 22 April 1817, ibid. p. 183.
72 Reproduced in G. Newton, *Shades of Light*, p. xi.
73 Hammond, *The Camera Obscura*, p. 7.
74 Macdonald, 'Gregory Blaxland's Reward Land Grant'.
75 'Gregory Blaxland', *ADB*.
76 Ibid.
77 Blaxland, 'Daily Journal' (the copy sent to Sir Joseph Banks) and *A Journal of a Tour of Discovery*. Both appear in Richards, *Blaxland—Lawson—Wentworth*.
78 Blaxland, *Journal of a Tour*, p. 76. Subsequent quotations are from, respectively, pp. 68–9, 71, 73.
79 Field, 'Journal of an Excursion', p. 129.

PASSAGE TWO

1 G. Evans (attrib.), *A View of Sydney N. S. Wales on entering the heads the distance Seven Miles* (c. 1809). Mitchell Library, Sydney Ref. PXD 388–3 f.1.
2 G. Bull, 'The Artistic Background' in McCormick, *First Views of Australia*, p. 24.
3 William Westall, *Port Jackson, Sydney* (1804). Victoria and Albert Museum, London.
4 B. Smith, *European Vision and the South Pacific*, p. 220.
5 See Hoorn, *The Lycett Album*.
6 Collins, *An Account of the English Colony in New South Wales*, vol. I, p. 451.
7 Paz, 'Walt Whitman' in *On Poets and Others*, p. 10.
8 Fabian, *Time and the Other*, p. 32.
9 Ibid., p. 11.
10 Darwin, 'Journey Across the Blue Mountains' in Mackaness, *Fourteen Journeys*, p. 229.
11 Tench, *A Complete Account of the Settlement*, p. 146.
12 Willey, *When the Sky Fell Down*, pp. 72–3.
13 Collins, *Account of the English Colony*, p. 496.
14 Kohen, *The Darug and their Neighbours*, p. 15.
15 Ibid., p. 13.
16 Barrallier, 'Barrallier's Journal', *HRNSW*, vol. V, p. 753.
17 Evans, 'Evans's Journal' in Mackaness, *Fourteen Journeys*, p. 27. Subsequent quotations are from, respectively, pp. 21, 23, 27, 28, 30.
18 Collection of the National Gallery of Victoria, Melbourne.
19 Collection of the Geelong Art Gallery, Geelong.
20 *Illustrated Melbourne Post*, 3 January 1863, p. 11.
21 Darwin, 'Journey Across the Blue Mountains', p. 232.
22 *Argus*, 29 December 1862, p. 5.
23 *Illustrated Melbourne Post*, 3 January 1863, p. 11.
24 Bonyhady, *Images in Opposition*, p. 78.
25 D. Thomas, Introduction to Bruce, *Eugen von Guérard*, p. 13.
26 Von Guérard, *Australian Landscapes*.
27 Sayers, 'The Shaping of Australian Landscape Painting' in E. Johns et al, *New Worlds From Old*, p. 56.
28 Gelder and Jacobs, *Uncanny Australia*, p. 23.
29 'Missing Tourists', *Blue Mountains Echo*, 16 October 1925.

30 Hurley, *The Blue Mountains and Jenolan Caves*, pp. 33, 32.

31 Andrews (ed.), *The Devil's Wilderness*, p. 75.

32 *Tourist Map of the Blue Mountains Including Jenolan and Wombeyan Caves*, New South Wales Department of Lands, 1981.

33 Descartes, 'Rules for the Direction of the Mind' in *The Philosophical Writings of Descartes*, vol. 1, p. 20.

34 Andrews, *The Devil's Wilderness*, p. 83.

35 Banks to Under Secretary King, *HRA*, Series I, vol. II, p. 231.

36 Ibid., p. 232.

37 Barrett, *Life in the Burragorang*, p. 1.

38 Jamison, 'Journal of the First Excursion', Jan. 1834, p. 58.

39 Jamison, 'Journal of the First Excursion (Concluded)', Feb. 1834, p. 111.

40 Ibid., pp. 114, 117.

41 Blaxland, *Journal of a Tour*, in Richards, *Blaxland—Lawson—Wentworth*, p. 70.

42 R. Mitchell, 'Bass's Land Explorations', pp. 245–7.

43 Macquarie, 'Tour over the Western or Blue Mountains, 1815' in Mackaness, *Fourteen Journeys*, p. 67.

44 Cited in Searle, 'Caley's Repulse', p. 3.

45 Ibid., p. 6.

46 Ibid., p. 8.

47 Cited ibid.

48 Stockton, 'Aboriginal Art in the Blue Mountains' in *Blue Mountains Dreaming*, p. 72.

49 Carter, 'Culture of Coincidence' in *Living in a New Country*.

50 Antill, 'Journal of an Excursion over the Blue or Western Mountains' in Mackaness, *Fourteen Journeys*, p. 86.

51 R. H. Mathews, 'Some Mythology of the Gundungurra Tribe', pp. 203–6. Subsequent quotes from this source.

52 J. Smith, *Aboriginal Legends*, p. 7.

53 Mathews, 'Some Mythology and Folklore of the Gundungurra Tribe', National Library of Australia MS 8007/3/7.

54 Ellis, *Aboriginal Music Education for Living*, p. 90.

55 J. Smith, *Aboriginal Legends*, p. 63.

56 Bellingham, *Ten Years with the Palette, Shot Gun & Rifle*, p. 27. Subsequent quotations are from, respectively, pp. 26, 26, 34, 13, 13, 13.

57 Borges, 'The God's Script', in *Labyrinths*, pp. 203, 206.

58 Borges, 'The House of Asterion', ibid., p. 172.

PASSAGE THREE

1 R. H. Mathews, 'Some Mythology of the Gundungurra Tribe', p. 204.

2 Collection of the National Gallery of Victoria. The spelling *Kosciusko* is the Australianised *Kosciuszko*. The mountain has been officially renamed using the Polish spelling.

3 Cited in Bonyhady, *Images in Opposition*, p. 64.

4 Burke, *A Philosophical Enquiry*, pp. 16, 58, 128.

5 Taylor, *Australia*, p. 129.

6 *North-east view from the northern top of Mount Kosciusko* (1863), oil on canvas, 66.5 × 116.8 cm. Collection of the National Gallery of Australia.

7 Bonyhady, *Images in Opposition*, pp. 93–5.

8 Kaluski, *Sir Paul E. Strzelecki*, p. 30.

9 Cited ibid., p. 32.

10 Ibid.

11 Strzelecki, *Physical Description*, p. 57.

12 Andrews (ed.), *The Devil's Wilderness*, p. 52.

13 Strzelecki, *Physical Description*, p. 57.

14 Strzelecki, ibid., pp. 58–9 (note).

15 Kaluski, *Strzelecki*, p. 23.

16 Andrews, *The Devil's Wilderness*, p. 27.

17 Nancy Phelan, personal communication.

18 Andrews, *The Devil's Wilderness*, p. 84.

19 Ibid., pp. 73–4.

20 Andrews, 'The Carmarthen Hills and Thereabouts', p. 8.

21 Andrews, *The Devil's Wilderness*, p. 86.

22 'Exploration of the Mountains', 2 November 1805, *HRA.*, Series I, vol. V, p. 727.

23 Bateson, *The Convict Ships 1787–1868*, pp. 70, 74.

24 Hawkins, 'Journey from Sydney to Bathurst' in Mackaness (ed.), *Fourteen Journeys*, p. 106.

25 Tench, *A Complete Account of the Settlement*, p. 224 (note).

26 Ibid., p. 155.

27 Reproduced in Hunter, *An Historical Journal*.

28 In describing geometrical solids as a product of 'ideology', the physicist B. K. Ridley waggishly suggested they might be composed of a material known as *utopium*. See Ridley, *Time, Space and Things*.

29 Tench, *A Complete Account of the Settlement*, p. 224 (note).

30 B. Smith, 'Coleridge's *Ancient Mariner* and Cook's Second Voyage' in *Imagining the Pacific*, p. 148.

31 See Wood, 'Lieutenant William Dawes and Captain Watkin Tench', pp. 13–14.

32 Collins, *An Account of the English Colony in New South Wales*, vol. I, p. 73.

33 Caley to Banks, 10 Dec. 1804, *HRNSW*, vol. V, p. 508.

34 Tench in *Sydney's First Four Years*, p. 158.

35 Phillip to Sydney, *HRA.*, Series I, vol. I, p. 19.

36 Tench in *Sydney's First Four Years*, p. 280.

37 Cited in McAfee, *Dawes's Meteorological Journal*, p. 8.

38 Davison, *The Unforgiving Minute*, p. 16.

39 Troy, *The Sydney Language*, p. 14.

40 Tench in *Sydney's First Four Years*, p. 206 (note).

293

41 Ibid., pp. 207–8.
42 See Wood, 'Lieutenant William Dawes', p. 7.
43 King to Hobart, 28 October, 1802, *HRA*, Series I, vol. III, p. 691.
44 Tench, *A Complete Account of the Settlement*, p. 246.
45 King to Hobart, 9 May 1803, *H.R.A.*, Series I, vol. IV, p. 85.
46 *Sydney Gazette*, 12 March and 19 March 1803.
47 *Sydney Gazette*, 26 March 1803.
48 Foucault, *Discipline and Punish*.
49 *Sydney Gazette*, 3 July 1803.
50 Ibid.
51 Hunter to Portland, 15 February 1798, *HRNSW*, vol. III, pp. 360, 361.
52 Collins, *An Account of the English Colony*, vol. II, pp. 43, 214.
53 Ibid., vol. I, p. 356, vol. II, pp. 214–15.
54 *HRNSW*, vol. III, pp. 207–8.
55 Collins, *An Account of the English Colony*, vol. II, p. 43.
56 Hunter to Banks, 21 August 1801, *HRNSW*, vol. III, p. 820.
57 'Journey into the Interior', ibid., pp. 820–28.
58 Chisholm, *The Romance of the Lyrebird*.
59 'Journey into the Interior', pp. 820–21. Subsequent quotations are from, respectively, pp. 821, 822, 825, 826, 827.
60 T. Whitley, 'The Reputed Passage of the Blue Mountains', p. 190.
61 Cambage, 'Exploration Beyond the Upper Nepean', pp. 35–6.
62 Carter, *The Road to Botany Bay*, chapter 10.
63 See J. B. Harley, 'Maps, Knowledge and Power' in Cosgrove and Daniels (eds), *The Iconography of Landscape*.
64 Garryowen, *The Chronicles of Early Melbourne, 1835–1851*, cited in Behan, *Mr Justice J. W. Willis*.
65 Lattas, The New Panopticon, p. 90.
66 Ibid., p. 103. Citations from *Sydney Gazette*.
67 Cited in Lattas, 'Savagery and Civilisation', p. 41.
68 Agamben, *Infancy and History*, p. 24.
69 Ibid. p. 25.
70 See Dunmore, introduction to *Fragmens du Dernier Voyage de la Pérouse* (original spelling and capitalisation). Subsequent quotations are from, respectively, pp. vi, 35, 35–6, 36, 6.
71 Dunmore, *Utopias*, pp. 10–11.
72 Ibid., p. 6.
73 Taussig, *Mimesis and Alterity*, pp. 13, 7–8, 19.
74 Jay, *Downcast Eyes*, pp. 36, 65.
75 Cited ibid., pp. 37–8.
76 Sider, 'When Parrots Learn to Talk', p. 8.
77 Carter, *The Sound In-Between*, p. 73.
78 Carter, *Living in a New Country*, p. 93.
79 Hunter, *An Historical Journal*, pp. 106–7.
80 Cambage, 'Exploration Beyond the Upper Nepean in 1798', p. 4.
81 Tench, *A Complete Account of the Settlement*, p. 228.
82 'Barrallier's Journal', *HRNSW*, vol. V, p. 823.
83 Gibson, *The Diminishing Paradise*.
84 Dumaresq, 'A Ride to Bathurst, 1827', in Mackaness, *Fourteen Journeys*, p. 188.

PASSAGE FOUR

1 J. Smith, 'Blue Mountains Myths and Realities' in P. Stanbury (ed.), *The Blue Mountains*, p. 187.
2 Anon., *Souvenir of the Blue Mountains*.
3 *Blue Mountains Echo*, 6 July 1928.
4 Hurley, *The Blue Mountains and Jenolan Caves*, p. 2.
5 *Sydney Morning Herald*, 25 June 1992.
6 M. Ward in J. Smith, *Aboriginal Legends*, p. 11.
7 Ibid., p. 73.
8 Calasso, *The Marriage of Cadmus and Harmony*, pp. 147, 136.
9 Wentworth, *Australasia*, p. 15.
10 R. H. Mathews, 'Some Mythology of the Gundungurra Tribe', p. 204.
11 Smith, *Aboriginal Legends*, p. 49.
12 R. H. Mathews, 'The Aboriginal Fisheries at Brewarrina'.
13 J. Mathews, *The Opal that Turned into Fire*, foreword.
14 Elkin, 'R. H. Mathews' (Part II), p. 132.
15 Nietzsche, *Twilight of the Idols*, p. 26.
16 Kant, *The Conflict of the Faculties*, p. 199.
17 Davies and Stanbury, *The Mechanical Eye in Australia*, p. 106.
18 Collection of the Macleay Museum, University of Sydney.
19 Crary, *Techniques of the Observer*, pp. 125, 127.
20 Cited ibid., p. 127.
21 Bonyhady, *The Colonial Earth*, pp. 200–201.
22 Crary, *Techniques of the Observer*, p. 125.
23 Davies and Stanbury, *Mechanical Eye*, p. 106.
24 Collection of the Macleay Museum, University of Sydney.
25 'A Mountain Sensation', *Sydney Morning Herald*, 9 July 1906.
26 J. Smith, *Blue Mountains Walking Track Heritage Study*, p. 8.
27 A. Burke, 'Awesome Cliffs, Fairy Dells and Lovers Silhouetted in the Sunset' in Stanbury, *The Blue Mountains*, p. 106.
28 Smith, *Blue Mountains Walking Track Heritage Study*, p. 73.
29 Anon., 'A Legend of the Blue Mountains: The Orphan Rock', *Blue Mountains Echo*, 30 April 1910. Reprinted in Smith, *Aboriginal Legends*, p. 14.
30 Ibid., p. 15.
31 Pierce, *The Country of Lost Children*, p. xii.
32 Ibid. pp. 198–201.

33 Photos are held in the Mel Ward Archive, Australian Museum.
34 M. D. McPaul to M. Ward, 12 August 1947, Mel Ward Archive (AN 93/2), Australian Museum.
35 G. P. Whitley, 'Melbourne Ward', p. 19.
36 *Reader's Digest*, June 1957.
37 Mel Ward Archive (AN 93/2), Australian Museum.
38 Griffiths, *Hunters and Collectors*, p. 39.
39 Ibid., p. 130.
40 Mel Ward Archive (AN 93/2), Australian Museum.
41 Mauldon, *Melbourne Ward's Gallery*, p. 37.
42 Smith, *Aboriginal Legends*, p. 73.
43 Ward, *Legend Walk*, p. 2.
44 Ryan, *Reminiscences of Australia*, pp. 3–5.
45 For example, see Maureen Brecknell, 'Shades of Grey: Early Contact in the Blue Mountains' in Stockton (ed.), *Blue Mountains Dreaming*.
46 Taussig, *The Magic of the State*, p. 10.
47 Pearce, *On Collecting*, pp. 347, 348.
48 J. Fenton, 'The Pitt Rivers Museum, Oxford'. Cited in Clifford, *The Predicament of Culture*, p. 216.
49 Healy, *From the Ruins of Colonisation*, p. 50.
50 Fabian, *Time and the Other*, p. 11.
51 'Three more sisters for Katoomba', *Blue Mountains Gazette*, 9 June 1966.
52 Smith, 'Blue Mountains Myths and Realities' in Stanbury, *Blue Mountains*, p. 196.
53 Interview with June Barker.
54 'Double-Yew', *The Jumbly history of Parramatta*, p. 4.
55 Interview with June Barker.
56 Jackson, *At Home in the World*, p. 1.
57 Also titled *Homage to Catalina*. From hereon referred to as 'Homage' (radio version).
58 Goodall, *Invasion to Embassy*, p. 279.
59 From an interview with 'a real queen, Betty, of the Katoomba Tribe'. *Telegraph*, 4 October 1922.
60 Low, *Pictorial Memories*, p. 88.
61 Longdin and Meadows, 'Catalina: Wild Heart of Katoomba', p. 114.
62 'Death of Former Mountains Mayor', *Blue Mountains Advertiser*, 5 June 1969, pp. 1, 13.
63 Walford to Miss Campbell, 2 September 1957. Collection of Jim Smith.
64 Rotary Club of Katoomba, *Old Leura and Katoomba*, p. 301.
65 As broadcast in 'Homage' (radio version). Subsequent Stanger quotations from this source unless otherwise stated.
66 Attenbrow, *Katoomba Falls Creek Valley*.
67 Interview with Bill Boldiston.
68 Smith, 'Katoomba's Fringe Dwellers' in Stockton (ed.), *Blue Mountains Dreaming*, p. 123.
69 Smith, *Aborigines of the Burragorang Valley 1830–1960*, p. 7.

70 Smith, 'Katoomba's Fringe Dwellers', p. 123.
71 Jean Murphy in 'Homage' (radio version).
72 Lolita Martinez in Sheridah Melvin, 'The Mirror of Waranjari'.
73 Reported as 'The destruction of Frog Hollow', *Blue Mountains Echo*, 15 November 1988.
74 Govett, *Sketches of New South Wales*, p. 4.
75 Smith, *Aborigines of the Burragorang Valley*, p. 9.
76 Pearce, *Rabbit Hot, Rabbit Cold*, p. 23.
77 Hugh Doggett, 'Homage' (radio version).
78 Blue Mountains City Council Archives, Box 5, File 11965.
79 Interview with Hugh Doggett.
80 Deed between the Blue Mountains City Council and the Blue Mountains Sporting Drivers Club Ltd, 8 July 1957. Minutes of the Blue Mountains City Council, 8 July 1957, p. 3.
81 Doug Macarthur, 'Homage' (radio version).
82 Smith, 'Katoomba's Fringe Dwellers', p. 133.
83 Bill Boldiston, 'Homage' (radio version).
84 T. A. Humphries to *Blue Mountains Courier*, 2 May 1957.
85 'The Reader Writes', *Blue Mountains Courier*, 25 April 1957.
86 'Keen Interest Shown in Racing Track', *Blue Mountains Courier*, 2 May 1957.
87 Attachment A to Minutes of Special Council Meeting, 24 November 1970, p. 1745. Blue Mountains City Council Archives.
88 Supreme Court of New South Wales file 498/70.
89 'Walford Park controversy goes back years', *Blue Mountains Gazette*, 12 May 1982.
90 Bill Boldiston, 'Homage' (radio version).
91 R. H. Mathews, 'Some Mythology of the Gundungurra Tribe', p. 206.

PASSAGE FIVE

1 This and subsequent quotations are drawn from the coronial records of the Local Court, Katoomba. Details withheld to conceal the identities of the deceased.
2 The opinion of Sir T. Mitchell. Cited in A. Potts, 'William Romaine Govett' in Govett, *Sketches of New South Wales*, p. xxix.
3 Cited in Andrews, 'Govett's Luck', p. 264.
4 The myth is cited in Potts, 'William Romaine Govett' (biographical sketch) in Govett, *Sketches of New South Wales*, pp. xxvi–xxxi.
5 Trollope, *Australia and New Zealand*, p. 206.
6 Cited in Potts, 'William Romaine Govett', p. xxxi.
7 Z., 'The History of Govett's Leap', *The Nepean Times*, 3 March 1882.
8 Z., 'The History of Govett's Leap' (continued), *The Nepean Times*, 10 March 1882.

9 Roberts, 'Bells Falls massacre', p. 627.
10 Ibid., p. 615.
11 See Cunningham, *Featuring Australia*.
12 Sartre, *Being and Nothingness*, p. 29. Sartre attributes the comment to Kierkegaard.
13 State Records of New South Wales: Attorney General and Justice—Coroners' inquests, CGS 345 (13/8459 No. 2389). Inquest into the death of Vere Gordon Childe, 1957. Typographical errors have been corrected. Subsequent quotations concerning Childe's inquest from this source.
14 Collection of the Mitchell Library, ML Ref. A330 opp. p. 6.
15 Govett, *Notes and sketches, Blue Mountains: 1830–1835*, pp. 6–7.
16 Govett, *Sketches of New South Wales*, p. 71.
17 Ibid., pp. 2–3.
18 Trollope, *Australian and New Zealand*, p. 206.
19 Govett, *Sketches of New South Wales*, p. 4.
20 Payne, 'Lookouts', p. 19.
21 Andrews, 'The Naming of Govetts Leap', p. 7.
22 Trollope, *Australia and New Zealand*, p. 206.
23 T. Mitchell, *Three Expeditions*, vol. II, p. 154–5.
24 See Macqueen, *Back from the Brink*, ch. 6.
25 Mitchell, *Three Expeditions*, vol. II, p. 154.
26 Bonyhady, *The Colonial Earth*, pp. 193–8.
27 The opinion of du Faur. Cited in Newton, *Shades of Light*, p. 56.
28 Ibid, p. 56.
29 Macqueen, *Back from the Brink*, ch. 21.
30 In Mitchell, *Three Expeditions*, vol. II.
31 Bachelard, *Air and Dreams*, p. 94.
32 Anderson, *Suicide in Victorian and Edwardian England*, pp. 219–223.
33 Drawn from the coronial records of the Local Court, Katoomba.
34 Alvarez, *The Savage God*, p. 185.
35 Camus, *The Myth of Sisyphus*, p. 11.
36 Alvarez, *The Savage God*, p. 69.
37 Waller and Williams, *Criminal Law*, p. 131.
38 *Coroners Act 1980*, 44 (3), New South Wales Statutes. The coroner is entitled to permit publication if it is deemed 'desirable in the public interest'. See section 44 (4).
39 'Body of Professor Found 1,000 ft Below Top of Cliff', *The Sydney Morning Herald*, 21 October 1957.
40 Interview with Ernest Constable.
41 Green, *Prehistorian*, p. xix.
42 Mulvaney, 'V. G. Childe 1892–1957', p. 93.
43 Childe, 'Retrospect', p. 73.
44 National Archives of Australia: ASIO; Series A6126/25, Item 279 and Series A6126/XR1, Item 65.
45 National Archives of Australia: ASIO; Series A6126/25, Item 279.

46 Camus, *The Myth of Sisyphus*, p. 12.
47 Green, *Prehistorian*, p. 30.
48 Mulvaney, ' "Another university man gone wrong" ' in Harris (ed.), *Archaeology of V. Gordon Childe*, p. 58.
49 Childe, 'Retrospect', p. 69.
50 Green, *Prehistorian*, p. 35.
51 Ibid., p. 40.
52 Childe, *How Labour Governs*, p. 181.
53 Childe, 'Retrospect', p. 70.
54 Ibid., p. 70.
55 Piggott, 'The Dawn: and an Epilogue', p. 75.
56 Green, *Prehistorian*, p. 51.
57 See Childe, *Skara Brae*.
58 Piggott, 'The Dawn: and an Epilogue', p. 77.
59 Green, *Prehistorian*, p. xxi.
60 Mallowan, *Mallowan's Memoirs*, p. 235.
61 Green, *Prehistorian*, p. 8.
62 H. Kilbride-Jones in Harris, *Archaeology of V. Gordon Childe*, pp. 136, 137.
63 Green, *Prehistorian*, p. 7.
64 Mulvaney, ' "Another university man gone wrong" ', p. 62.
65 Green, *Prehistorian*, p. 146.
66 Cited ibid., p. 151.
67 Cited ibid., p. 145.
68 Childe, 'Retrospect', p. 74.
69 Childe, 'Valediction', *Bulletin of the London Institute of Archaeology*, I, p. 1.
70 Childe to Soviet Archaeologists, 16 December 1956. Published in Harris, *The Archaeology*, pp. 95–99.
71 Green, *Prehistorian*, p. 121.
72 J. Lindsay, foreword to Green, *Prehistorian*, p. xvii.
73 Lindsay, *Life Rarely Tells*, p. 130.
74 Alvarez, *The Savage God*, p. 225.
75 Seiden, 'Where Are They Now?', p. 205.
76 Haglund to editor, p. 86.
77 Stewart to editor, p. 87.
78 Grimes to editor, p. 1.
79 Childe to Grimes, p. 1. Childe made an error in dating this letter. Presumably it was written on 19 October.
80 Ibid., pp. 2–3.
81 Low, 'New Light on the Death of V. Gordon Childe'.
82 Cited in Trigger, *Gordon Childe*, p. 11.
83 Mulvaney, 'Afterword' in Gathercole et al (eds), *Childe and Australia*, p. 212.
84 Cited in Agamben, *Infancy and History*, p. 17.
85 Borges, 'The House of Asterion', in *Labyrinths*, p. 173.
86 Trigger, *Gordon Childe*, p. 148.
87 Mallowan, *Mallowan's Memoirs*, p. 235.
88 Freud, 'The Uncanny'.
89 Cited in Mulvaney, 'Afterword', p. 213.
90 F. B. Smith, foreword to Childe, *How Labour Governs*, p. ix.

296

91 Mulvaney, 'From "The Dawn" to Sunset', p. 30.
92 Trigger, *Gordon Childe*, p. 68.
93 Pickett and Alder, *Layers of Time*, p. 23.
94 Nicholas, *Charles Darwin in Australia*, p. 43.
95 Hurley, *The Blue Mountains and Jenolan Caves*, p. 8.
96 Mulvaney, 'V. G. Childe, 1892–1957', p. 93.
97 Childe, *Man Makes Himself*, p. 9.
98 Ibid.
99 Childe, 'Guest of Honour', ABC Radio broadcast.
100 Cited in Mulvaney, 'Afterword', p. 215.
101 Mulvaney in discussion of 'Another University Man Gone Wrong', p. 72.
102 Cited in Griffiths, *Hunters and Collectors*, p. 90.
103 Cited ibid.
104 C. Renfrew, 'Concluding remarks' in Harris, *Archaeology of V. Gordon Childe*, p. 129.
105 Trigger, *Gordon Childe*, pp. 50, 100.
106 Childe, *The Dawn of European Civilization*, p. xiii.
107 Trigger, *Gordon Childe*, p. 57.
108 M. Rowlands, 'Childe and the Archaeology of Freedom' in Harris, *Archaeology of V. Gordon Childe*, p. 37.
109 Childe, *Social Evolution*, p. 75.
110 Childe, *Society and Knowledge*, p. 84.
111 Ibid., p. 85.
112 Engels, *The Origin of the Family, Private Property and the State*, p. 467.
113 Trigger, 'Childe's Relevance to the 1990s' in Harris, *The Archaeology*, p. 18.
114 Trigger, ibid., p. 17.
115 Childe, 'Changing Methods and Aims in Prehistory', p. 4.
116 Cited in Trigger, *Gordon Childe*, p. 66.
117 Gathercole in introduction to *Childe and Australia*, p. xv.
118 Childe, *History*, pp. 3, 6.
119 Gathercole, 'The Relationship Between Vere Gordon Childe's Political and Academic Thought—and Practice' in Gathercole et al *Childe and Australia*, p. 96.
120 Trigger, *Gordon Childe*, p. 104.
121 Childe, 'Retrospect', p. 73.
122 W. Peace, 'Vere Gordon Childe and the Cold War' in *Childe and Australia*, pp. 131, 132, 132.
123 Trigger, *Gordon Childe*, p. 121.

124 Peace, 'Vere Gordon Childe and the Cold War', p. 138.
125 Green, *Prehistorian*, p. 121.
126 Hardy, *But the Dead Are Many*.
127 Cited Green, *Prehistorian*, p. 122.
128 Ibid., p. 126.
129 Kilbride-Jones, 'Postscript', p. 136.
130 Harris, *The Archaeology of V. Gordon Childe*, p. 110.
131 Frontispiece to ibid.
132 Cassirer, *The Philosophy of Symbolic Forms*, pp. xvii, xvi.
133 Childe, *Society and Knowledge*, p. 130.
134 Freud, 'Mourning and Melancholia', p. 163.
135 Cited in Camus, *The Myth of Sisyphus*, p. 19.
136 Koestler, 'The God that Failed', p. 15.
137 Ibid., p. 74.
138 Camus, *The Myth of Sisyphus*, p. 96.
139 Stockton, *Blue Mountains Dreaming*, p. 5.

CODA

1   Tench, *A Narrative of the Expedition*, p. 61.
2   Thompson & Perkins, 'The Wild Cattle of the Cowpastures Revisited', p. 16.
3   Discussion with Gavin Andrews, December 1993.
4   Berndt, *The World of the First Australians*, p. 155.
5   Hardy, *The Return of the Native*, pp. 6, 13.
6   Cited in Todorov, *Mikhail Bakhtin*, p. 96.
7   Levinas, *Entre Nous*, p. xii.
8   O'Reilly, *Cullenbenbong*, p. 31. Subsequent quotations are from, respectively, pp. 31, 37, 32, 42, 43, 45, 46, 47, 48, 48, 50, 51, 52.
9   Hindmarsh, 'Wild Cattle', p. 29.
10 Kim de Govrik (Area Manager, National Parks and Wildlife Service of NSW) to Steve Johnston, 10 February 1998. Collection of Steve Johnston.
11 Campbell, 'Enigmas in Cave and Stone' in *David Campbell: Collected Poems*, p. 239.
12 Lyon and Urry, 'Bull Shelter', p. 39.
13 Campbell, 'Enigmas in Cave and Stone', p. 239.
14 Miller, Bull Cave, p. 18.
15 Mansell, 'Yarmul: For the lies we sing', pp. 28–34.
16 O'Reilly, *Cullenbenbong*, p. 10.
17 Péron, *A Voyage of Discovery*, p. 286.

ILLUSTRATIONS

299

ILLUSTRATIONS

SELECT BIBLIOGRAPHY

ABBREVIATIONS OF REFERENCE WORKS

ADB: Australian Dictionary of Biography
HRA: Historical Records of Australia
HRNSW: Historical Records of New South
    Wales
JRAHS: Journal of the Royal Australian Historical
    Society

ARCHIVAL COLLECTIONS

ASIO Records, National Archives of Australia.
Attorney General's and Coronial Records, State
    Records of New South Wales.
Australian Broadcasting Corporation Archives.
Mel Ward Archive, Australian Museum (AN93/2).
R. H. Mathews Papers, National Library of
    Australia (MS8006).
Records of the Blue Mountains City Council.

ORAL HISTORY AND TAPE ARCHIVES

(a) Interviews conducted by Martin Thomas
Recordings made in the Blue Mountains for The
    Gully Oral History Project, March 1999.
    Tapes in possession of the author. Gwenda
    Doggett, Hugh Doggett, Ken Duff, Doug
    Macarthur, John Stanger, Lynette Stanger,
    Neil Stuart.
June Barker of Lightning Ridge recorded in
    September 1999. Tape in the collection of the
    Cultural Heritage Division, National Parks
    and Wildlife Service of New South Wales.
(b) Recordings by other researchers
Ernest Constable, interviewed by Maryanne
    Quinn, Speaking of the Past: Oral History
    Project, 1984, Blue Mountains City Library
    Local Studies Collection.

Transcripts from Sheridah Melvin, 'The Mirror of
    Waranjari' Oral History Project, 1987, Blue
    Mountains City Library Local Studies
    Collection.

FILM AND RADIO PRODUCTIONS

Chauvel, Charles (director), Jedda, Charles
    Chauvel Productions, 1955.
Childe, Gordon, 'Guest of Honour', broadcast on
    ABC Radio, 13 October, 1957.
Thomas, Martin (producer), Homage to Catalina.
    Broadcast on 'Hindsight', ABC Radio
    National, 1999.
—— (producer), This is Jimmie Barker. Broadcast on
    'Radio Eye', ABC Radio National, March 2000.
Weiley, John (director/producer), The Edge, 1996.

BOOKS, MANUSCRIPTS AND OTHER
PRINTED MATERIAL

Agamben, Giorgio, Infancy and History: The
    Destruction of Experience, London: Verso, 1993.
Alvarez, A., The Savage God: A Study of Suicide,
    London: Weidenfeld and Nicolson, 1972 (1971).
Anderson, Benedict, Imagined Communities:
    Reflections on the Origin and Spread of
    Nationalism, London: Verso, 1983.
Anderson, Olive, Suicide in Victorian and Edwardian
    England, Oxford: Clarendon Press, 1987.
Andrews, Alan E. J. (ed.), The Devil's Wilderness:
    George Caley's Journey to Mount Banks 1804,
    Hobart: Blubber Head Press, 1984.
—— 'The Carmarthen Hills and Thereabouts',
    JRAHS, vol. 69, no. 1, 1983.
—— 'Govett's Luck: Assistant Surveyor Govett
    and the Southern Tributaries of the Colo
    River', JRAHS, vol. 63, no. 4, 1978.

—— 'The Naming of Govetts Leap', *Newsletter of the Royal Australian Historical Society*, March 1976.

Anon., *Memoirs of William Cox, J. P., etc.*, Sydney and Brisbane: William Brooks, 1901.

Anon., *Souvenir of the Blue Mountains, N.S.W., Australia*, Sydney: Hans Herzog & Co. for the Carrington Hotel, Katoomba, 1903.

Attenbrow, Val, *Katoomba Falls Creek Valley: Investigation of Pre-European and Post–Contact Aboriginal Sites*, Sydney South: Australian Museum Business Services, 1993.

Bachelard, Gaston, *Air and Dreams: An Essay on the Imagination of Movement*, trans. Edith R. Farrell and C. Frederick Farrell, Dallas: Dallas Institute Publications, 1988 (1943).

Baker, D. W. A., *The Civilised Surveyor: Thomas Mitchell and the Australian Aborigines*, Melbourne: Melbourne University Press, 1997.

Barrell, John, *The dark side of the landscape: The rural poor in English painting 1730–1840*, Cambridge: Cambridge University Press, 1980.

Barrett, Jim, *Life in the Burragorang*, Glenbrook: Published privately, 1995.

Batailles, Georges, 'The Labyrinth' in *Visions of Excess: Selected Writings, 1927–1939*, trans. Allan Stoekl, Minnesota: University of Minnesota Press, 1985.

Bateson, Charles, *The Convict Ships 1787–1868*, Glasgow: Brown, Son & Ferguson, 1969.

Behan, H. F., *Mr Justice J. W. Willis*, Glen Iris: published privately, 1979.

Bellingham, Sid R., *Ten Years with the Palette, Shot Gun & Rifle on the Blue Mountains, NSW*, Sydney: P. Offer, 1899.

Benjamin, Walter, *Illuminations*, trans. Harry Zohn, New York: Schocken Books, 1968 (1955).

Berman, Morris, *The Reenchantment of the World*, Ithaca: Cornell University Press, 1981.

Berndt, Ronald M. and Catherine H., *The World of the First Australians: Aboriginal Traditional Life: Past and Present*, Canberra: Aboriginal Studies Press, 1992.

Bonyhady, Tim, *Images in Opposition: Australian Landscape Painting 1801–1890*, Melbourne: Oxford University Press, 1991.

—— *The Colonial Earth*, Melbourne: Melbourne University Press, 2000.

Borges, Jorge Luis, *Labyrinths: Selected Stories and Other Writings*, Harmondsworth: Penguin, 1964.

Bruce, Candice, Comstock, Edward and McDonald, Frank, *Eugene von Guerard 1811–1901: A German Romantic in the Antipodes*, Martinborough: Alister Taylor, 1982.

Bruce, Candice, *Eugen von Guérard*, Sydney: Australian Gallery Directors Council, 1980.

Burke, Edmund, *A Philosophical Enquiry into the Origin of our Ideas of the Sublime and the Beautiful*, London: R. & J. Dodsley, 1759.

Calasso, Roberto, *The Marriage of Cadmus and Harmony*, trans., Tim Parks, New York: Alfred A. Knopf, 1993.

Cambage, R. H., 'Exploration Beyond the Upper Nepean in 1798', *JRAHS*, vol. 6 no. 1, 1920.

Campbell, David, 'Enigmas in Cave and Stone' in *David Campbell: Collected Poems*, (ed.) Leonie Kramer, North Ryde: Angus and Robertson, 1989.

Camus, Albert, *The Myth of Sisyphus*, trans., Justin O'Brien, London: Hamish Hamilton, 1979 (1942).

Carter, Paul, *Living in a New Country: History, travelling and language*, London: Faber and Faber, 1992.

—— *The Road to Botany Bay: An Essay in Spatial History*, London: Faber and Faber, 1987.

—— *The Sound In–Between: Voice, Space, Performance*, Sydney: New South Wales University Press and New Endeavour Press, 1992.

Cassirer, Ernst, *The Philosophy of Symbolic Forms: Mythical Thought*, trans. Ralph Manheim, vol. 2, New Haven: Yale University Press, 1964 (1955).

Childe, V. Gordon, 'Retrospect', *Antiquity*, vol. 32, no. 126 June 1958.

—— *Social Evolution*, London: Watts & Co, 1951.

—— *Society and Knowledge*, New York: Harper & Bros, 1956.

—— 'Changing Methods and Aims in Prehistory: Presidential Address for 1935', *Proceedings of the Prehistoric Society*, 1, 1935.

—— 'Valediction', *Bulletin of the London Institute of Archaeology*, 1, 1958.

—— *History*, London: Cobbett Press, 1947.

—— *How Labour Governs: A Study of Workers' Representation in Australia*, Melbourne: Melbourne University Press, 1964 (1923).

—— Letter to W. F. Grimes, *Antiquity*, vol. 54, no. 210, March 1980.

—— *Man Makes Himself*, London: Watts & Co., 1965 (1936).

—— *Skara Brae: A Pictish Village in Orkney*, London: Kegan Paul, Trench, Trubner & Co, 1931.

—— *The Dawn of European Civilization*, London: Kegan Paul, Trench, Trubner & Co, 1925.

Chisholm, Alec, *The Romance of the Lyrebird*, Sydney: Angus and Robertson, 1960.

Clare, John, *Bodgie Dada & the Cult of Cool*, Sydney: University of New South Wales Press, 1995.

Clark, C. M. H., *A History of Australia I: From the Earliest Times to the Age of Macquarie*, Melbourne: Melbourne University Press, 1963.

Clifford, James, *The Predicament of Culture*, Cambridge, MA: Harvard University Press, 1988.

Collins, David, *An Account of the English Colony in New South Wales*, Sydney: A. H. & A. W. Reed, 1975 (1798).

Conrad, Joseph, *Heart of Darkness*, New York: New American Library, 1980 (1902).

Cosgrove, Denis and Daniels, Stephen (eds.), *The Iconography of Landscape: Essays on the symbolic representation, design and use of past environments*, Cambridge: Cambridge University Press, 1992.

Crary, Jonathan, *Techniques of the Observer: On Vision and Modernity in the Nineteenth Century*, Cambridge: October Books, 1995.

Cunningham, Chris, *The Blue Mountains Rediscovered: Beyond the Myths of Early Australian Exploration*, Kenthurst: Kangaroo Press, 1996.

Cunningham, Stuart, *Featuring Australia: The Cinema of Charles Chauvel*, Sydney: Allen & Unwin, 1991.

Currey, J. E. B. (ed.), *Reflections on the Colony of New South Wales: George Caley*, Melbourne: Lansdowne Press, 1966.

Davies, Alan and Stanbury, Peter, *The Mechanical Eye in Australia: Photography 1841–1900*, Melbourne: Oxford University Press, 1985.

Davison, Graeme, *The Unforgiving Minute: How Australia learned to tell the time*, Melbourne: Oxford University Press, 1993.

Descartes, René, *The Philosophical Writings of Descartes*, vol. 1, trans. John Cottingham, Robert Stoothoff, Dugald Murdoch, Cambridge: Cambridge University Press, 1985.

Doob, Penelope Reed, *The Idea of the Labyrinth from Classical Antiquity through the Middle Ages*, Ithaca: Cornell University Press, 1990.

Double-Yew (Frank Walford), *The Jumbly history of Parramatta: in commemoration of nothing in particular*, Parramatta: Frank Walford, 1915.

Dunmore, John (ed.), *Fragmens du Dernier Voyage de la Pérouse*, Canberra: National Library of Australia, 1987 (1797).

—— *Utopias and Imaginary Voyages to Australasia*, Canberra: National Library of Australia, 1988.

Durkheim, Emile, *Suicide: A Study in Sociology*, trans. John A. Spaulding and George Simpson, London: Routledge & Kegan Paul, 1963 (1897).

Elkin, A. P., 'R. H. Mathews: His Contribution to Aboriginal Studies Part II', *Oceania*, vol. 66, no. 2, 1975.

Ellis, Catherine J., *Aboriginal Music Education for Living: Cross-cultural Experiences from South Australia*, St Lucia: University of Queensland Press, 1985.

Emerson, Ralph Waldo, *Nature and Other Writings*, Boston: Shambhala, 1994.

Engels, Frederick, *The Origin of the Family, Private Property and the State* (1884) in *Marx Engels: Selected Works*, Moscow: Progress Press, 1986.

Fabian, Johannes, *Time and the Other: How Anthropology Makes its Object*, New York: Columbia University Press, 1983.

Falconer, Delia, *The Service of Clouds*, Sydney: Picador, 1997.

Foster, David, 'A Walk in the Southern Blue Mountains' in Michael Duffy (ed.), *Crossing the Blue Mountains: Journeys through two centuries from naturalist Charles Darwin to novelist David Foster*, Potts Point: Duffy & Snellgrove, 1997.

—— *The Glade within the Grove*, Sydney: Random House, 1996.

Foster, William C., *Sir Thomas Livingston Mitchell and his World 1792–1855*, Sydney: Institution of Surveyors NSW, 1985.

Foucault, Michel, *Discipline and Punish: The Birth of the Prison*, trans. Alan Sheridan, London: Penguin, 1991.

—— *The History of Sexuality: An Introduction*, trans. Robert Hurley, London: Penguin, 1984 (1976).

Freud, Sigmund, 'Mourning and Melancholia' 1917 in *Collected Papers*, vol. 4, London: Hogarth Press, 1956.

—— 'The "Uncanny" ' 1919 in *Collected Papers*, vol. 4, London: Hogarth Press, 1956.

Gathercole, Peter, Irving, T. H. and Melleuish Gregory (eds), *Childe and Australia*, St Lucia: University of Queensland Press, 1995.

Gelder, Ken and Jacobs, Jane, *Uncanny Australia*, Melbourne: Melbourne University Press, 1998.

Gibson, Ross, *The Diminishing Paradise: Changing Literary Perceptions of Australia*, Sydney: Sirius, 1984.

Gilmore, Mary, *Old Days, Old Ways: A Book of Recollections*, Sydney: Angus and Robertson, 1986 (1934).

303

Goethe, Johann Wolfgang von, *The Sorrows of the Young Werther*, trans. Michael Hulse, Harmondsworth: Penguin, 1989 (1774).

Goodall, Heather, *Invasion to Embassy: Land in Aboriginal Politics in New South Wales, 1770–1972*, Sydney: Allen & Unwin in association with Black Books, 1996.

Govett, William Romaine, *Notes and sketches, Blue Mountains: 1830–1835*. Mitchell Library MS, A330.

—— *Sketches of New South Wales*, Melbourne: Gaston Renard Publisher, 1977.

Green, Sally, *Prehistorian: A Biography of V. Gordon Childe*, Bradford-on-Avon: Moonraker Press, 1981.

Griffiths, Tom, *Hunters and Collectors: The Antiquarian Imagination in Australia*, Cambridge: Cambridge University Press, 1996.

Grimes, W. F., Letter to Editor, *Antiquity*, vol. 54, no. 210, March 1980.

Guérard, Eugene von, *Australian Landscapes: A Series of 24 Tinted Lithographs, etc.*, Melbourne: Hamel & Ferguson, 1866–67.

—— *An Artist on the Goldfields: The Diary of Eugène von Guérard*, ed. Marjorie Tipping, Melbourne: Melbourne University Press, 1982.

Gurr, T. Stuart and Harrowsmith, Gwen, *Blue Mountains Story*, Sydney: Shakespeare Head Press, 1949.

Hacking, Ian, *The Taming of Chance*, Cambridge: Cambridge University Press, 1990.

Haglund, Laila, 'Memories of Gordon Childe', *Australian Archaeology*, 30, 1990.

—— Letter to Editor, *Antiquity*, vol. 53, no. 208, July 1979.

Hamilton, George, *The Journal of an Overlander*. National Library MS4299C.

Hammond, John H., *The Camera Obscura: A Chronicle*, Bristol: Adam Hilger, 1981.

Hardy, Frank, *But the Dead Are Many: A Novel in Fugue Form*, Sydney: Bodley Head, 1975.

Hardy, Thomas, *Jude the Obscure*, London: Macmillan, 1974 (1896).

—— *The Return of the Native*, London: Macmillan & Co, 1949 (1878).

Harris, David R. (ed.), *The Archaeology of V. Gordon Childe: Contemporary Perspectives*, London: UCL Press and University of Chicago Press, 1994.

Healy, Chris, *From the Ruins of Colonisation: History as Social Memory*, Cambridge: Cambridge University Press, 1997.

Hindmarsh, W. L., 'The Wild Cattle of the Cowpastures of New South Wales', *Australian Veterinary Journal*, vol. 45, January 1969.

Hoberman, John M., 'Kierkegaard on Vertigo' in Robert L. Perkins (ed.), *International Kierkegaard Commentary: The Sickness unto Death*, Macon: Mercer University Press, 1987.

Hoorn, Jeanette, *The Lycett Album: Drawings of Aborigines and Australian Scenery*, Canberra: National Library of Australia, 1990.

Houison, J. K. S., 'John and Gregory Blaxland', *JRAHS*, vol. 22, no. 1, 1936.

Hudson, Arthur, *Over the Blue Mountains*, North Sydney: Schools Publishing House, 1958.

Hume, David, *The Life of David Hume Esq. Written by Himself*, London: W. Strahan and T. Cadell, 1777.

Hunter, Captain John, *An Historical Journal of Events at Sydney and at Sea 1787–1792, etc.*, Sydney: Angus & Robertson, 1968 (1793).

Hurley, Frank, *The Blue Mountains and Jenolan Caves: A Camera Study*, Sydney: Angus and Robertson, 1952.

Jackson, John Brinckerhoff, *A Sense of Place, A Sense of Time*, New Haven: Yale University Press, 1994.

Jackson, Michael, *At Home in the World*, Durham: Duke University Press, 1995.

Jamison, Sir John, 'Journal of the First Excursion up the Warragamba', *New South Wales Magazine*, Jan. 1834.

—— 'Journal of the First Excursion up the Warragamba Concluded', *New South Wales Magazine*, Feb. 1834.

—— *Explorations*, 1818. Mitchell Library MS C131–2.

Jay, Martin, *Downcast Eyes: The Denigration of Vision in Twentieth-Century French Thought*, Berkeley: University of California Press, 1994.

Johns, Elizabeth et al, *New Worlds From Old: 19th Century Australian & American Landscapes*, Canberra: National Gallery of Australia and Wadsworth Atheneum, 1998.

Kafka, Franz, *Metamorphosis and other stories*, trans. Willa and Edwin Muir, London: Penguin, 1961.

Kaluski, Marian, *Sir Paul E. Strzelecki: A Polish Count's Explorations in 19th Century Australia*, Melbourne: A. E. Press, 1985.

Kant, Immanuel, *The Conflict of the Faculties*, trans. Mary J. Gregor, New York: Abaris, 1979.

Kendall, Henry, *Poems of Henry Clarence Kendall*, London: Longmans, Green, & Co., 1903.

304

Koestler, Arthur, 'The God that Failed' in Richard Crossman (ed.), *The God that Failed*, New York: Harper Bros, 1949.

Kohen, James, *The Darug and their Neighbours*, Blacktown: Darug Link in association with Blacktown Historical Society, 1997 (1993).

Langton, Marcia, 'What do we mean by wilderness?: Wilderness and *terra nullius* in Australian Art'. Paper presented at The Sydney Institute, 12 October 1995, not paginated.

Lattas, Andrew, 'Savagery and Civilisation: Towards a Genealogy of Racism', *Social Analysis*, 21 August 1987.

—— The New Panopticon: Newspaper Discourse and the Rationalisation of Society and Culture in New South Wales 1803–1830, PhD thesis: University of Adelaide, 1985.

Levinas, Emmanuel, *Entre Nous: On Thinking-of-the-Other*, trans. Michael B. Smith and Barbara Harshav, London: Athlone Press, 1998.

Lindsay, Jack, *Life Rarely Tells: An Autobiography in Three Volumes*, vol. I, Ringwood: Penguin, 1982.

Longdin, Ruth and Meadows, Elida, 'Catalina: Wild Heart of Katoomba', *Public History Review*, 1998.

Low, John, 'New Light on the Death of V. Gordon Childe', *The Hummer*, no. 8, Feb–Mar 1985.

—— *Pictorial Memories: Blue Mountains*, Crows Nest: Atrand, 1991.

Lyon, K. and Urry, J. 'Bull Shelter: a Cow Pastures' conundrum', *Australian Institute of Aboriginal Studies Newsletter*, no. 11 March 1979.

Macdonald, W. A., 'Gregory Blaxland's Reward Land Grant', *JRAHS*, vol. XXIV, no. 2, 1938.

Mackaness, George (ed.), *Fourteen Journeys Over the Blue Mountains of New South Wales 1813–1841*, Sydney: Horwitz-Grahame, 1965.

Macqueen, Andy, *Back from the Brink: Blue Gum Forest and the Grose Wilderness*, Springwood: privately published, 1997.

Mallowan, Max, *Mallowan's Memoirs*, London: Collins, 1977.

Mansell, Chris, 'Yarmul: For the lies we sing', *Imago*, vol. 5, no. 3, December, 1993.

Mathews, Janet, *The Opal that Turned into Fire*, (ed.) Isobel White, Broome: Magabala Books, 1994.

Mathews, R. H., 'Some Mythology of the Gundungurra Tribe, New South Wales', *Zeitschrift für Ethnologie*, Heft 2, 1908.

—— 'The Aboriginal Fisheries at Brewarrina', *Journal and Proceedings of the Royal Society of New South Wales*, vol. 37, 1903.

—— 'The Gundungurra Language', *Proceedings of the American Philosophical Society*, vol. 60, no. 167, 1901.

Mauldon, Verena, Melbourne Ward's Gallery of Natural History and Native Art, MA thesis: University of Sydney, 1989.

McAfee, Robert F., *Dawes's Meteorological Journal*, Canberra: Australian Government Publishing Service, 1981.

McCormick, Tim, *First Views of Australia 1788–1825*, Chippendale: David Ell Press, 1987.

Melbourne, A. C. V., *William Charles Wentworth*, Penrith: Discovery Press, 1972 (1934).

Meredith, John, *The Last Kooradgie: Moyengully, Chief Man of the Gundungurra People*, Kenthurst: Kangaroo Press, 1989.

Miller, R. D., Bull Cave: Its Relevance to the Prehistory of the Sydney Region, Honours thesis: Dept of Archaeology, University of Sydney, 1983.

Mitchell, R. Else, 'Bass's Land Explorations', *JRAHS*, vol. 37, no. 4, 1951.

Mitchell, T. L., *Field, note and sketch book*, 1828–30. Mitchell Library MS C42.

—— Minutes given in evidence, 'Report from the Commissioners Appointed to Inquire into the Surveyor General's Department', *Votes and Proceedings of the Legislative Council during the Session of the Year 1855*, Sydney: Government Printer, 1856.

—— *Three Expeditions into the Interior of Australia, etc*, London: T. & W. Boone, 1839 (1838).

Mitchell, W. J. T. (ed.), *Landscape and Power*, Chicago: University of Chicago Press, 1994.

Moffatt, Tracey, *Fever Pitch*, Annandale: Piper Press, 1995.

Mudrooroo, ' "Tell them you're Indian" ' in Gillian Cowlishaw and Barry Morris (eds), *Race Matters: Indigenous Australians and 'Our' Society*, Canberra: Aboriginal Studies Press, 1997.

Muecke, Stephen, Benterrak, Krim, and Roe, Paddy, *Reading the Country: Introduction to Nomadology*, Freemantle: Freemantle Arts Centre Press, 1996 (1984).

Mulvaney, D. J., 'From "The Dawn" to Sunset: Gordon Childe in Melbourne, 1957', *Australian Archaeology*, 30, 1990.

—— 'V. G. Childe 1892–1957', *Historical Studies: Australia and New Zealand*, vol. 8, no. 29, 1957.

New South Wales National Parks and Wildlife Service in association with Environment Australia, *The Greater Blue Mountains Area World Heritage Nomination*, Canberra, 1998.

305

Newton, Gael, *Shades of Light: Photography and Australia 1839–1988*, Canberra: National Gallery of Australia, 1988.

Nicholas, F. W. and J. M., *Charles Darwin in Australia*, Cambridge: Cambridge University Press, 1989.

Nietzsche, Friedrich, *The Birth of Tragedy out of the Spirit of Music*, trans. Shaun Whiteside, London: Penguin, 1993 (1872).

—— *Thus Spoke Zarathustra: A Book for Everyone and No One*, trans. R. J. Hollingdale, Harmondsworth: Penguin, 1969 (1883–92).

—— *Twilight of the Idols or How to Philosophize with a Hammer*, trans. R. J. Hollingdale, Harmondsworth: Penguin, 1968 (1889).

O'Reilly, Bernard, *Cullenbenbong*, Sydney: Envirobook, undated (1944).

Ovid, *Metamorphoses*, trans. Mary M. Innes, Harmondsworth: Penguin, 1955.

Oxley, John, *Journals of Two Expeditions into the Interior of New South Wales: undertaken by order of the British Government in the Years 1817–1818*, London: John Murray, 1820.

Payne, Cathie, 'Lookouts' in Cathy Payne, Peter McCarthy and Kurt Brereton (eds), *Australian Mythological Sights • Sites • Cites*, Sydney: Third Degree, 1986.

Paz, Octavio, *On Poets and Others*, trans. Michael Schmidt, New York: Arcade Publishing, 1986.

Pearce, Owen W., *Rabbit Hot, Rabbit Cold: Chronicles of a Vanishing Australian Community*, Woden: Popinjay Publications, 1991.

Pearce, Susan M., *On Collecting: An investigation into collecting in the European tradition*, London: Routledge, 1995.

Péron, M., *A Voyage of Discovery to the Southern Hemisphere*, London: Richard Phillips, 1809.

Perry, T. M., *Australia's First Frontier: The Spread of Settlement in New South Wales 1788–1829*, Melbourne: Melbourne University Press, 1965.

Pickett, J. W and Alder, J. D., *Layers of Time: The Blue Mountains and their geology*, Sydney: NSW Department of Mineral Resources, 1997.

Pierce, Peter, *The Country of Lost Children: An Australian Anxiety*, Cambridge: Cambridge University Press, 1999.

Piggott, Stuart, 'The Dawn: and an Epilogue', *Antiquity*, vol. 32, no. 126, June 1958.

Pliny the Elder, *Natural History*, vol. X, trans. E. E. Eicholz, London: William Heinemann, 1971.

Poe, Edgar Allen, *The Unknown Poe: An Anthology of Fugitive Writings by Edgar Allan Poe*, San Francisco: City Lights, 1980.

Read, Peter, *Belonging: Australians, Place and Aboriginal Ownership*, Cambridge: Cambridge University Press, 2000.

—— *Returning to Nothing: The meaning of lost places*, Cambridge: Cambridge University Press, 1996.

Richards, Joanna Armour (ed.), *Blaxland—Lawson—Wentworth*, Hobart: Blubber Head Press, 1979.

Ridley, B. K., *Time, Space and Things*, Cambridge: Cambridge University Press, 1994.

Roberts, David, 'Bells Falls massacre and Bathurst's history of violence: local tradition and Australian historiography', *Australian Historical Studies*, vol. 26, no. 105, 1995.

Rohdie, Sam, *The Passion of Pier Paolo Pasolini*, London: British Film Institute Publishing, 1995.

Rolls, Eric, *A Million Wild Acres*, Ringwood: Penguin, 1981.

Rose, Deborah Bird, *Nourishing Terrains: Australian Aboriginal Views of Landscape and Wilderness*, Canberra: Australian Heritage Commission, 1996.

Rotary Club of Katoomba, *Old Leura and Katoomba: a collection of historical background articles*, Katoomba: The Club, 1982.

Rothenberg, Jerome, 'Indians & Wilderness', *Dialectical Anthropology*, 5, 1980.

Ryan, James T., *Reminiscences of Australia*, Sydney: George Robertson and Company, 1894.

Sartre, Jean-Paul, *Being and Nothingness*, trans. Hazel E. Barnes, New York: Gramercy Books, 1994.

Schama, Simon, *Landscape and Memory*, London: HarperCollins, 1995.

Searle, A. E., 'Caley's Repulse'. Unpublished MS in the Local Studies Collection, Blue Mountains City Library.

Seiden, Richard H., 'Where Are They Now?: A Follow-up Study of Suicide Attempters from the Golden Gate Bridge', *Suicide and Life-Threatening Behaviour*, vol. 8, no. 4, 1978.

Sider, Gerald, 'When Parrots Learn to Talk, and Why They Can't: Domination, Deception, and Self-Deception in Indian-White Relations', *Comparative Studies in Society and History*, 1987.

Smith, Bernard, *European Vision and the South Pacific*, Melbourne: Oxford University Press, 1989 (1960).

—— *Imagining the Pacific: In the Wake of the Cook Voyages*, Melbourne: Melbourne University Press, 1992.

306

Smith, Jim, *Aboriginal Legends of the Blue Mountains*, Wentworth Falls: published privately, 1993.

—— *Aborigines of the Burragorang Valley 1830–1960*, Wentworth Falls: published privately, 1991.

—— *Blue Mountains National Park Walking Track Heritage Study*, Sydney: NSW National Parks and Wildlife Service, 1998.

—— *What is happening to the Blue Mountains?* Katoomba: Megalong Books, 1981.

Speirs, Hugh, *Landscape Art and the Blue Mountains*, Sydney: Alternative Publishing Co-operative, 1981.

Stanbury (ed.), Peter, *The Blue Mountains: Grand Adventure for All*, Sydney: Macleay Museum and Second Back Row Press, 1988.

Stewart, Eve, Letter to Editor, *Antiquity*, vol. 53, no. 208, July 1979.

Stockton, Eugene (ed.), *Blue Mountains Dreaming: The Aboriginal Heritage*, Winmalee: Three Sisters Publications, 1993.

Strzelecki, P. E. De, *Physical Description of New South Wales and Van Diemen's Land*, London: Longman, Brown, Green and Longmans, 1845.

Taussig, Michael, *Mimesis and Alterity: A Particular History of the Senses*, New York: Routledge, 1993.

—— *The Magic of the State*, New York: Routledge, 1997.

Taylor, Griffith, *Australia: A study of warm environments and their effect on British settlement*, London: Methuen, 1945.

Tench, Watkin, *A Complete Account of the Settlement at Port Jackson*, in L. F. Fitzhardinge (ed.), *Sydney's First Four Years*, Sydney: Angus and Robertson, 1961 (1793).

—— *A Narrative of the Expedition to Botany Bay*, in L. F. Fitzhardinge (ed.), *Sydney's First Four Years*, Sydney: Angus and Robertson, 1961 (1789).

Thomas, Martin (ed.), *Uncertain Ground: Essays Between Art & Nature*, Sydney: Art Gallery of NSW, 1999.

—— 'Centennial Dreamings: The Tyranny of a Discourse', *The Age Monthly Review*, Dec. 1987–Jan. 1988.

Thompson, Jack and Perkins, John, 'The Wild Cattle of the Cowpastures Revisited', *JRAHS*, vol. 77, no. 4, 1992.

Tipping, Marjorie (ed.), *An Artist on the Goldfields: The Diary of Eugène von Guérard*, Melbourne: Melbourne University Press, 1982.

Todorov, Tzvetan, *Mikhail Bakhtin: The Dialogical Principle*, Manchester: Manchester University Press, 1984.

Trigger, Bruce G., *Gordon Childe: Revolutions in Archaeology*, New York: Columbia University Press, 1980.

Trollope, Anthony, *Australia and New Zealand*, Melbourne: George Robertson, 1873.

Troy, Jakelin, *The Sydney Language*, Canberra: Australian Dictionaries Project, 1993.

Walford, Frank, *Twisted Clay*, London: Horwitz, 1962 (1933).

Wallace-Crabbe, Chris, 'Stones' in *Overland*, 135, Winter 1994.

Waller, L. and Williams, C. R., *Criminal Law: Text and Cases*, Sydney: Butterworths, 1993.

Ward, Mel, *Legend Walk: Australian Aboriginal Legends*, Waramanga: Geoff Bates, 1979.

Webster, John, *Metallographia: or, An History of Metals*, London: Walter Kettilby, MDCLXXI.

Weiss, Allen S., *Unnatural Horizons: Paradox and Contradiction in Landscape Architecture*, New York: Princeton Architectural Press, 1998.

Wentworth, W. C., *Australasia: A Poem written for the Chancellor's Medal at the Cambridge Commencement, July 1823*, London: G. and W. B. Whittaker, 1823.

Werriberrie aka Russell, William, *My Recollections*, The Oaks: The Oaks Historical Society, 1991 (1914).

Whitaker, Ann-Maree, 'The Convicts who Conquered the Blue Mountains', *Descent*, March 1993.

Whitley, G. P., 'Melbourne Ward', *Proceedings of the Royal Zoological Society of N. S. W.*, 24 February 1967.

Whitley, Thomas, 'The Reputed Passage of the Blue Mountains in 1798 and Incidents connected with its Story', *JRAHS*, no. 10, 1904–5.

Willey, Keith, *When the Sky Fell Down: The Destruction of the Tribes of the Sydney Region 1788–1850s*, Sydney: Collins, 1979.

Willmot, Eric, *Pemulwuy the Rainbow Warrior*, Sydney: Bantam, 1988 (1987).

Wittgenstein, Ludwig, *Notebooks 1914–1916*, trans. G. E. M. Anscombe, Chicago: University of Chicago Press, 1979 (1961).

307

INDEX

Page numbers in italics indicate illustrations

308

311

313